**Damson By The Pound**

To my wife who has given me invaluable support over the past 50 years. Also to my cousin Jim without whose help there would be considerable gaps in the content and photographic detail.

# Damson By The Pound

## Memories of a Warwickshire Family
## 1900 — 1939

### by

## Stanley J Beavan

BREWIN BOOKS

First published
by Brewin Books, Studley, Warwickshire, B80 7LG
in February 1993

© Stanley J. Beavan

All rights reserved

ISBN 1 85858 008 0

British Library Cataloguing in Publication Data.
A Catalogue record for this book is available from the British Library

Typeset in Times by Avon Dataset, Bidford on Avon, Warwickshire, B50 4JH
and made and printed by The Cromwell Press, Broughton Gifford, Melksham, Wiltshire.

Queen Victoria celebrated her Golden Jubilee, a prodigious period in our history. In Solihull, as in so many other towns and villages, an oak sapling was planted to commemorate the occasion. In Solihull it was planted at the junction of Station Road and Blossomfield Road, henceforth the spot became known as, "Jubilee Oak". Several members of my family attended the occasion.

The doughty Queen created a mighty lineage during her reign in the 19th century, as did Great Granny Street. Her progeny, the Beavans, Butlers, Streets and Blizzards established themselves as Warwickshire families in the surrounding districts.

The last decade of the 20th. century will shortly fade into the shadows of history with many of its achievements and the people who played a role in them. The author resolved to record its passing and the part Elmdon and its inhabitants played in its scenario.

The spectre of early death from what are now little known health and social problems were constantly with us in those days. Despite that we possessed an innocent vision of the coherence of a social, domestic, industrial and agricultural whole which would continue in perpetuity. Those of us who are given to watch the inexorable passing of time are only too aware of how transitory that period was.

Yesterday

Today, I walked to yesterday
And trod a path I knew,
The years bequeathed a limping step
Autumn days are left but few.
I searched in vain for remembered face
Of childhood, long since gone,
Strangers passed on every side
They did not stop, not one.
Twilight cast its dusky cloak
As I wandered down the lane
A wreath of smoke, above the trees,
I would see our home, again.
Around the bend, I hurried
As eager as a boy,
The glow of fire, within the hearth
When pleasures, did not cloy.
There was nothing there before me,
All trace of home had gone
No welcome at the window,
No door to knock upon.
Damned eyes, that they grow misty,
My footsteps faltered on,
I walked today, to yesterday,
But yesterday was gone.

# CONTENTS

1. My Forebears Chase a Star. — 1
2. My Parents. — 7
3. Our first Home. — 13
4. Lugtrout Lane c1920. — 21
5. The New House. — 23
6. Damson Lane and The Pound. — 27
7. Walnut Tree Cottages. — 37
8. Keeping the Wolf from the Door. — 47
9. The Elmdon Estate. — 55
10. A Keepers' Year. — 67
11. The Farming Year. — 75
12. Off to School. — 87
13. Hobbies and Sports. — 93
14. The Pound. — 103
15. Solihull Gas Works — The Wharf. — 109
16. Solihull Gas Works — Mill Lane. — 119
17. I Spread My Wings. — 125
18. Family Leisure in the 1920's and 30's. — 133
19. The Wireless Arrives in Elmdon Heath. — 147
20. Fate casts a Shadow. — 155
21. We Gain our Wheels. — 163
22. Welcome to the Fairer Sex. — 181
23. An Electrifying Experience. — 187

## *Acknowledgements*

Solihull Library (Sue Bates)
The National Motorcycle Museum Ltd.
British Motor Industry Heritage Trust
Mrs. Mary Dalloe
Marie Lines
K. Morris

# Chapter 1
# My Forebears Chase a Star

From the middle of the 18th century significant changes were taking place in the central region of England, particularly around a small town known as Birmingham. Until that time the economic base of the United Kingdom had been agriculture and the establishment of our Empire overseas. It had been successful on both counts and enjoyed considerable prosperity. The education system was of a very high order and in consequence the products of this system began to question and experiment with known scientific theories and principles.

Messrs Watt, Boulton, Telford, Stevenson and MacAdam and many others were applying themselves to the needs of the nation; in return for which we could acquire many of the riches waiting to be exploited from our colonies and dominions. The only motive force was the horse and continued to be for another century or more. Watts simple experiment with a kettle was ultimately to provide this country with the means of becoming the workshop to the world.

To exploit that invention, unlimited supplies of coal, iron and water were required. All of those base materials had been discovered near to the small town in the Midlands. The area was to acquire the name of, "the black country", and would become synonymous with the industrial revolution. A further accolade was the recognition that it was the home of a "1001 trades"!

As the coal mines, smelting ovens, iron foundries and mills and workshops were built and began to operate, word soon got round the Midland counties that there was well paid work to be had. That news soon meant that lowly paid farm labourers and other workers began a migration from their areas to the new eldorado. The men found work in the new factories and their womenfolk went to work for the owners and managers of the mills and factories in which their menfolk worked. George Beavan, a young wagoner from Ross-on-Wye, later to become my grandfather, was one of those men.

My Grandfather was not a good communicator, I was never to establish how or why he had come to be in Solihull. In the case of my paternal Grandmother there was no problem in that regard, she spent long hours reminiscing with a small lad who had a voracious appetite for knowledge.

Her parents, a Mr. and Mrs. Street, with their offsprings, formed part of the cottage industry in Redditch and its surrounding areas manufacturing fish hooks and needles. The work was hard and unrelenting, the adults made the blind needles from lengths of steel wire, many hundreds and thousands of them each year. They were then passed to other members of the men's families to stamp in the eyes and form the points. The last job of polishing the finished article was the children's task. When they were gleaming, the youngest, in our case, my grandmother, had to pack them in small black paper packets ready for sale locally or for dispatch around the world. Almost all of the work was carried out as a cottage industry over long hours. When daylight failed, they resorted to tallow candles placed behind a bottle of water to magnify the light output from the meagre source.

The tools used by the workers to produce the articles were hammers, anvils, chisels, candles and last but not least, the Jewellers rouge, used to polish the finished item. All had to be provided by the workers with little or no help from the factory owner.

The wages paid for the work was very low. The children received none at all, and my grandmother told me that her mother was paid one penny for each 500 perfect needles delivered to the factory manager! They were then dispatched to the lace and stocking factories in Leicester and Nottingham.

The route between Astwood Bank and Birmingham does not appear to pass through Warwick, nevertheless, that was where my grandmother's family found themselves one fine summer morning as they made their way to a promised land. They had walked many miles before they were attracted by a large gathering, they stopped, and sat down to take a rest. The gathering was outside the imposing gates of Warwick Jail. To help my grandmother to see what was going on, my great grandfather lifted her onto his shoulders. The sight that met her eyes was at first confusing. The gates were wide open and just inside was a platform with a scaffold rising above it with a strong rope hanging from it. She saw movement in the yard behind the platform and shortly several men ascended steps and gathered beneath the noose at the end of the rope. She could see that one of the men had his hands tied behind his back and his head was covered by a black bag. At that moment the crowd became impatient and began to chant, "Get on with it. Let him drop"! At that moment the little girl could see the man had the noose around his neck and was standing on a trap door. With a loud report, the trap swung down and the man fell through to disappear below the platform. She was very frightened and covered her eyes, and after a short while she asked her father what had happened. He told her that the man had done a terrible thing and that was what they did to those sort of people. He added, "He had probably stolen a sheep to feed his family"!

On their journey they were fortunate in that they had not been accosted by footpads, a common and frequent hazard then. It had not been an easy journey, three days on the road, sleeping under the hedge or in barns and eating only what could be found at the roadside or taken from farmers fields. At last they arrived, tired, hungry and dishevelled and in trepidation of what the future held. They learned that they had fetched up in Solihull. Great grandfather found work and good beer in the pubs so they settled down and lived fairly happily ever after.

The reason why it was only a fairly happy life was because my great grandfather, an ex seaman, liked his beer and the rough and violent sports, that were popular at that time. After a bout of drinking he would be involved in shin kicking, bare knuckle boxing and any other activity which tested his strength and pugnacity. The bloody bouts used to be held regularly on the spare ground at the bottom of Drury Lane by the cottages which stood there. He also used to spend long hours in the various pubs in the village and it was a common sight when my great grandmother, a small, slight lady, would breach the men only retreat of either the Maltshovel, Masons or Gardeners Arms snugs, to remove her unwilling husband who would be scolded for his insobriety and lack of thought for his family. Needless to say, after a few days he could be found once again in his favourite haunts, boasting of his exploits as a press ganged seaman in his youth.

The establishment of good road and rail networks around the ever expanding manufacturing centre encouraged developers to move in and build whole new towns and villages on the outskirts of Birmingham. In Warwickshire, the stage coach roads to Warwick, Stratford and Coventry together with the newly laid railway tracks provided excellent access and so extensive building began. The old roads were repaired and updated and that great man, Isambard Kingdom Brunel built the Great Western Railway between London and Birmingham. The establishment of stations at Solihull, Olton and Lapworth ensured that those villages grew very quickly indeed.

The families who came to live in the new houses required staff to look after them, maids, cooks, gardeners, coachmen, grooms and later, chauffeurs. The local councils also required many more workers to provide the essential services which the new arrivals now demanded. To fill those jobs and posts, men who had no skills as engineers filled the more strenuous ones and their womenfolk filled the remainder.

My maternal grandmother moved from her home in Allbrighton, near Wolverhampton, to Moseley to find work as a cook. She brought her daughter, Elsie with her. She quickly moved to Solihull to take up a similar position. My knowledge of Emma and Elsie Morris's early life are unknown because of my mother's early death at the age of 30 when I was but a boy of ten tender years.

George Beavans' move to the Midlands did not improve his prospects, he settled for his previous job of wagoner on one of the farms in Elmdon Heath. His future now secure, he met and married my grandmother and they set up house in a cottage near to Yew Tree Farm which stood at the bottom of Yew Tree Lane where the dairy now operates. Their children were born there. William, Alice, George, Harry and finally, my father, Joe. At the turn of the century George must have changed his job and went to work for Charlie Lea at Foredrove Farm. As a result, the family also moved into 4 Walnut Tree Cottages. My grandparents continued to live there until their deaths in the mid 1930's.

My Forebears. Back row from left — Harry, Emma, "Pem", Alice, William and George. Centre row — George and Jane Beavan. Front row — Joe Beavan, the authors father.

My mothers presence in Solihull meant that my father met her at some juncture, they became attracted to each other, and after several years of courting and with the added impetus of World War I. they were married in 1916. After the war I was born in 1920. I recall a very close relationship between my mother and my grandmother, and one in which I also found deep pleasure. Because Emma was in service, her free time was limited to one afternoon each week which she spent with us in the cottage in Lugtrout Lane. I see her still, all in black, walking briskly towards me, a warm smile on her face. She always brought me a titbit, something which she had cooked, usually a chocolate eclair. After a hug and kiss she would produce the goody from the large black fur muff she always wore.

Toward the end of her life she came to live with us. In failing health, and despite all the care my mother lavished on her, she was eventually admitted into Meriden Cottage Hospital where she died and was subsequently buried in Hampton-in-Arden churchyard. The year was 1924.

It was after a visit to see her that I learnt my first lesson in road safety. To visit her we caught an open-decked, solid tyred bus at the junction of Yew Tree Lane and Hampton Lane. It took us to Meriden via Hampton. On arrival in Meriden we disembarked and walked across the Green, past the obelisk which marks the centre of England to the hospital. It once stood at the junction of the Coventry Road and The Meriden Mile, it is now a row of cottages. On our return from what had been a depressing visit I leapt off the bus and dashed across the road in front of it. Fortunately in those days there was little traffic on the roads and so I was lucky. When mother alighted, she grabbed me by the arm, shook and severely admonished me for being so foolish to run out without looking first to see if the road was clear. It was a lesson well learned.

# Chapter 2

# My Parents

My parents were married in 1916 soon after my father had joined the army. Shortly afterwards he found himself on board a troop ship bound for foreign climes, but meanwhile my mother found that she was going to bear their first child. Whether it was the trauma of my father's departure so soon after the wedding, or for some other reason, she lost their first born. In 1919 father returned from the war, was demobilised and resumed his peacetime activities. While he was away, mother had acquired a small cottage in Lugtrout Lane which was to be their home for some time. In 1920 they were blessed with their second child.

My father was a chap of average build, five foot ten inches tall and reasonably well built. He possessed a pleasant disposition, but a little Victorian in some of his attitudes. He could be very outspoken if provoked, but was a very good husband and father. He did not seek friendships and was not particularly close to other members of his family. The exception to that was his devotion to his mother. When one got to know her it was easy to understand why he felt so close to her. I would later fall under her spell.

My mother was an excellent match for him, they made a very happy couple. She was a tall person for a woman of that era when the stature of most working people was only of an average height of five foot six inches. She was at least five foot nine inches. Very good looking, she carried herself well and enjoyed a feature of high fashion of that time, a truly fabulous head of hair. It was jet black, luxuriant with a high sheen and maintained by constant attention to it. My earliest memories of her are each morning as she stood in the bedroom window brushing and combing it, from the top of her head down to her waist in long, sensuous movements. I was born at one o'clock on the 7th. November 1920, upstairs in the small bedroom of the cottage. Both father and mother took great pleasure in later years teasing me about the timing of my arrival into the world. They were wont to inform me that, "we were worried that because of the delay, our Sunday dinner would be spoiled"! My arrival formed a close and loving family giving each of us much pleasure.

Our home was our world and everything in my parent's power was done to make it comfortable and happy. They did not possess many material things, though the small house was well furnished. On his return to civilian life, Dad returned to his job as a gardener at Elmdon Hall. My mother was now a wife and mother and her place was in the home as the Victorian order decreed. It was not considered

My parents, Joe and Elsie Beavan, a wedding photograph, c1916.

chauvinist by any one, as it was traditional. The woman of the house dedicated all her time and energies to the home. The acceptance of that way of life was held in the knowledge that she enjoyed the love and devotion of the man who would provide for the family.

My father's commitment to that ideal was total. To ensure that his plans for the family was attained he devoted a great deal of his time to earning sufficient money to achieve that goal. He quickly realised that the old order and pre-war life of near feudalism was fast becoming unsupportable. Death duties and other financial problems resulted in Elmdon Estate being sold and the loss of my father's job. He found a job at Packington Hall but left soon afterwards when he could see that there

The author at 3 years.

were better opportunities in other work. He sought a more secure future and better pay. That was not particularly easy as many other men in similar situations were also now being thrown onto the job market.

The heavy losses of men during the war included many of the sons and husbands of the landowners who pre-war had provided many of the jobs in the shires and also those in the industrial workforce. The losses resulted in large and catastrophic death duties payable by those same landowners' estates. In many cases it proved an impossible task, the only solution was to sell the estate. An action which wreaked devastation on the landed gentry and their loyal workers who found themselves out of work and out of their tied cottages, and without the necessary skills needed in the new mechanised world.

With the outbreak of hostilities in 1914 my father tried to join up with his colleagues but was rejected because he was found to have broken his left instep, the consequence of which, had made him flat footed and therefore, medically unfit for active service. Dejected, he returned to his job but continued to pay frequent calls to the recruitment office in the hope that he would be accepted. During the Great War, if a young, apparently healthy man was seen in the village not in uniform, he was instantly identified as a conscientious objector. To show displeasure toward such men, a white feather was placed in their buttonhole. The fact that many men like my father, and others, had been medically discharged from the Services because of wounds they had suffered, mattered not. Fortunately in World War II the practice was not common, thank goodness.

The war wore on, losses escalated and the need for many more men as replacements resulted in men with medical conditions and previously rejected, were now accepted. They were allocated to an Army Corps or services where their condition did not prevent them from playing a full part in waging the war. My father was trained and posted to the Army Service Corps, it was later to receive royal recognition and became the Royal Army Service Corp, (R. A. S. C. ). The training, despite an urgent need to fill the gaps in the front line, was very comprehensive and thorough. He successfully completed the course of motor mechanic and was posted to a unit in London which supplied drivers and mechanics to Staff Officers. He often told me how he enjoyed that period of his service. His main duties were to drive the officers all over the country in a range of large staff cars, many the best that the British motor industry could produce. Rolls Royces, Daimlers, and a particular favourite was one which some of his mates considered to be a forbidding monster, a Vauxhall 14/90 tourer. A drop-down hood, chain drive and a very powerful engine that required careful nursing when being driven in a town environment. He often described to me the difficulties he faced when driving it through London. "When we drove through the city I had to keep it in second gear otherwise it would have become uncontrollable. If I tried to change up into third gear I couldn't keep the speed down. I was stopped several times by the police when I did try to use a higher gear". His other favourite was a Daimler Straight 8. Its name gives a clue to what was under the bonnet. A huge eight cylinder engine, the cylinders in line and fitted with sleeve valves. At that time most cars were built to obtain maximum power from fairly primitive designs. Daimler introduced sleeve valves to provide high performance with emphasis on silenct and smooth running when under power. The result was very impressive indeed. To illustrate what he was trying to convey father told me that he often demonstrated the smoothness of the engine by standing a pencil on end on the top of a quietly running engine; invariably it remained rock steady and did not fall off! That was in 1916! The proven excellence of the design was recognised by Royalty and the aristocracy.

After a short while he was posted to the Middle East where he initially joined an

# MY PARENTS

My fathers army unit in Palastine, c1916.

A Douglas motor cycle similar to that used by World War I Dispatch Riders.

anti-aircraft unit. He soon left it to join a pool of drivers for staff officers as he had done in England. In those duties he found himself driving General Allenby, including that man's triumphant entry into Jerusalem when it fell to British forces. He remained with the General and took him to Damascus and was there when the war ended.

One of the General's staff officers, also a General, whose name was Stanley, tried to persuade my father to go with him to Australia at the end of the war to establish a sheep farm there. Although he was sorely tempted, my mother said, "No", and so he had to refuse the offer. I later learnt that when I was christened Stanley Joseph in the small church in Catherine de Barnes, my first name came from my father's erstwhile commanding officer and of course the second from his own. I am happy to enjoy two illustrative christian names.

My father's training in mechanical engineering and the internal combustion engine gave him a head start in the search for new work. The development of housing estates and commercial properties in the Solihull area required men with the right qualifications to drive the vehicles needed to deliver the materials to the sites. Men were also required with the right skills to install the new sources of energies in those new properties. The most common of these new energies, gas, and the means of producing it, was easily achieved with a minimum of skill. However the installation of it safely into a house required a high degree of skill or aptitude, both of which my father possessed in good measure. He applied for a job with Solihull Gas Company and initially was given a job in the works as a stoker. He quickly moved up to the laying of the gas mains throughout the district and then became a fitter before completing his career with the company as a meter inspector.

# Chapter 3
# Our First Home

During my father's absence in the army, my mother acquired a small cottage in Lugtrout Lane. It was to become a very cosy and welcoming home for her family. There are many occasions which I recall with delight, distress, fondness and sadness. The earliest recollection I have is that of my father entering the living room one Sunday morning in his army uniform. I judge that I was about two and half years old at the time. It transpired that he had been attending a Remembrance Day service at the memorial in Solihull on Armistice Day in that year. For some reason it was not the unusual clothes that he wore but the rifle which he carefully stood in a corner of the room. That was the only time I saw him in uniform.

Built in the 18th. century by a farmer for his men, the cottage stood, as it still does today, in its own grounds behind tall hedges. Since those days it has acquired a garage and a coat of white paint and no doubt internal renovation. There was not a great deal of room inside. Two small rooms downstairs and one bedroom and the top of the stairs as another was just enough for father, mother and I. How the large Victorian families coped in such restricted accommodation I have no idea.

The main room was entered by the front door which opened straight onto the lane, another led into a smaller room at the bottom of the stairs. There was a brewhouse, "brewhus", beyond where all the washing, butchering and wine making was carried on near to the copper which stood in a corner. A well by the back door provided all the water and a dirt privy at the bottom of the garden completed the downstairs offices. Upstairs, a bedroom of modest size which was the main one, another which formed the top of the stairs was the children's room. The stairs were narrow and wound round in a tight bend, very difficult to negotiate when not in good health for anyone of advanced years.

In the main bedroom I was conceived, born and nursed through a broken arm. My mother recuperated from scarlet fever in it and my father endured several debilitating bouts of malaria in it. When my maternal grandmother came to visit, and finally when she became ill, I was taken into my parents room while she used the small room.

Downstairs, the living room was a place of constant surprise and delight for a young child. My mother's exceptional standards in the culinary arts were put to good use on the large, scrubbed white table top. She often referred to a recipe book which she constantly updated when new ones came to her notice. Below I copy an example which was used to good effect when feeding hungry men from the threshing yard or on a shooting day.

"Two penny dinners, the following proportions serve for 120 dinners (pints) of Irish Stew".

|  | s. | d. |
|---|---|---|
| "Three 6 lbs tins of Australian Mutton" | 10 | 0 |
| "Six pecks of Potatoes" | 6 | 0 |
| "Six packets of Pea Flower" | 1 | 0 |
| "Three pennyworth of Flower" |  | 3 |
| "Three lbs of Rice" | 1 | 0 |
| "Carrots, Turnips & Celery Tops" | 1 | 0 |
| "Pepper and Salt" |  | 3 |
|  | £1 0 | 0 |

"The above I know will stick to a fellows ribs."

There are many more of these old, easy and appetising meals in her book which I often refer to when I try to emulate her at the stove!

It was at Christmas when the small living room came into its own. The festive season was yet to become commercialised as it is now. Food, drink, presents, (in moderation) and celebrations were very important but were not allowed to obscure the true purpose of, "the Day". The church played an all embracing part in the festive season.

At least six weeks before Christmas my mother stocked up her larder with all ingredients required to make the many special meals to celebrate the occasion. Each Saturday evening she took father and I to Solihull to buy them. The shops stayed open in the late evening and it was magical to walk along the Warwick Road, The Parade, (now Poplar Road), and the High Street. The cold, crisp air caused our breath to make smoky grey patterns in the pools of flickering yellow light beneath the gas lamps. The shops which my mother was most interested in were of course the grocers, Wrensons, Longs, Conibears. That was all very well for her, but a young lad needed some excitement too. I was impatient to look at all the enticing toys in Miss Deebanks window and also in Peggs where the new bikes, air guns and the like stood waiting to fill someone's stocking. On the way down the High Street father always made a point of going into Fosters while mother went into Waldens to see if she could find a nice piece of cloth or material. Jasper Halls, the chemist, could be relied upon for gifts of soap and toilet goods, strangely he didn't have a display of large glass containers filled with red, green and blue liquid as did his competitor Winfield the chemists on the corner of the High Street and Poplar Road. It was there that sometimes we went our separate ways again, she to Bancrofts for the odd thing that she had not obtained at Waldens, while we made our way along to

Twiggs, the bookshop in the row of shops on the Parade. A day or two before Christmas Day we would make a bee line to Ravens, the butchers, to select a piece of beef to have as a relief from poultry. Both Tustins and Ravens had silver iron bars running along the top of their windows on which were hung turkeys of all sizes, their heads many tied in paper bags with black feathers protruding from them. Those were the old breed which could be seen strutting around any farm yard, but especially Billy Markhams. They were more tasty, though with a drier flesh, than the more bland birds sold today. I often wonder why so many birds could be hung outside, in all weathers, without us falling foul of all the diseases which seem to be so prevalent today, despite our supposedly higher standards of living and more hygienic environment!

When I grew older we used to go to Birmingham to look at the bigger shops and the wider choice of goods. We walked to the Barley Mow, and stepped on the open topped Midland Red bus for town. A rough ride on solid tyres and many cobbled streets before we heard the driver revving his engine and crashing his gears as he climbed the highly polished cobbles alongside St. Martins Church.

As we dismounted, the shouting coster-mongers attracted our attention to their colourful barrows heavily laden with fruit, vegetables, toys and various knickknacks, all with a tantalising vision of what could be found at the bottom of a stocking hung from the bottom of the bed. Dad always ushered us past them as he suspected that they were, " fools gold", so it was into the Market Hall and the crush of many other families shopping for the special occasion. After several hours in the throes of the milling, excited crowds in Lewis's, Greys, and the 3d and 6d store of Woolworths, we made our way back down the Bull Ring, the stall holders still vociferously pleading with the passers by to come and look at what they had to offer. The black canopy of night was now lit by a conglomeration of lights, mostly the paraffin goose necks fixed to the top of the many stalls as they clung to their respective spots along the pavement from the Market Hall down the hill as far as The Flea Market. Now clutching our bulging parcels we climbed onto the bus back to Solihull and after a short walk, the quiet and peace of Elmdon Heath.

In the warm, cosy living room of the cottage we once again began to live the relaxed form of life so natural then. With the hectic and expensive expeditions behind us mother began in earnest to prepare for Christmas. I always helped her in the preparation of the various ingredients for the cake and puddings. Chopping peel, splitting almonds, making sweets with the strong homemade marzipan. After covering the cake with it she then made sweets for us all, potatoes, strawberries, apples, pears and grapes. Each of them in their correct colours with the addition of some cocoa in which the potatoes were rolled to make them look as if soil was still adhering to them. She always made many more than we could reasonably eat so that I would have some to use as currency as an entry fee to Joe Culls magic lantern show in his grandfathers barn which was just across the lane from the cottage.

On Christmas Day the small living room was a wonderland. Paper decorations hanging from the low ceiling, a tree, specially dug up by Dad from a secret place. Small candles in their holders which flickered in the firelight, sugar pigs and mice chasing each other round the bottom of it. In the evening the decorations twisted and swayed in the heat from the oil lamp standing on the table and from the fire in the shining black grate.

The morning passed so quickly as I played with my presents and all too soon it was time to sit down to the feast of the year. Cockerel, goose or pheasant, all the vegetables and Christmas pudding, each one of us eagerly searching for a "joey" in the piece set before us. The joey was the small silver three'penny bit which was still in use.

Tea that day was tinned salmon, trifle, jelly and blancmange, this homemade, and the large iced cake from which I frequently stole the silver balls. During the evening, I played with my new toys while my parents sat each side of the fire and recalled days that had gone. Despite the large meals which we had enjoyed up to that time, there were still opportunities to partake of the sweets, petit-fours and nuts. I also looked forward to one of the sugar mice from beneath the tree, now lit with the candles. That was also when father and mother would make a toast to the future in home-made wine, beetroot, elderberry or perhaps the potent parsnip. For me it was home made lemonade or ginger beer.

The small Dames school which served the children of the Elmdon Estate was put to good use at that time of the year. In the main room a party was held for the children. I remember so well my first party in it. My mother and I walked from our home up Damson Lane, across The Church Field, through the Park and past the Terrace to the entrance to the school. Greeted by one of the party givers, we were ushered in, divested of our heavy outer garments and led into the main class room. A large fire blazed in the hearth adding to the light provided by several large oil lamps and many garlands that the children who attended the school had made. The parents and teachers hurried about replenishing what must have seemed a famished army of youngsters, more cakes, tarts, jellies and, "Can I have some more of that pop please"! Eventually we were all satisfied and the table and chairs were cleared away for the games to begin. Someone played the piano so that we could play musical chairs, several large enamelled water filled bowls were set on chairs into which were put apples for an apple dunking contest. All too soon there were calls for we children to collect our clothes from the cloak-room ready to go home. Just as mother and I were leaving, a party organizer stopped us and told me that I had won a prize in the raffle. Turning to the rest of the party she announced that I had won a lovely, Blue Beveren rabbit, as the prize. That made my day.

Once outside we retraced our steps below the overhanging branches of the tall Wellingtonians in which the local pheasants were roosting. It was by the Fish Pool that the local poachers used to lure the birds before they perched, by spreading raisins, liberally laced with whisky, beneath the trees. Shortly after roosting they fell into the waiting bags of the poachers.

My father was waiting for us with a roaring fire when we got home, I could not contain myself to remove my coat and hat before I recounted what a grand time we had all had, but I had been the lucky one and had scooped the prize, a bunny. If I recall correctly his first words were, "that's good, it will come in for next Sunday's dinner!" He said that with a broad grin on his face. A few days later we collected the rabbit from one of the small cottages in Lode Lane that now stand almost opposite the Land Rover plant. A hutch was built and secured against the back wall of the scullery. I became very fond of the animal, so much so that on one freezing afternoon on our way home from a visit to Solihull I found a swede which had fallen from a cart at the junction of Wherrets Well Lane and Lugtrout Lane outside Cox's farm. Picking it up, with some difficulty as it was very heavy, I carried it back for the rabbit.

The small living room in the cottage provided a bright and sunny retreat in the summer and a warm, cosy and very welcoming one in the dark days of winter. A focus of all the families' activities. My mother frequently sang to me as we sat near the fire, one particular song I was very fond of and it brings back very tender memories to me. I cannot remember all the words but here are those that I do remember.

The song went something like this:

> "Sally go round the Sun
> Sally go round the Moon
> Sally go round the chimney pots
> On a Sunday afternoon."

Yet another one which she sang often was:

> "Let the Great big World keep Turning."

As she sang she slowly twined a wisp of my hair through her fingers as I sat near her feet beside the fire.

The loss of their first born meant that they took extra care with my health. I escaped many of the common complaints that were fatal then. Their care, however, did not extend to protection from my own folly or bravado. There were two such occasions. The first was when I ignored my father's advice not to try to use his fork when we were in the garden. The result, a tine through my big toe! Fortunately it did not seem to be too bad and after washing and dressing it I was none the worse. The second happened as I played with other children in the hay field opposite the cottage. The farmer was in the process of building a hay rick in the far corner of the field, it was about 4 feet high and made an excellent base as a castle for we boys to guard against all comers.

In the heat of the moment I missed my footing and fell awkwardly. Climbing to my feet I felt something in my eye but when I tried to wipe it with my left hand I found that the arm was much to painful. With streaming eyes and a very painful ache in my arm I hurried home across the field to the comfort that I knew would await me. My main concern was the irritation in my eye which I wished to alleviate as soon as possible but to my concern, my mother and grandmother were far more interested in my arm. At last my eye was dealt with and then mother explained to me that I had broken the arm. As it was a Sunday my visit to the doctors had to wait until the following morning.

In an attempt to ease the pain my mother collected a small bottle of olive oil from her bedroom and gently rubbed it into the broken limb. The oil was held in high regard as an healing agent as well as its qualities as a cosmetic and culinary aid. The following day I was taken to see Doctor, "John", Whitehouse in his surgery on the corner of Lode Lane and The Warwick Road. It would not be the only visit to that haven for the ailing.

He was held by many in such high esteem that as a small boy I thought I would be healed by a benevolent deity. On inspection he told my father that he had no need to break it again, a frequent requirement, but he would like me to have it X-rayed to make sure that everything was alright.

The following day we made our way to the General Hospital in Birmingham. The journey was quite different to those when we went shopping. It was, as always, a bumpy ride except I now felt each bump an a painful experience. We walked from the Bull Ring up Bull Street and down Steelhouse Lane to the Hospital. My condition made me notice the many poorly dressed, unwashed and unshaven men who lined the pavements, some with limbs missing, most wearing their war medals. They were all trying to make a little money by selling matches, boot laces and other small knick knacks from home made trays suspended from their bent shoulders. There were others who did not have the will to do more and sought relief from their despair by seeking solace in drink. Some were staggering around while others were so drunk, they lay half on and half off the pavements, others were shouting and cursing their luck and those who had sent them to war.

At the hospital we were led to a special room, all dark and claustrophobic. After my details had been given I was taken to another room which was even darker and had a large orange object hanging from the ceiling, the X-ray machine. The electro-medical sciences were in their infancy and the potential hazards were not fully understood. Safety procedures and precautions for both operator and patient were minimal. There was a bed in the centre of the room below the orange, bulbous device hanging from the ceiling. A nurse carefully removed my jacket and shirt and arranged the arm on a metal plate on the bed. The device was then brought down to within a few inches of my arm. A shade was taken from a small window in the end of the device. The nurse then told me to remain perfectly still as she disappeared behind a blue curtain. A slight pause, another request to remain perfectly still and then a whirring sound. The nurse reappeared and told me that I could go, she redressed me and took me back to father in the waiting room. We returned home and since that day I have experienced no problem with the arm.

Shortly after that episode we moved from Lugtrout Lane to a new house just over the hedge from my grandmother's garden in Damson Lane. That's another story.

## Chapter 4
# Lugtrout Lane c1920

The cottage in which we lived from 1920 to 1925 was one of several in Lugtrout Lane. An old route linking The Pound and its junction of several lanes to Catherine de Barnes. Near to its junction with Wherrets Well Lane and a small farm, a stream ran across it and shortly afterwards emptied into the canal. Near to it were a collection of Edwardian houses and three very old cottages forming a small hamlet. The hamlet did not have an identity, it was always considered to be part of Elmdon Heath. Our cottage was situated in the centre of the cluster of houses. Along the lane on the right another cottage standing end on was the home of the grandsire of Joe Cull, a pal of mine. He ran the local milk round from a few cows which he kept in a field opposite. Just beyond his cottage a narrow, sandy lane known as Tuckers Lane gave access to a gravel pit and farm before it joined the Hampton Lane opposite Ravenshaw Lane. Lugtrout Lane continued in parallel with the canal until it too joined Hampton Lane in Catherine de Barnes, known locally as Catney.

The lane was a typical country one, its purpose to serve the local farms and people living along it. Its surface was rutted by constant use by heavy wagons and deep water filled puddles in winter, during the hot summer months it became dry and dusty. In all seasons of the year there was the additional hazards of farm animals and their droppings as they were led between field to farm for milking or other needs.

The conditions of the highways were reflected in the clothes people wore. The long dresses so fashionable with the ladies, which dragged the floor, had a strip of calico sown along the bottom edge of them, it could easily be taken off for cleaning. A common item, worn in different styles, were tall, strong, well made boots. The men's were laced with leather laces, the women and young children's were buttoned some way up their legs. Known as high boots, they gave very good protection from the wet, muddy, and filthy conditions in which we lived. To secure the button boots, a special domestic tool was used, known as a button hook. They were found in every home, some a simple item, a hook at one end and a small handle at the other. There were others made from silver and enamel and which are now quite valuable,

The lane was frequently used by the ambulance from the Isolation Hospital situated in Henwood Lane at Catney. The first one that I recall was a horse drawn one, later it was replaced by one which was driven by a motor with a brown, wooden body. In later years I was able to give it close scrutiny. I found it to be a Ford, the rear wheels driven directly without a differential gear in the back axle. To start such a vehicle it was necessary to jack the rear wheels off the ground before the engine could be turned. The pedal arrangement was also quite different to that now used. Later, a modern Morris Commercial version was used.

No one was anxious to make use of these vehicles, nevertheless, they were in constant use. As it passed, most watched its slow passage as if mesmerized, all wishing its incumbent a happy return! The three fevers were very common, scarlet, diptheria and the dreaded typhoid. My mother had good reason to thank God for the provision of both ambulance and hospital when she caught scarlet fever. Happily she survived, others didn't.

Each week it was our custom to call on Gran to ensure that both she and my grandfather were still in good health. It was just a short stroll along Lugtrout Lane to Swinglers shop where we turned into Damson Lane, right over the iron bridge and up to their cottage. In the summer, the sun was high in the sky, the smell of new mown hay heavy in the air, large numbers of butterflies and moths fluttered around, and we could hear the song of many birds before they went to roost. In the winter months, a very different picture, especially the journey home. Pitch black in the absence of a moon. Stepping out from the comfort of her home was quite a shock, particularly if it had begun to freeze. I was always very pleased to see the moon's bluish white light throwing shadows of the tall walnut trees across the lane and providing a very good light for our journey back home. As we walked along my parents discussed the health and well-being of my grandparents. My grandfather had ceased to work for some time and their only income was the old age pension. Gran kept fowl, as almost every cottager did then. Before we left, she always offered my father a dozen eggs which he accepted and made sure that Gran also accepted payment for them. As we walked I frequently heard a whispered question by Mother, "How much did you give her for them Joe?" "I gave her two shillings, (ten pence), Lass. Swinglers would have been selling them for two and six pence, (twelve and a half pence)!" They would also discuss my grandfathers inconsiderate attitude toward my grandmother. He was not an easy man to either understand or to get along with and as a small boy I could sense that my father had little feeling for him. At last, Dad was opening the front door and there in the grate was the welcoming fire and warm room, a drink of cocoa and then, "Up the wooden hill to Bedfordshire"!

## Chapter 5

# The New House

August, 1925. our time in the cottage in Lugtrout Lane came to an end and we moved into a new house in Damson Lane which had been built on the other side of my grandmother's garden hedge. It made me very pleased, as it did my parents, to be so near her.

Down a short path from the lane and round to the back of the house, the first door opened into a lavatory complete with water flush. No more struggling through snow or wet grass in the dark with only a candle lantern to guide one to the dirt privy at the bottom of the garden. No more visions of odd-goblins' shadows dancing in the weak light as I sat trembling there. The next door was the back one which opened into the kitchen with its red tiled floor. Scrubbed every wash day, newspaper laid on it to protect it from dirty boots accompanied by plaudits to, "Keep off it. I have only just washed that"! A hurried retreat and several minutes passed before I would venture in to ask for something to eat. A fireplace with a black, shining grate and hob which shone after many applications of Zebo Black Lead and much elbow grease. Under a large window was the brown, glazed sink with brass water tap above. No more having to go out to pump water from the well on cold winter mornings before washing, Hurrah!

The great War had created many problems, not the least of which was the need to get the country back on its feet and its industry geared to civilian needs and the economy. To accomplish that, the government of the day considered that housing should take priority and introduced a Bill for that to be implemented.

Local councils were charged with the task of providing sufficient housing of a high standard to meet the demand. The effect of that was the emergence of the council house. Solihull played its part and in the early 1920's built four in Elmdon Heath, in the then Rural District Council. They were built by Braggs, whose yard occupied a place at the bottom of Churchill. In their day they were recognized as one of the best firms in the area.

Those first 4 houses were built in Damson Lane in a field near to the canal bridge and were all occupied at the same time. The first houses to be built in the lane for some considerable time they were given a new numbering system, the one nearest to the canal was number 1 and then 3, 5 and 7. A family from up north named Pickles with their two sons, Robert and Tom moved into number 1. The Churchill family went into 3 while number 5 was occupied by a Mr. William "Ginty" Street, his wife Alice and their two daughters, Trixy and Rosie and their son, Arthur and Spot the fox terrier. In number 7, the last of the four became Joe Beavans family home.

Members of the original Street family were now beginning to assemble in Elmdon Heath. In Walnut Tree Cottages lived my grandparents. My grandmother Jane was a Street before her marriage. Next door in Number 5, lived George Blizzard, wife Marion and son James. George was the son of Gran's sister who had acquired the name Blizzard in marriage. At Number 5, Damson Lane, Ginty Street was another of the family Street. So, my father, Ginty and George Blizzard were all related, as was Jim, his son, Ginty's children and me.

To add to those, another of the Street girls had married a Butler and lived in a cottage on the Common.

The families' associations were much deeper than at first appears obvious. My father, Ginty, and George were all employed by the Elmdon Hall estate. Dad and George as gardeners and Ginty as a bricklayer. Furthermore, Alice, Ginty's wife worked in the Hall as one of the staff. George's wife Marion's father was the Head Game keeper and Harry Beavan, my father's brother, was a gamekeeper under him. In one of the small cottages in the terrace in the park lived Lizzie Drinkwater, another of the Street sisters. She also worked for Squire Alston. The Beavans, Blizzards, Butlers and Streets were one of the founder families in Elmdon and its Heath.

I soon settled in my new home with its improved amenities and with my cousins so close to play with. The kitchen was the centre of all our activities. Although houses built to the standards of that period are now considered to be lacking in essential amenities, they were very comfortable and cheap to run. In the kitchen was the fire and its grate and hob. It was quite capable of providing all the heat necessary to heat the room, to do the cooking on and to supply constant hot water. Leading off it was a small bathroom, very innovative compared with conditions common in country cottages. In it was a full sized bath and by its side a gas boiler with a system whereby the hot water could be siphoned off straight into the bath! Next to the bath room was a pantry with a cold slab. How much easier to use than the modern cupboards which can only be used if one goes down on bended knee! The only other ground floor room was the front room, the Holy of Holies, in which one could only set foot on special occasions, funerals, baptisms and annual festive occasions. It was a very comfortable room, with a nice fireplace and sufficient room for furniture and people. Upstairs were three bedrooms, a large one in the front for the bread winner and his wife, a second one for the eldest child and a smaller one for the youngest in the family. The former two both enjoyed the use of a fire, the last did not. My bedroom was the second one at the back of the house with its outlook over the fields to Bills Moor wood and the country beyond. I believe that the scene from the window in that room provided the base for my lifelong penchant for all things wild and natural.

The scene that met my gaze from the window was of the canal bank as it sloped down into the field and hidden ditch where the moisture encouraged long grasses to grow even in the hottest of summers. On the bank we played as children in sight of our parents . We picked buttercups, holding them beneath our chins to see if we liked butter, we also picked, "Bacon and Eggs", or to be more scientific, Common Birds Foot Trefoil. With our parents we picked mushrooms in late summer and dug caves in the rabbit warren and sandpit which we had created from it.

A gate near the pig sties led from the cottages into the field in which Gran used to let her fowl run, truly free range. One was a very aggressive Rhode Island Red cockerel, a superb specimen who claimed the field as his domain and those who entered it, did so at their peril. As soon as he heard the latch on the gate lifted, his head rose and a beaded eye latched onto the unfortunate intruder. Even Gran carried a stick when she called them in at the end of the day. He ultimately signed his own death warrant and ended his days in the pot for Christmas. In the lower centre of the field stood a magnificent Turkish Oak and in the corner of another field was an English Oak in which I spent many happy hours just living a part of nature. That oak still stands at the junction of Walsgrave Drive and Draycote Close in Damsonwood.

Beyond the meadow at the back of our house were other fields and Bills Moor wood. In a corner of a field and the wood was an old barn in which barn owls nested each year. Along the edge of the field and wood, corncrakes nested and in the evening, as I lay in bed, I was serenaded by their very distinctive, raucous calls, "rack, rack, rack, rack". That continued all summer long and lulled both me and cousin Jim to sleep on many occasions. The nightingales also occupied the wood and added to the cacophony of bird song from it. It was frequently disturbed by a loud report from the keepers alarm gun as it fired to distract predators of the reared pheasants which were also to be found on the edge of the wood.

In the small back room I successfully overcame a number of common childish complaints and also at least one or two not so common. One morning in 1926 I felt ill and was put to bed and soon I became very yellow. Dr. Whitehouse called and diagnosed yellow jaundice which was suspected all along. Had it merely been that I would have recovered quickly but it developed into a serious case of hepatitis from which I was lucky to recover. I still recall the look of relief on my father's face when he saw me emerge from a night of delirium and very high temperature.

The next summer I was laid low with whooping cough, quickly followed by measles and then chicken pox. The latter was not a conventional attack and Dr. John Whitehouse had recourse to call in a second opinion as he suspected it to be smallpox. On close examination it was decided that it was the usual childrens complaint. Recuperating from that illness I went with my grandmother to collect firewood, a regular chore. On the way home across the meadow I attempted to climb a barbed wire fence only to rip a "V" tear in a finger on my left hand. She dressed it and scolded me at the same time for being so careless. I still carry the scar which served me well when asked if I had any distinguishing features.

Dr. Whitehouse made regular calls to see my father who suffered with bouts of malaria each year. We both found it necessary to visit him in his surgery for treatment for whitlows, a common enough complaint then but not often seen these days. I believe it to be a hazard for people who work on the land. Abscesses beneath the finger nail was the symptom, the cure could either be slow and reasonably comfortable, or swift and very painful. In my case the finger was dressed and eventually the nail became so loose that it could be pulled off quickly with just a sharp stab of pain. My father was not treated so gently, Dr. John warned him that, " This is going to hurt, Joe!", and with that he would pull off the nail immediately without it becoming loose from treatment. My father endured that twice and afterwards exclaimed, "That burnt a bit"!

Dr. John attended all the family for many years. He brought all of my aunts and uncles into the world, as he did my father and I. A typical country doctor who possessed great skill and a very good manner which immediately put one at ease. It was well known that he often refused to charge for his treatment if he knew that money was scarce. Always well dressed, morning coat, wing collar, striped trousers and white spats over highly polished shoes. In the early days he paid visits in a horse and trap. For some time my Uncle George served as his coachman. In the 1920's when I knew him first he had a Rover car and often took me to school if his visit coincided with me going to school. He continued in practice for many years. I last spoke to him in the early '50's by which time he must have been 90 years young.

## Chapter 6
# Damson Lane and The Pound

Elmdon and its Heath, an Anglo-Saxon name given to a settlement and recognized by "The Hill of The Elms" was first occupied about 800 A.D. The first task of those early settlers was to clear the land of trees so that it could be planted. It is thought likely the site selected was where Whar Hall Farm stood until its recent demolition; alas, the Georgian farmhouse and buildings have been replaced by a public house, community centre and numerous houses. Progress?

If one stands where the narrow lane leads to Elmdon church and allows one's imagination to wander, it is possible to envisage what confronted those settlers. At its highest point of what is a long ridge, the ground falls away on all sides except along its southern route toward Elmdon Heath where it terminates at The Pound. The ridge was very important to the early settlers because the land along it is heavy, red clay, difficult to work with their primitive tools. Also, without adequate drainage the crops would have rotted in the high water table. They were well aware of the problems and carefully chose the clearance site well so that the natural fall of the land assisted drainage and labour. The settlement was successful, went from strength to strength and became of sufficient importance for it to be recorded in the Doomsday Book. At that time "Roger holds of Turchil in Elmddune half a hide. The arable employs half a plough. Yet there are in the demesne 1 plough ans 5 acres of meadow and wood 1 furlong long and another broad. It was and is worth 5s"!

The successful use of the land increased the ridges importance and it became a well used route and subsequent highway up to the present day.

When we moved into our new home, the world in which we lived was one of well laid hedges, fields farmed with various crops and narrow lanes tended by lengthmen. These were employed by the council to tend the lanes and roads, to keep them swept and clean, grass verges trimmed and the whole pleasant to negotiate and walk along despite the pot-holes and ruts in the old surface.

The lanes and roads were not lit as they are today, only in the towns and villages and at most crossroads where they lit the wooden sign posts. In the winter months it was pitch black outside, the sole relief was the moon and stars as they shone through the scudding clouds. The days became longer and the clocks were put forward, the sun hung longer in the heavens and at dusk, fire-flies danced around us as we played or made our way home from a shopping trip. The smell of new mown hay assailed our noses and crickets chirruped in the banks of the lanes. The sheet lightening, rare now, provided considerable light, the whole sky suffused in a warm glow and the silhouettes of tall elms, oaks and walnut trees threw shadows across our paths. In their crowns, bats darted and flitted in their search for food. It all gave us so much pleasure then.

Despite the lack of light in the dark days of winter, we encountered few difficulties. The horse-drawn carts, cabs and early motors had oil lamps fitted on each side of the front merely to warn oncoming traffic rather than to provide illumination of the road ahead.

Damson Lane rose from The Pound up a short incline topped on the rise by an old cottage, home for the Cranmer family. Mr and Mrs, and their three sons. Tom, the father, was the chauffeur and gardener for the people who lived in Ivy Hall which used to stand in Beechnut Lane. He was a friend of my fathers' and made a fine sight as he rode to work on his tall cycle dressed in his uniform. He wore dark green livery, black, highly polished leggings, and a peaked cap, as he proudly rode up the lane. His cottage was old and protected from prying eyes by a thick hedge and a large outhouse. Robert, one of his sons, and I were about the same age and frequently walked to and from school together. Invariably his mother would be waiting as we arrived at their gate. Although reserved, she was a very nice person and not unlike my mother in appearance. The charming old cottage no longer stands guardian over The Common as it once did. Like Ivy Hall and many other valuable and aesthetic buildings, it was demolished and is now the site of two nondescript bungalows.

On the Common below the Cranmers cottage, a row of artisans cottages stood along the lane opposite a field and allotments. Built in the 19th century they possessed no significant features. My Uncle George and Aunt Lottie lived in the third one down with their son, Walter and daughter, Mary. Aunt Lottie kept a small shop for many years as a means of supporting her family as uncle George worked only occasionally. He was crippled with the "screws" a common name for arthritis or rheumatism. The family blamed his army service for his condition. He joined the Grenadier Guards in the latter end of the last century and saw service in South Africa in the Boer War as well as in France in the Great War. Two doors below them lived Harry Frosts' family. Harry sustained serious wounds during World War I and he suffered considerable pain from them. He was a postman, as was his eldest son, also named, Harry. Charles, who was about my age, was also a friend of both me and cousin Jim. A few doors below them, a passage gave access to the rear of the cottages. On one side lived my great aunt, Mrs. Butler and her family. On the other side of the passage lived Jack Cotton and his family. He was the blacksmith, his forge stood behind the last cottage in the row where the McVie family lived.

A field separated the last cottage and Lugtrout Lane. Between Lugtrout and the canal, a slaughterhouse stood back from the lane. In the summer months one

## DAMSON LANE AND THE POUND

quickly recognized the fact by the obnoxious smell that emanated from it.

Opposite the end of Lugtrout Lane stood Swinglers shop, it, and Aunt Lotties served the whole neighbourhood. A fairly large house, one half occupied by the shop, the other by living quarters for the family. It was a typical shop of the period, one could buy all one required from it. There was an "L" shaped counter behind which, Mrs. Swingler and her daughter provided a very good service. There were many items on display commonly used then — Sunlight Soap, Robin Starch, Reckitts Blue — all essential for the weekly Wash. Pears and Lux toilet soap also there to care for the body beautiful. To maintain the high standards in the home Zebo Black Lead polish was bought and applied once a week to the fire grate and fenders and fire irons so that they shone and glistened in the fire light.

Behind the counter, standing on wooden pallets were sacks of flour, sugar, both brown and white, cereals and pulses of many sorts. On the top of the counter stood the grand scales, shining brass pan and round platform on which the brass weights measured the correct weight of each loose item. Above hung sides of cured bacon, either smoked or plain, taken down and sliced by hand on the large, dangerous slicer. As a small boy I used to stand in awe as the bright blade sang as it sliced through meat and bone and the rashers fell, one by one, onto the strategically placed sheet of grease-proof paper. Ham was also served off the bone. Behind the servers were shelves standing from floor to ceiling in which were all sorts of foodstuffs, mostly the tinned variety. Strangely in those days, tinned salmon, pineapple, and cream were acceptable and much sort after as treats for Sunday tea; yet tinned vegetables were frowned upon, the thought being that a housewife worth her salt could provide all the families needs from her husbands garden.

All the fats were lined up in the corner of the short arm of the counter. There was local lard, Cheddar, Double Gloucester, and Leicestershire cheeses, butter all in large blocks from which the customers requirements were cut, weighed and wrapped in grease-proof paper. The sugar was taken from a sack with a small brass shovel and poured into a blue paper bag on the scales. When the correct weight was measured the bag was tied together with white sugar string. The bags were excellent for me to take my lunch in to school. As a young boy I experienced difficulty in pronouncing my, "S"s, in consequence, my friends pulled my leg when I told them that, "I had my wunch in a wugar bag"!

In the summer months ice cream was sold and my father made it in the early years, I often went with him knowing that it was in my interest to do so. The machine was taken from the shed and thoroughly cleaned. It comprised a wooden barrel about the size of a large bucket. Across the top was a metal support for handle, gears and paddle and these were removed to give access to a smaller, metal barrel. To make the much sought after treat, ice delivered that morning from the ice factory in Digbeth was poured into the wooden barrel. The metal one was then pressed down into the ice and filled with the essential ingredients. Real cream, an egg or two, and a tablespoonful of glycerine which ensured that it remained frozen but soft. The support with gears and handle was fitted on the top and all was ready. Father always started the process by slowly turning the handle, easy at first when the contents of the small barrel were still in liquid form, as the process developed it became more difficult to turn. I always found it stiff to turn but enjoyed taking part. After about half an hour the top was removed and the product inspected. If it was just right it was taken out of the machine and put into an ice box in the cool room at the back of the shop. Mrs. Swingler would ask Father if he thought I had done my bit and with a smile put the question, "Have you paid your helper, Joe"? He always replied in the negative so she would scold him and taking a wafer tub from a shelf, filled it to overflowing and offered it to me saying, "Here lad, take this for your morning's work and I hope to see you next week". I did not need any encouragement to put in an appearance. In some shops the ice cream was made with ice cream powder and the finished product had a very yellow colour. Most of us didn't like it, but I suppose some must have, it was certainly no cheaper than the true cream variety.

Swinglers sold their ice-cream in tubs, (similar to the top of a cornet), at just one or two pennies each. Excellent, value for children with little pocket money. There were also cornets, wafers (very common) and if like our family, basins. The cornets and wafers were priced at two pence and four pence each and the pint basin which I was frequently sent to fetch for Sunday tea, six pence.

Beyond the shop and their garden was the original iron bridge over the canal. It was made from large iron girders, those providing the top rail were at least foot wide and provided adequate seating for all the children in the lane, the only problem was the large rivet heads which could make it uncomfortable after a little while. At each end were large red signs. These were made from lengths of rail which provided the supports on top of which were triangular iron signs displaying the penalties that would be imposed if the weight restrictions on the bridge were exceeded. I believe the figures were five and ten tons. In later years I often wondered how the heavy traction engines and steam rollers managed to avoid the limitations!

At the end of the bridge on its right hand side, a path led off along the top of the canal bank to three cottages where the Peaches, Smiths and Cricks lived. Beyond, the path continued across the fields along the bank until it emerged at Catney. The path was known as, "The Gossies", as several large patches of Gorse grew near it, especially near to the bathing hole in the canal.

Above the bridge the pot-holed, rutted lane meandered below a tall, thick canopy of beech, elm and oak to the Coventry Road at Elmdon. Until 1924, a field and pit was all that stood between the bridge and Walnut Tree Cottages; after that date four council houses were built in the field, the first houses to be built in the lane for many decades.

On each side of the lane were deep, wide ditches surmounted by well laid hedges

# DAMSON LANE AND THE POUND

The Grand Union Canal looking toward Catherine de Barnes
from The Iron Bridge in Damson Lane.

protecting fields with names like, "The Hill Field, The Water Meadow, Ten Acre", and many more, farmed by Les Nock and Billy Markham and the chap who lived in Dunstans Farm at the top of the lane. Les Nock and his family lived in Foredrove Farm where I spent many happy hours following the plough, mower, drill or binder with George Peachy perched up on the iron seat driving a pair of Shires. On the other side of the lane from the farm were four spinneys which had been established in the last century as coverts for game birds reared on the Elmdon state. The first one began just beyond what is now Coppice Road and each of the others were separated by five barbed gates into fields. These are now the entrances

*The pit in "Chubby". Once part of the much larger Hampton Copse.*

to Inchford, Dalescote and Oakslade roads. The uneven and twisting footpath along that stretch of Damson Lane began as a track which we children made 60 years ago as we played through the spinneys. A track which led from the gate where Oakslade Drive is now was once the approach to a brick works which ceased production in the mid-19th, century. The two large pits which can still be seen on each side of the wood we knew as "Chubby", were the source of material for the bricks. The wood with dense ground cover of rhododendrons and an adjunct to Hampton Copse, was also an important part of the Estate and its game rearing activities.

Beyond Foredrove farm, but on the opposite side of the lane, stood the imposing Georgian farm house known as Whar Hall Farm. Billy Markham and his family farmed it in the period of which I write as did his father before him. A startling drift of snowdrops beneath a large damson tree grew between the house and the lane. On the opposite side of the lane was a clap gate giving access to a path across the Church Field and to another clap gate onto the church drive. Sweet chestnuts and mushrooms were there to be picked at the right time of the year as we walked to church.

In a paddock adjoining the farm Billy kept flocks of fowl, turkeys and guinea-fowl, the two latter provided excellent attentive and raucous guards for the farm. Quite a few of the birds laid away — in other words, they laid their eggs under bushes and trees and hedges around the paddock. A tall holly tree on the bank between the lane and the paddock, was the favourite place for a turkey, she laid her eggs in that spot for several years in succession. The fact did not go unnoticed by we lads. It was from that nest that I took my turkeys egg for my egg collection. A sandpit beneath the tree was also the communal dust bath for all the birds in the paddock. Where the farm stood now stands a "modern", pub, and where we walked across the church field Land Rover now use the area as a test track.

A large traffic island and double carriageway now spills fumes and noise where new mown hay and the clink of horses hooves were the only distractions to the peace and quiet in Elmdon. The original lane still provides access to Dunstan Farm and a one way access onto the Coventry Road. Fred Pratley, a school friend and pal for many years of my father, lived in one of the small cottages on the corner of the lane at that point.

At its southern end the lane, together with several others, formed a junction known as The Pound. It was originally an enclosure in which straying animals could be confined until claimed by their owners. It became simply a small triangular grass island at the junction of four roads and the site of a wooden sign post.

Early in 1927 Elmdon Heath again resounded to many sounds of frenetic activity. The last time was when William Jessop employed hundreds of Irish navvies to cut a canal from London to Birmingham in the late 18th century. The sounds of horses iron shod hooves and bright, shining martingales mingled with the sounds of the picks and shovels wielded by shouting and swearing navvies subscribing to the cacophony that witnessed the final ravaging of our once peaceful corner of England.

Opposite the four houses, one of which we lived in, four more were built to the same specification. A little later we awoke one morning to find a steam roller standing by the iron bridge, hissing and chuffing, impatient to begin to rip the lane apart. First the hedge along the lane opposite the artisans cottages was ripped out and a road, to become Alston Road, was cut across The Common. Houses were then built along it and from its entrance up over The Common almost to the Pound.

To operate one of those large, hot, steaming and sometimes, dirty monsters, the men who drove them lavished a great deal of care and attention on them. They were in constant need of coal and water and their working parts needed to be oiled regularly if they were not to come to a grinding halt. The driver went round pouring oil into the brass oil reservoirs and cleaned the engine down with oily rag as he did so. The brass and copper work shone from much attention, the only dirty parts were the chimneys and road wheels. Each morning, before work began, the fire had to be rekindled. It was raked clear of clinker and ash and fresh coals fed onto it for it to leap into new life ready to maintain the steam pressure required to drive the engine all day. Once started, as the engine was driven along it produced many odours that people of my generation will recall with immense nostalgia. The evocative smell of steam mixed with hot oil and tar, tobacco from clay pipes and twist spat from hard chewing mouths as the men were urged to work harder. Sweat from horses straining to pull heavy loads. Bran and corn in their nose bags and dust as it billowed from their hooves. The new roads were cut across virgin land or older lanes were made wider to accommodate the ever increasing numbers of vehicles now replacing the farm, council and tradesmens carts and vans.

The development of Elmdon Heath required a more efficient care of the environment and the disposal of rubbish and other noxious detritus produced by the rapidly expanding population. The four council houses in which we lived were provided with outside water closets which emptied into individual cesspools. Until that time all the cottages and farm houses in the lane had dealt with their own, "night soil", — a time honoured procedure by taking the ash from the fire place each morning and throwing it onto the contents in the dirt closet through the flap at the back. The slops collected from the bed chamber pots were treated in the same way. At the end of the week, the dung-hill was cleared out and its contents distributed over the garden. It was very efficacious in maintaining the productivity of the land, albeit, unpleasant.

A motorised tanker emptied the cesspools each Monday morning. The engine of the tanker drove a pump and the contents were collected and when full was driven away to dispose of its load. At that time, the council introduced a method of collecting the night soil, from the old cottages. A cylindrical tank, complete with lid, mounted on a horse drawn cart and hauled by a Welsh cob, also arrived each Monday morning. A little man named Joe, who was both deaf and dumb, collected the large galvanised buckets which had now been provided and emptied them, one at a time, into the waiting tank by the gate. His route to the tank took him past the back doors of the cottages but, he never closed the lid, no doubt because it was too much trouble. It is not difficult to imagine the apprehension of our families as each Monday morning dawned. A short figure staggering beneath an open, swilling, obnoxious bucket, a broad grin as he carried out his unpleasant task. Much to the relief of everyone who lived in Damson Lane in the early '30's, a sewer was laid and all the houses and cottages were connected to it. Whew, what a relief!

About that time the greater part of the top gardens of the cottages were taken, fenced off, and houses were built in the field above them. At the same time, water, gas, electricity and telephone services were laid and the lane was widened and its surface improved and the new tarmac surface replaced the puddles which had provided we children with the excuse to get our feet wet. My father installed gas in my grandmothers cottage and also arranged for water to be laid into it. That brought to an abrupt end the need to fetch water from the pump, fill the oil lamps each week and to clean the glass chimneys and shades on them more frequently, at least twice a week. Mantles still had to be replaced when they broke and the flame, either from oil or gas, escaped and blackened the chimneys or shades.

# DAMSON LANE AND THE POUND 35

I recall quite vividly when the water pipe was laid into my grandmothers cottage, a trench was cut across the small garden plot in front of it. Looking into the trench one morning I was very surprised to see a row of very large sandstone blocks in the bottom, they were obviously very old and had been the base support for a very substantial building. I asked my father if he knew what they were but he declared ignorance of them. My belief that the cottages were of a considerable age were confirmed for me with that find.

The metamorphosis of our quiet and peaceful corner of England had really begun. As well as the development of the Pound and Alston Road, more houses and shops were built in the lane and near to it. A row of shops were built opposite the end of Alston Road, an outdoor, a greengrocers, a butchers, a grocers and a "snob", a cobblers. The cobbler was a Mr. Harding who had previously occupied a workshop at the top of an old wooden staircase that ran up the outside of a wall of the "Spike", a nickname for the Union or Workhouse which stood in Union Road. His coming removed the need for men like my father to carry out their own boot repairs. This was a regular operation, usually on a winter evening. He would take a boot last, a three legged, iron device, and at the end of each leg, a foot-shaped mould on which the shoe or boot to be repaired, was placed. Father bought pieces of leather, nails, tacks, tips and tachen-end in preparation for the job. After soaking the leather overnight to make it soft and pliable and fitting the worn item on the last, he began the operation. Placing the piece of leather on the worn sole he cut it to the correct shape then nailed it in place. Sometimes he used the tachen-end, a strong twine which had been soaked in pitch and was therefore waterproof. He invariably used it to sew and repair my mother's more dainty shoes.

The shop on the end of the row near Lugtrout Lane was the Outdoor. Run by the Toppings, their son was a pal of mine and he often entertained us as we sat on the bridge in the warm, summer evenings. He could play the harmonica, he would not agree that it was a mouth-organ, it was a far superior instrument. He was also very good at mimicking a well liked performer of the time, Stanley Holloway. He used to recite monologues, "Sam, Pick up thy Musket", and "Albert on a visit to Blackpool Zoo", both of which were recited in a north country dialogue. As the Toppings came from the area it was not difficult for him to do so. That is not to disparage his excellent performances.

Yet another shop, together with several houses was built between Cranmers cottage and The Pound. The shop was a fish and chip shop. In the garden, Mr. Jackson, the owner, built a model of Solihull church and a small model garden. The church could be lit at night and inside he placed a small loudspeaker so that on Sunday evenings he could relay the evening service from his wireless in the shop. A very popular display.

The development of Elmdon Heath encouraged The Midland Red bus company to introduce a regular service between The Pound and Birmingham. I believe the first was numbered 133, then it became the 182 for many years. All the facilities of Solihull and Birmingham were now within easy reach.

# Chapter 7
# Walnut Tree Cottages

Up a short incline from the iron bridge stood three cottages behind a picket fence and tall walnut trees — hence their name — built end on, to the lane in the 17th century. Two of the occupants lived rent free as they were, "tied cottages". The first, in which my grandparents lived, number 4 was tied to Foredrove Farm and the last of the three, number 6, Frank Norwood and his families home, was tied to Whar Hall Farm. The centre one, number 5, was occupied by George Blizzard, his wife, Marion and their son, James. George did not work for one of the local farmers so did not enjoy the accommodation, rent free, as did the others. He worked for Brigadier Ludlow in Lovelace Avenue among other large houses in the area. My grandfather had worked as a wagoner on Foredrove Farm for Charlie Lea and then later, for Les Nock. When he became too old to do the job he could have been evicted, but that was not the way Les Nock or Billy Markham operated. If they were able to help their workers, they did so.

The three cottages were all essentially the same in the number of rooms in each, although their disposition was different. If I describe my grandparents in detail it will provide an accurate picture of the other two. It will also portray a farm labourers home of the late 19th and early 20th centuries.

The approach to the cottages was by a path which led along the back of them to the pigsties and dirt privies at its end. My grandparents cottage enjoyed the use of another path which led from the gate straight to its front door. There was a small triangular flower bed between the two paths and a long kitchen garden running down to the left. A trellis Porch gave shelter where one could shake the snow and rain from one's heavy coats and scrape the manure and mud from ones boots. In the early summer a large spiraea thrust its tall spikes of cream flower heads through the trellis. On the wall to the left a goldfinch, bullfinch or linnet, caught in the fields, sang and trilled in a wooden cage to the wild birds that visited the gardens.

A large iron ring hung from the latch on the front door. Lift and turn and one stepped into a warm, welcoming, sweet smelling living room. The perfume came from the bunches of lavender, sage, and other herbs which were hung to dry to be used frequently in the many receipts that the family enjoyed. In the winter, a roaring fire in the wide open inglenook imposed its welcoming presence, and even in the summer there was always a fire in the grate as it was the only source of heat. Just inside on the right, a door led down three stone steps into a cool, dark larder.

# DAMSON BY THE POUND

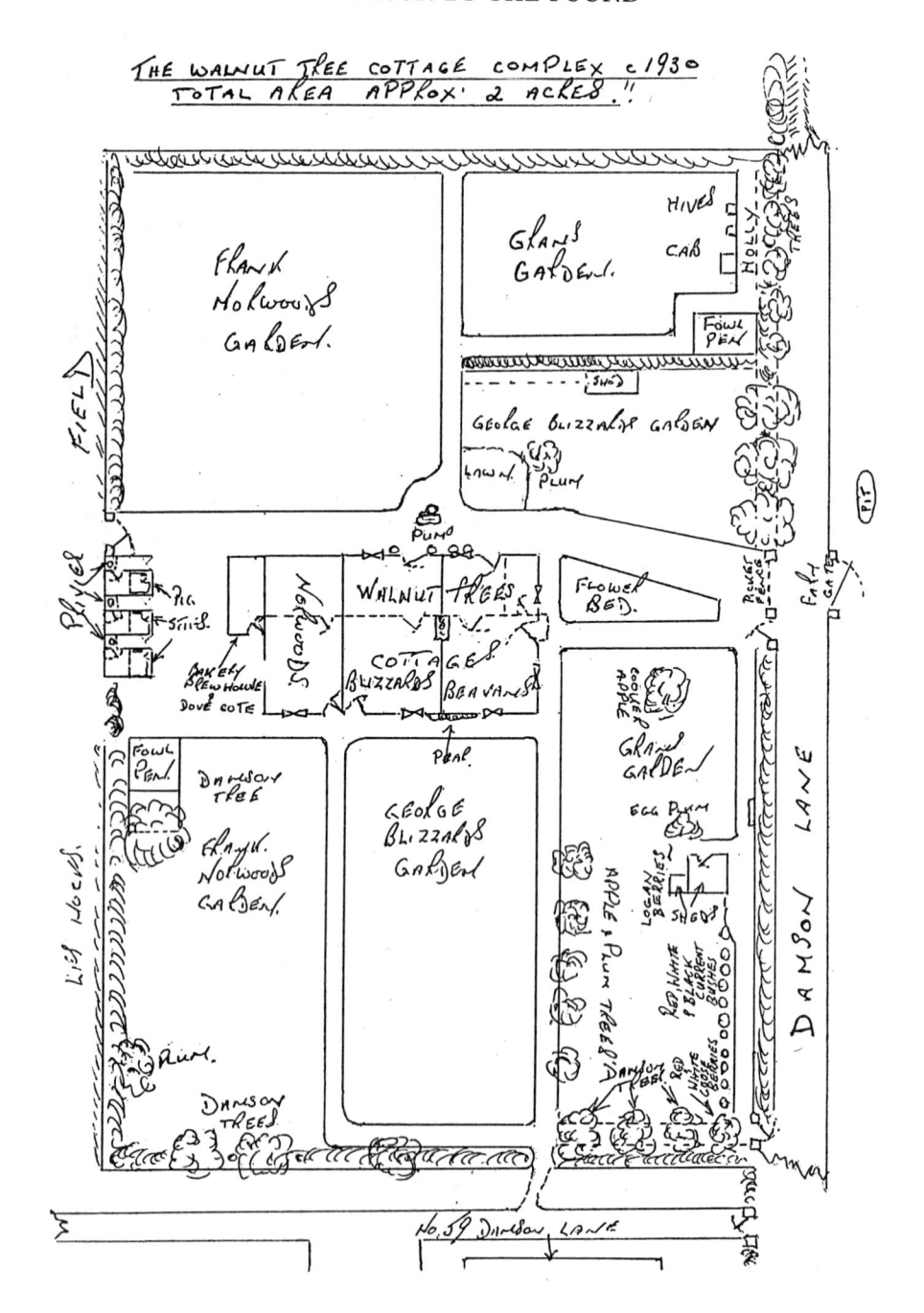

*The Walnut Tree Cottage Complex c.1930. Total area approx. 2 acres.*

# WALNUT TREE COTTAGES

Numbers 4, 5 and 6 Walnut Tree Cottages, c1925.

This was built into what had been the original north wall of the house to ensure a cool ambience throughout the year.

Here was perhaps the most important room in the cottage as far as a young, healthy, rapidly growing lad was concerned. A stone flagged floor with two long settles running the length of two walls and each standing a foot above the floor to aid the cooling process. In the space beneath, vegetables were stored after being dug out of the clamps outside. Above the settles were shelves loaded with cooked and raw food which required cool conditions. The front edge of the shelves had hooks from which hung rabbits, hares, and other pieces of meat; larger iron hooks in the ceiling were used for geese, turkey, pork and bacon and sometimes, venison. The latter came from uncle Harry when he was a keeper at Castle Ashby in Northamptonshire.

On the settles were an assortment of barrels, jowls, (large, brown, wide open-topped crock vessels), and jugs, some containing liquid refreshment. The wooden barrels from which large wooden taps protruded, wooden bungs, some with fine white muslin wrapped around them preventing a complete seal on top, protected home-made wine in varying stages of fermentation, or "working", as we preferred to call it. If one stood quietly, the gentle hiss and pop as gas escaped could be heard, a very satisfying and tempting sound which heralded future happy times.

The wines produced from the workings in the larder were from the fruit, flowers and vegetables in both garden and field. The wine was made throughout the year as various ingredients became available. In the Spring, dandelions and cowslip, then elderflower. As the summer ripened the fruit plum, damson and gooseberry were used. In the autumn, beetroot, elderberry, potato and parsnip, this last one was the most potent of them all and was treated with considerable reserve by those in the know. At the end of the year, after Jack Frost had fully ripened them, we picked Sloes from the hedge-rows to make Sloe Gin. Gin was very cheap unlike now.

The beet and damson were kept and invariably offered to callers in the winter months. Gran would mix it with a little warm water in a small barrel shaped wine glass. She considered that its potency was enhanced by so doing. She was

My grand-parents ouside number 4 Walnut Tree Cottage.

George and Marion Blizzard, Mrs Cook and My cousin Jim.

proved right on many occasions much to the embarrassment of the imbiber. Her parsnip was the frequent undoing of many unwary caller — it was a brave man who ignored the warnings that it had "a kick in it", and they were always advised not to go outside if they had drunk too much. I can remember several unfortunates hanging onto the trellis by the front door. Fortunately in those days, the mode of transport was often by horse, and in many cases it knew the way home better than its master.

Up from the larder in the living room, on the right standing against the wall, was a large, well polished mahogany sideboard. On it was a glass display case protecting a barn owl and a long tailed tits nest. The owl had been killed by my grandfather with a horse's bridle as it perched on a gate post near Bills Moor wood. The nest was one that my father took from a gorse bush, on the canal bank behind the cottages after the young had flown.

In the centre of the room was a large, well scrubbed kitchen table with several chairs standing round it. When not being used for meals it was covered with a dark green chenille cloth. The large ingle-nook fireplace occupied almost the whole of one wall. In it was the grate in which a fire always burnt to provide the heat required for cooking, tea making and warmth. A large, oak beam, blackened by centuries of smoke from the fire below, carried the wall and staircase above. A wide shelf was fixed to it and was the mantle shelf. On it were several tins and jars which held a fascination for me. Gran always seemed to find something in them to soothe, cure or pacify for those in need. My favourites were the square biscuits covered with hard icing of different colours. There were also "Victory 'V's" and hot peppermints. On the under side of the beam were iron hooks one was extra large and was used frequently when a large goose or turkey or joint of meat had to be roasted. They were first fixed onto a length of rope which in turn was hung from a "Jack", and that in turn was hung from the hook in the beam. Another use it was put to was the separation of honey from its comb when the hives were raided for their nectar.

On either side of the fire were brick extensions on which one could sit and above them were two small cupboards.

On the right, near where Gran sat, it was used to store the large bricks of salt and other items that required warm, dry conditions. The one on the other side near the foot of grandfather's chaise-longue contained jars and bottles of ointments, liniments and potions which were used in an attempt to alleviate the pain from his "screws". Most of the farm labourers in days gone by suffered with rheumatism and arthritis, the result of spending many hours out in the very wet and cold conditions without benefit of good, weatherproof clothing. One of those potions was a "Whites of Oils". As it was home-made I suspect that it was no more than a weak mixture of horse lineament which Grandfather had used to cure similar problems in animals in his care when he worked them.

It was almost a nightly ritual for my grandmother to massage his swollen and tender knees with one or other of the pain relievers. After the massage she then placed a piece of flannel, soaked in oils on his affected joints and then tied it in place with more cloth. After the attention he acquired a better mood and was not so difficult. As I am now, long in the tooth, and also suffer with the "screws", I recognize his discomfort and to a degree, sympathise with him.

A highly polished fender and fire irons stood in front of the fire. Each morning before anyone else had risen, Gran would have attended to the fire, riddled the ash and would have it blazing by the time the house became alive. Under the fresh coals, the large, black kettle was quietly hissing as if impatient to be making the refreshing early morning cup of tea. With several pages of yesterdays Daily Graphic, she busied herself polishing the fender and irons which shone and glistened in the glow from the fire. Each Friday the whole of the fire place and its metal parts were attacked with black lead at the end of which they were the pride of the household and remained spik and span for yet another week.

A rag rug always lay in front of the fire. Common then, they were made from odd pieces of worn out clothing, cut into strips and worked into a piece of hessian and they made a very good fire side rug. Each Spring there was some dispute between me and a piglet for the favoured spot.

A large Welsh dresser occupied the wall by grandfather's chaise-longue. At one end hanging from the wall, a grandmother clock, hand wound, which chimed the hours. At the other end, stood a majestic grandfather clock, driven by heavy lead weights and rewound each Friday night before Gran retired. It recorded time, day of the month and phases of the moon. On a warm afternoon in summer with sunlight slanting through the window by the fire, or on a winter's afternoon, a large roaring fire in the grate and a rib sticking repast, the rhythmic, "tick-tock", from each clock quickly produced a somnolent haven in which the hard-worked labourer soon surrendered.

The shelves of the dresser displayed plates, cups and saucers and several commemorative mugs. Queen Victoria's Jubilee, her visit to India as Empress, King Edward VII and King George V coronations were some of the events held in high esteem by the man in the street in those days.

The stairs led from the side of the fire-place around the inglenook to a small landing at the top, and that feature alone established the cottages as being of at least 17th. century origin. There were three bedrooms, the floors were wide elm boards scrubbed white over many decades. Exposed beams supported the roof above. Low windows overlooked the surrounding countryside and a sweet, clean smell assailed one's senses as one ascended the stairs. On the beds, there were patchwork quilts that added to the homely scene. In the winter months an item now frequently seen hanging as a decoration was put to good use then. From the wall by the front door a bed warmer was taken down and each night was used to warm the beds. Ice on the trough beneath the pump, a bright, clear moon shining through the windows, it was time to take extra care to ensure a good nights sleep. A large stone taken from the garden for the purpose, was placed in the oven to warm. After about half an hour it was removed, put into the copper pan, which was then wrapped in a piece of old blanket then placed in the main bed. It was moved around beneath the bedclothes with the long handle until the bed was well and truly comfortable. The long, woollen nightdress and cap which Gran wore, and the thick, woollen night-shirt and woollen hat that grandfather wore ensured a warm and pleasant nights sleep until they rose at 5 o'clock once again to begin the daily routine.

Another table stood between the grandfather clock and the front door, and on it stood a wind up gramophone and several boxes of records. It was bought as a Christmas present by my father for his parents shortly before World War I. Imagine his chagrin when he played the first record, Peter Dawson singing, "The Road to Mandalay", and his father rejected it off-hand because he could not understand how it worked. His opposition to it remained all his life, even when I played it in the '30's he still objected to it.

The table in the centre of the room and the imposing fire place beyond, made a very great impression upon those who were privileged to have enjoyed the scene. In the evenings, as dusk began to fall, it took on that of a comfortable retreat from the cares and concerns of everyday life. As the light began to fade, Gran took a spill from a holder near the fire. The oil lamp was taken from its resting place on the dresser and put in the middle of the table. A good lamp, one with the advantage of a mantle, which meant that it gave a much better light than those with wicks only. With glass chimney and shade removed, and the spill lit from the fire, as it touched the exposed wick a flame ran round it. The mantle was lowered, and after a short time to allow the lamp to warm up, the chimney and shade were replaced. Now the wick was turned up to provide a very good light and the family could settle down for quiet reflection of the days activities. A bright fire in the highly polished grate, Grandfather on his couch below the curtained window, and Gran sunk deep in the cushions of her chair by the fire, a haven of Victorian cottage serenity.

Near the bottom of the stairs, a door led into the brewhouse, a local term for a scullery but one which also had a ring of truth. There was an earthenware sink with a hole at one end to allow water to run down into an outside drain. A draining board provided a surface on which to place items from the sink. In the far corner, a large copper in which all the families washing was boiled and cleaned; at various times it also served to boil the various coloured liquids which became potent home-made wine. The odours in that claustrophobic chamber were many, washing soda, soap, starch and wet cloth; subtle fragrances of cooked fruit also wafted on the laden air.

The rear roofs of the cottages were long and sloped down at about a 60 degree angle, at the bottom of which was a long gutter running the length of them. At intervals, short pipes fed large rain water butts. They were covered with a sack and a wooden top to keep their contents clear. Needless to say the mosquitoes found a way in and cousin Jim and I often watched their larva floating up and down. The beautiful, soft water from them was used for washing one's hair and the weekly wash. A communal pump stood just across the path which provided all the water used for drinking and cooking before mains water was laid on in the '30's. Opposite the far end of the cottages, across a small open space, were the pig sties and dirt closets; Gran's was the first, the Blizzards next and finally the Norwoods. Each unit comprised an earth closet, a small, white-washed sanctum with scrubbed white seat across one end. In the wall dividing the closet from the sty was a trap door which gave access to a storage area above the sty. Below was the covered area in which a pig could shelter from the wind, (pigs hate it). They slept and farrowed in it also. In the front was the open pen secured by a very strong wooden door. The bedding material, slaughter bench and sundry tools were kept in the store above the sty.

At the back of each privy, a small hatch at ground level provided access to remove the night soil. That chore, usually carried out in the early morning, was when the contents were deposited on the garden and dug in. The gardens for the cottages had a fine, black, friable tilth which resulted from such treatment over many generations of occupants. At the end of each week the same procedure was undertaken with each pig sty.

A path led from the cottage down to a hedge over the other side of which was my home. Fruit trees lined it, a mixture of egg and victoria plum, ergmont russet and worcester permain apples. I enjoyed each walk down that path!

From just inside the front gate, a path also led down on the other side of the garden by the boundary hedge between lane and garden. At the bottom, in the corner, a small gate gave access for a path which led down from Frank Norwoods' cottage. On the garden side of that path were many currant bushes, white, red and black. Gooseberries, small red ones with hairy skins, good for tarts, gooseberry fool and wine making. There was also a large, yellow dessert variety.

About halfway down the path against the hedge was a home-made timber bench and opposite the bench were two sheds, one larger than the other. The larger of the two served as a store for all the garden tools, a Beetle, a large mallet, its head made from apple wood, and used when driving in fence posts; its special feature was that it did not split the posts. A large scythe, wooden hay rake and a pitch fork were among many more. Outside by the door stood a large grindstone and the small water bath beneath the stone, it was used very often to sharpen all the edged tools and the knives from the house.

When he was "in residence", Grandfather sat for hours, dozing, reliving his past life and monitoring everything that happened in his neighbourhood. In the fine, summer months he divided his time between shed and bench. It was woe betide Jim or I if we dared to interrupt his reverie by running or playing near him. To fail to recognise his domain was to invite instant retribution and a bawling out, accompanied by the aggressive waving of his walking stick. In his high, semi-Welsh voice, he ordered us to "Get off there you damn kids. Get off with you. I'll give you what for if I catch you"! There was of course no danger of that but it would have alerted Gran who came and by some magic, pacified him until the next time.

In the garden opposite the window which looked out onto the lane, a tall, old, cooking apple tree stood, its fruit was conical and green shading to yellow. They made excellent pies, tarts, charlottes, but better than all of those were the, "Tittiovies", that both Gran and Mother made from them. "Tittiovie", is an old Warwickshire name for the humble apple dumpling. Their resemblance to parts of the human anatomy had not escaped the robust descriptions so often used by country folk of old. Each Spring a robin built its nest in a hole in its trunk and successfully reared its brood despite the attention of Jim's cat, "Monty". The strong scent of jam in the making during the summer attracted hordes of wasps. Gran invariably hung a jam jar from one of the branches, in it was a cocktail of, jam, wine, sugar and a little water; the top was sealed by paper in which there was a hole just large enough for a wasp to get at the liquid below. It trapped many other insects besides the marauders, moths and, "Bobby-Howlers" being the other victims of the trap.

Near to the pump, another path led up to the top gardens. Jim's father tilled the garden between it and the walnut trees. A tall hedge divided his from Gran's other garden, her fowl pen and little further up, two bee hives and a shelter in which Mr Bratt, her lodger, used to sit. The shelter had once been the cab of a hansom cab and had seen better days, but now served its purpose as a shelter very well indeed. In the top corner of her garden, under a large holly tree was a large manure heap. When I was quite young she took me to it and told me that she had something to show me. With a stick, she carefully moved a piece of questionable material, and lo and behold! there in a slight depression were at least 20 soft, round, white eggs. She asked me if I could guess how they had got there? I told her I had no idea, she then told me that a grass snake had laid them. Naturally I said, "How will they hatch if they are not kept warm"? She then explained how the heat from the heap would do the job. That lesson was a good example to me of how we were constantly involved in the natural scheme of things.

The boiling of the dirty clothes, washing them, making the wine, and involvement in the annual slaughtering of the pig demonstrates very well the adage, and the very true one then, "A woman's work is never done"! All of that of course was in addition to cleaning the house, preparing and cooking the raw food stuffs, constantly feeding the fire with fuel and last, but by no means, least, bearing and rearing a house full of children. The modern escape in tranquillisers and sleeping pills were not available in those days before the emancipation of woman! What price our way of living now?

## Chapter 8
# Keeping the Wolf from the Door

We rely strongly upon a great deal of our food being freely available throughout the whole year, despite the elements. For most householders in the early part of the century it was necessary for them to provide most from their own resources. That method obviously restricted the variety and range of produce that could be grown.

To fend for themselves, each house or cottage had a long garden almost invariably used to grow vegetables and fruit, and a small front garden was devoted to flowers. Many also kept a range of animal and bird life which were included in their diet and stores. Pig sties, fowl pens, rabbit hutches and pigeon lofts were the most common of those. For those of us who lived in the country another source of food for both human and animal was the countryside and the local farms. It could be purchased or often collected, free, from the fields and hedgerows. Milk, eggs and such like often formed part of the workers wages for those who worked on the farms.

The "kitchen" garden, very descriptive, provided all the requirements for the householder. Vegetables were grown as earlies, second earlies, and main crop. They were rotated in different plots in the gardens to prevent diseases spreading among the crops. The earlies and second earlies were eaten as they became ready for use; the main crop was grown principally for storage both in their true form and as seed for future needs.

To store the main crop potatoes, a clamp was made in the garden. A shallow circular pit about nine inches deep and three feet across was dug, then it was lined with six inches of straw. To make the clamp, first a layer of potatoes, then a layer of straw and so on and slowly a pyramid of potatoes and straw was built until all the vegetables had been dealt with. The whole was now completely covered with at least six inches of straw and finally the same thickness of the soil which had been excavated for the pit. The needs of the families' potato supply for the next six months was now assured.

Other main crop vegetables such as beetroot and carrots were placed in boxes of fine ash or sand and put into a cool, frost free store. Onions were made up into strings and hung in the shed. Sometimes more were bought off the "Onion Man", a Breton who cycled round on an old bike calling out, "Any onions today lady?" in a strong French accent. They were a common sight along our country lanes pre-war. Shallots were pickled and used as onions. Parsnips, celery and the whole range of brassicas were left in the ground to be harvested when required. The coarser ash from the fire was spread along the rows to reduce slug and frost damage, in the latter case it made them easier to dig out as well.

While the men were planting, tending and harvesting the results of their labours, their womenfolk were not idle, they were processing all the items that were to be stored in one form or another.

Early in July immature walnuts were picked, with some difficulty because of the height of the trees, for pickling. It was imperative they were picked at exactly the right time, which was when the green husk surrounding the immature nut was firm but the shell of the nut had not yet formed or become woody. They were washed and immersed in a strong brine for seven to ten days during which time the brine was changed at least twice. Drained and placed on large, flat dishes, they were left to turn black and then put into jars and hot pickling vinegar poured over them. After several months in store they were much enjoyed with cold meat and ham. In October or early November, the mature nuts were harvested. A much simpler task as we waited for most of them to fall from the trees. Those that didn't, we left for the other thieves that were always in competition with us, the rooks, carrion crows and squirrels. Some of the nuts were still in their husks which were now a brownish green. They often broke open as they hit the ground. The lane beneath the trees at that time of the year was covered with husks, nuts and leaves in an array of colours that put shame to an Indian carpet. Our fingers soon became stained, tasted sour and were sore and painful for days after sessions peeling the stubborn husks which still clung to the nuts. Brushed to remove loose fibres they were stored in sand and salt until Christmas, and if we were not greedy they were still edible at Easter.

It was necessary to encourage the trees to maintain their yield. We employed a method first evolved by the Romans who it is thought introduced them into this country. The method was as described in an ancient rhyme;

"A woman, a dog and a Walnut tree,
the more you beat them, the better they be".

I can speak for the nuts and dogs, I have no knowledge of the first option!

In late summer it was the task, if one can call it that, for we children to collect hazel and filbert nuts from the hedgerows, hopefully before the squirrels and mice did so. They were stored in dry cupboard drawers again until the festive season. There were other much sought after delicacies to be had on those foraging expeditions if one looked carefully. In the same hedges were crab apples to be made into jelly. Wild cooking pears, stewed and served with home made custard made a very tasty supper.

The well manured fields provided very good harvests of mushrooms. Big ones as large as small dinner plates, black and mouth watering when cooked in white sauce in the oven. We picked considerable numbers of them early in the season for them to be made into ketchup. At other times, we picked only small numbers, usually on a Saturday evening to be eaten at breakfast the following morning. Favourite picking fields were the ones behind the cottages, the Church Field opposite Billy Markham's farm, the grassy area between Hampton Copse and Chubby, near where the charcoal burners used to work. Blackberries and elderberries were picked for jam and jellies, all taken from the roadside and the fields. I would think twice before picking them from the roadside these days.

As the fruit became ripe it was picked. The soft fruits first, then damsons and plums. The damson trees along the hedge which separated our house from Gran's cottage, and which incidentally were recognised as those from which Damson Lane was named, were reserved for cousin Jack to pick. He was a frequent weekend visitor when he willingly undertook odd jobs like picking fruit. Another task was for him to shave Grandfather because he could not shave himself and would not countenance my grandmother wielding an open razor under his nose. Jack was born in one of the cottages which stood on a short lane behind the Saddlers Arms before they were knocked down to make way for the "new" Magistrates court building. The Damsons were made into jam, wine and cheese and also eaten in pies. I like them very much indeed but unlike my father, I cannot eat them without custard. When he was served with them he always refused it saying, "I like to taste the fruit, I don't want custard". The egg plums and some of the Victorias went for jam or were made into pies, the greengages were always eaten as dessert fruit.

The strawberries, raspberries, loganberries and red, white and blackcurrants were also made into jams and jellies. Some of the jelly was put aside to provide pectin when strawberry, marrow and rhubarb jam was made as their pectin level was low and if one was not careful, the jams would not set.

After we had eaten our fill of broad, french and kidney beans, in that order, the remainder was left on the halm in the garden to fully ripen. The pods were collected and the beans removed and spread out to dry in the weak Autumn sun. It was done each year which shows the consistency of the weather then. The same procedure was adopted for the main crop peas, except when drying them precautions had to be taken to stop the birds from taking an easy meal, especially Frank Norwood's pigeons. He had fantails, rollers and racing varieties, they lived in a loft above the bread oven at the end of the cottages.

The long gardens attached to houses and cottages prior to World War II provided them with the space where fowl could be housed and their eggs and birds could supplement the larder. Needless to say, it was not that easy. They had to be fed every day and for every week of the year. The pens required constant attention to ensure that the fowl had good living conditions, otherwise they refused to lay or suffered from stress, and the result was feather pecking and other problems.

From June until the onset of winter, there was a steady yield of eggs, often more than could be eaten by the family. The surplus were preserved employing a long established method. An enamel or galvanised bucket, complete with lid, was filled with a solution made up to one of several recipe's, I give one taken from my mother's book of 1909;

"To preserve Eggs for Winter use."

1 lb. of lime in two lumps to every gallon of boiling water. Let the mixture stand until the next day. Stir it up and pour off through a thin mesh, the strong sediment at the bottom, reserve, and to every gallon of mixture crush two or three tablespoonfuls of salt. Put the eggs in straight from the nest!

signed, "Mother".

Yet another one instructs one to, "use 1 oz, or rather less of cream of Tartar to a gallon"!

The instruction to "crush" the salt was common in times when it was bought from the local shop in bricks, similar to a house brick. The salt came from underground sources in Wychbold and Bromsgrove, both in Worcestershire. I am sure that it had more taste than that in common use today. A problem was that if it was not kept dry it rapidly became damp and useless. That was overcome by storing it in the salt cupboards that could be found in the fireplaces of old.

My grandmother had a lodger in the latter part of the '20's and early '30's. His name was Mr. Bratt. I never found out what he did for a living except that it must have been a good job. Each morning he walked to Solihull station in pin striped trousers, black jacket and top coat, bowler hat and rolled umbrella with a small leather bag. A nice chap, self effacing type, well read as he spent some time each day doing the crossword in one of the better broad sheet papers. His demeanour was in considerable contrast to that of my grandfather, in fact it was like chalk and cheese. I believe he avoided any unpleasantness between them by keeping a low profile. Most of us did that in George Beavans presence!

Mr. Bratt took part in the preparations made for the lean months of the year. He kept bees and their honey was a very essential addition to the larder. His hives were in the top garden near the fowl pen. Near them he had placed a cab which had once formed part of an Hansom cab. He used it as a retreat from the atmosphere in the cottage and it was where he could also store the items he required when he opened the hives.

There were two hives. Each spring he spent some time looking around the neighbourhood for new swarms of bees. It was essential to maintain the health and strength of his stock and to do that he tried to renew it at suitable intervals. He was the first person to recite to me the following ancient adage in which he totally believed;

"A swarm of bees in May,
are worth a load of hay.

> A swarm of bees in June,
> is worth a silver spoon.
> A swarm of bees in July,
> let them fly by"!

As a young lad the process of collecting the honey never ceased to intrigue me. I spent many happy hours watching his careful preparations and handling of the bees. An afternoon was set aside, provided the weather was calm and still, to reap the first store of honey. Rummaging in the box attached to his cab he found hat, veil, gloves and smoke gun. Lighting some old cloth in the gun to make smoke, he removed the top from the hive. Slowly he then removed each comb, inspected them and also the condition of the bees clinging to them. His concern was for any dead or diseased insects or signs of mould or damage to the hive. If all was well he replaced the combs that were not full and then sealed it until his next visit.

The full combs were taken down to the cottage where Gran was waiting to extract the honey. She had placed a muslin bag over a wide mouthed crock bowl. Each comb was stood on end on the edge of the bowl and with a large kitchen knife, she cut the contents from the wooden frames. After all the combs had been cleaned they were put aside until later in the summer. The muslin bag was now tied with string and hung in front of the fire over a another bowl set on the hearth beneath. Slowly the liquid honey ran out leaving the wax in the bag. The extraction complete, the golden elixir was poured into jars, labels were stuck on them and then they also were stored ready to be eaten with scrumptious bread and butter or mixed with lemon and warm water to soothe sore throats in the coming winter months.

The wax which had been put on one side was now washed and heated in an old pan over the fire. The process effectively clarified it so that the smooth, white wax could be used in the home for many purposes. A piece wrapped in a cloth was used to rub the sole of the flat irons as they were taken from the front of the fire. Applied to obstinate drawers runners the wax made them run smoothly.

The housewife of yesteryear made use of almost everything that could be obtained, gathered or acquired from her own resources. So it was with bees wax as the base for a furniture polish. Two more recipes from my mother's book provides the means;

> "Furniture Polish".
> "1½ ozs of Bees wax dissolved in
> nearly ½ pint of turpentine,
> ½ oz. of Castile soap boiled in
> ½pt of soft water.
> Let the wax remain in the turpentine
> one night before adding the water and soap".
> signed "Mother"

Another one:

>"½ oz. Bees Wax,
>½ oz. White Wax,
>½ oz. Castile Soap,
>½ pint of soft-water boiling. Let stand
>on the stove till dissolved then add
>½ pint of Turpentine"
>This recipe is signed "Jessie".

The final laborious undertaking in preparation of the hard times ahead was killing the pig. The pig was kept because it would thrive on the scraps from its owner's table and with the minimum of attention. Another major advantage was that virtually all the animal could be eaten or used. An Italian reference to its fecundity is:

>"A pig is like Verdi's music,
>nothing is thrown away"!

It was with some misgiving that my grandmothers animals were slaughtered. As piglets they enjoyed the comfort of her home and fireside for the first month or two of their lives before being consigned to the sty, however, "When needs must, the Devil drives"!

The site where the deed took place was adjacent to the pump and the back doors to both her own brewhus, and that of Marion's. That was very important because large quantities of boiling water was needed.

On a cool, dry day, a local butcher appeared, armed to the teeth with his tools of the trade. The coppers had been fired up very early, water bubbling, smoke and steam issuing from every cranny of the brew-houses, pots and pans at the ready. The bench had been brought from its store above the sty and placed in front of the pump. The pig was brought from the sty, objecting strongly with squeals and grunts and flashing eye. A swift movement by the butcher with a sharp knife, its throat was cut and the deed was done. Bowls were thrust underneath to catch the valuable flow of blood as the menfolk quickly heaved the carcass up onto the bench. Before it could be butchered, the rough hair had to be removed, a laborious task that no one was keen on, but it had to done. Copious volumes of the boiling water was now put to good use. A tin bath was half filled with it and the carcass was rolled into it. After a few minutes all present, with sharp knives went to work scraping as hard as they could. In half an hour the carcass was lifted back up onto the bench, now pink, clean and hairless. The butcher then started his work in earnest.

The internal organs and its head were removed and placed on one side to be dealt with later. The carcass was then split down the middle to provide two sides. It was common for the butcher to settle for a side of the carcass as his payment for carrying out the job. That done he went on his way a happy man.

The work now began to butcher the remaining side and offal with alacrity. Although it was Autumn, the chance that the products could go off, was always present. The "side", and the "hams", were carefully washed, laid on a strong flat surface and treated with the following ingredients to preserve them;

"To Salt Back and Hams".
"¾ lb. Saltpetre,
1 Brick Salt, 6d.
Let it lie in the salt a fortnight.
Sprinkle half the saltpetre on first,
a little more on the hams & hocks &
then legs. Let as much salt as will lie".
Another recipe from my mothers book of 1909.

The procedure given above seems to be quite simple, however, it was far from that. Unless the work was carried meticulously rubbing the preserving mixture into every crevice and particularly along the bones, the meat would go off. Even so, when a ham was taken down there was a careful examination to see if there were any maggots near the bone, or if there was an unpleasant odour. To delay that eventuality it was customary for some of the meat, particularly the sides of bacon, to be smoked. That was achieved by hanging them in the wide chimney for months until they became quite black and to the uninitiated, very unappetising, but looks alone do not tell the true story. Other pieces of meat were wrapped in muslin and hung on the large hooks in the larder to mature.

Some of the hams required very detailed treatment much of it related to the individual tastes of the respective families. In our case, honey from the hives, and black molasses were the essential ingredients; and the hams steeped in the sweet, sickly smelling concoction for at least three or four weeks before also being hung in the larder. The results of the curing activity over many decades was very evident in the white powder and decaying brickwork around the larder walls where the salt had penetrated into the crumbling brickwork.

The essential and bulk of the carcass had been dealt with, the remainder of the other products were now processed. The first and most tiresome was stripping the intestines to provide the skins for sausage and black puddings. After scalding, the outer skin was stripped from the inner, usually a job for someone who had acquired the skill over the years. Often only a portion of them were so treated, the rest was left whole and were eaten as chitterlings. This was a common and much enjoyed Saturday dinner after being cooked for a considerable time and then served with vinegar and bread and butter. A long glass of cider was also very often an accompaniment to one of our favourite dishes.

When the skins had been separated they became two lengths of fine tubing, one was used for sausages, the other for the black puddings. The latter were made from the blood mixed with lumps of fat, pearl barley and seasoning and cooked. It was then fed into the large tube using a special machine, similar to the common mincing machine found in every home. The sausages were made from the less liked cuts of meat. First minced, it too was mixed with rusk and seasoning. I now enjoyed turning the handle of the machine as the mixture was forced through the tube which became a long, pink, wriggling snake. When full, the individual sausages were made by merely twisting the snake a couple of times at six inch intervals. At the end, several meals lay before one.

The "fry", or liver, was enjoyed with bacon and onions or layered with leeks and bacon in an enamel pie dish and cooked in the oven. It was also the main content of the faggots which were my favourite. To make those we used the "caul", the membrane that held the contents of the stomach, and which was used to serve the same purpose for the faggots. Someone was lucky to have the heart as a special treat. The trotters we ate for supper, always with a warm, wet cloth to hand to wipe sticky fingers. Yet another supper dish were the scratchings. This was the residue from the fat after straining it when making lard.

I always clamoured to get the bladder. A much prized item in those days. Balloons were rare and so the bladder replaced it in our games, when clean and blown up it was hung as a decoration at Christmas. In my case it was more often used as a balloon on a stick, as portrayed by Hogarth in his paintings lampooning 18th century royalty and pompous officials. We also played football with them but that was not very successful as they became hard and soon split.

At the end of the year and all the frantic activity, we felt confident that we could relax in the sure knowledge that the family would eat well and be kept warm and dry in the coming winter. In the evening, a fire blazing up the wide chimney, a small glass of the malevolent parsnip, warming damson or soporific beetroot or elder wine and all was right with the world!

## Chapter 9

# The Elmdon Estate

In the year 1250 A.D. the de Whitacre family built a parish church near to a Hall. The original Anglo-Saxon settlement now formed a well established hamlet. A larger Manor house was built in the reign of Henry VIII, replacing the old one. In 1760, after the death of The Countess, Dowager of Rosse, Abraham Spooner bought the Manor and rebuilt the church in 1781. He died on the 6th May, 1788 aged 98! The Hall was rebuilt in 1795 by his son, Isaac Spooner who died aged 80 in 1816. One of their daughters married William Wilbourforce in the church; it was he who introduced a Bill into Parliament which brought an end to the slave trade. The Spooners continued to occupy the Hall and Estate until the middle of the 19th century when it was sold to the Alston family. The hamlet continued as a active entity of the Estate until its disposal in a sale of the whole in 1920, the result of swingeing death duties after the Great War. The Georgian rectory continued in use well into the 1930's as the home of Canon Hayter.

The Estate was not a particularly large one. Its boundaries at the turn of the century were roughly from the Wheatsheaf hostelry along the Coventry Road to the Clock Inn at Bickenhill. From there it followed Clock Lane and Bickenhill Lane to Catherine de Barnes, "Catney", as it is known locally. From Catney, its southern border was Lugtrout Lane and Wherretts Well Lane to the Pound and then along Cornyx Lane and Moat Lane to Moathouse Farm. From there it followed Lode Lane, past Olton Hall, and on back to the Wheatsheaf. The area enclosed several farms with names that have survived as road names. Some come readily to mind, others have been lost. Moathouse, Tan House, Home, Castle Hills, Whar Hall, Foredrove, Dunstan, and Woodhouse farms are a few which I can recall with certainty. The Estate boasted a water mill and pool in Lode Lane, a section of the Grand Union Canal, and a brick yard which used to occupy a site next to a small extension to Hampton Copse which we knew as "Chubby" which has now assumed the title of the former! Between Tigers Island and The Clock Inn, The Cock Inn, a coaching inn stood on the stage route between Birmingham and Coventry. Adjacent to its low front door were a pair of stone steps used by those who visited the inn on horseback. They used to be a common sight, as did the horse troughs, at strategic points around the area. At the Cock was good stabling, victuals and comfort for the many people who used the stages. My grandmother often recounted in great detail how she watched the arrival of stage coaches with sweating horses, coachmen and

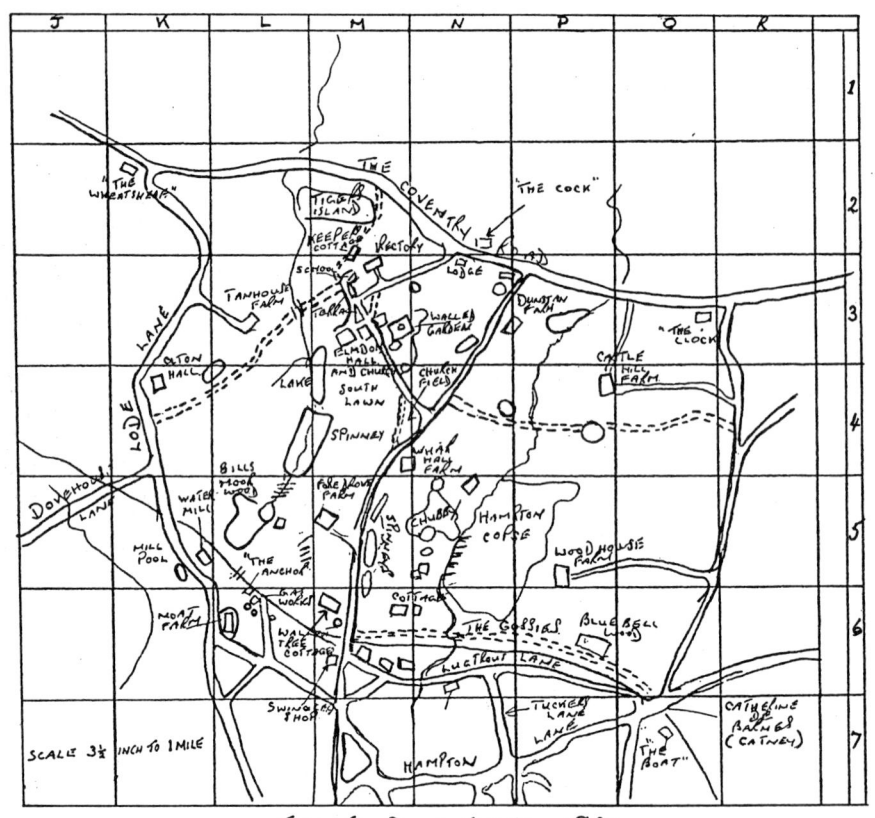

THE ELMDON ESTATE c.1890

postilions, with their often threadbare heavy cloaks and long copper horns. As the coach drew up with screeching brakes and shouts from the men, they immediately unhitched the sweating horses and led them to the stables where fresh ones were waiting. They quickly returned with the harnessed replacements, which were then installed in the empty shafts. Speed was of the essence if the company was to retain its route against the opposition. The travellers both in and on top of the coaches, were grateful for the stop so that they could stretch their legs and take a warming glass of Madeira or Porter. For those inside it was quite comfortable, but on the top, it was unpleasant, even in the summer months. Hazards such as over-hanging tree branches and the ever unpredictable weather. Refreshed, the coach and travellers left with the sounds of shouting and notes from the horn accompanied by the clatter of hooves as they wheeled out onto the stony road.

The heart of the estate was the Hall, church, rectory, Home Farm, Dame's school

Elmdon Hall, c1930.

and a row of terraced cottages, clustered on a knoll. The Hall stood on the summit of the knoll, next to the church and overlooking a lake, parkland and farmland. A South Lawn provided a superb view to the left over the greater area of the Park. It is now a public amenity enjoyed by Silhillians and many others. To the right, looking from the front of the Hall, a small copse ran down to the lake and boat house which housed pleasure craft and a large punt. On the left of the copse, about half way down, a spring was harnessed to provide electrical power to the Hall. Elmdon Hall was the first domestic building in the area to enjoy the use of such a facility. Squire Alston engaged a firm who specialised in obtaining the new, mystic energy from natural resources on estates like Elmdon. They employed a hydro-dynamic system which generated electric current to charge a bank of accumulators in the cellars of the Hall. Those in turn lit the house when required.

It was a simple system, worked by a weight and counterweight. A narrow brick lined well and culvert was built by Ginty Street where the spring emerged from the hillside. The well allowed the water from the spring to be controlled. The sequence of events was that the water filled a shallow, wooden bucket, whose natural position was at the top of the well, but was counter-balanced. When the bucket became full it sank to the bottom of the well, and as it did so, a cable attached to it turned a pulley mounted on the spindle of an electrical generator. The rotation produced sufficient power to charge the "Leyden jars", an early form of wet battery. Just before the bucket reached its lower limit, it hit a projection which tipped it, causing the water

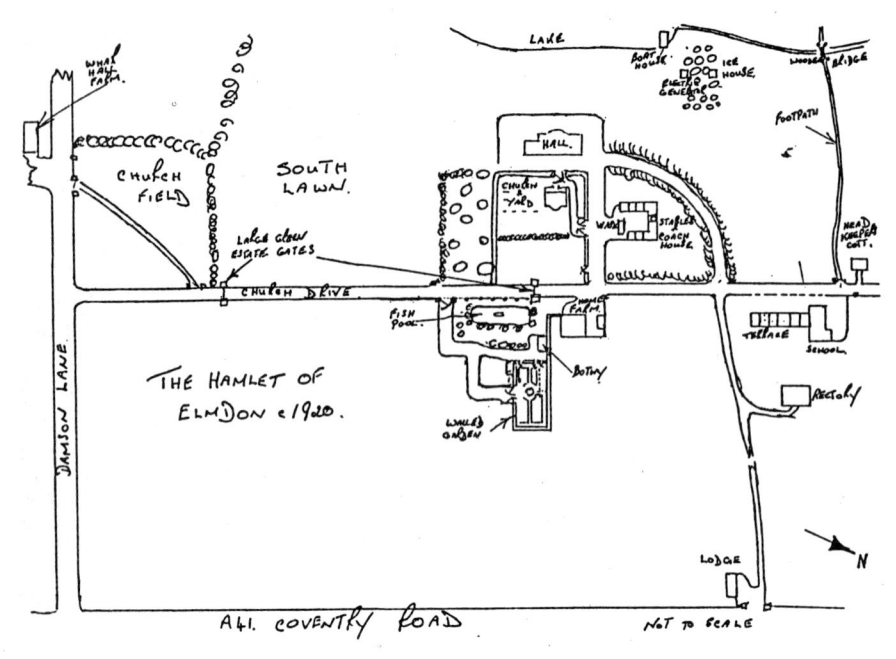

Elmdon Hall (line drawing)

to spill out and resume its age old route to the lake through the culvert. The loss of weight in the bucket resulted in the counter weight falling and returning the bucket to the top of the well. The action continued until halted by one of the estate workers. It provided a foolproof method of power, cheaply, economically and at no cost to the environment.

The early '30's when I first found the boat house and defunct remains of the hydro system, I was taken aback by the standards of living enjoyed by the Squire and his family in the early part of the century. The boat house was in dire need of repair as were the two boats inside. They were half submerged with rotting ropes hanging from them. On the rafters in the roof, the punt rested in reasonable condition.

On the opposite side of the copse and at the same level as the spring was an ice house. They were a common feature on the large estates of the period, and were the 19th century equivalent of our refrigerators and freezers. A large chamber about ten feet square and the same in depth, was sunk into a suitable hillside. The caverns were well designed, brick built with stone slab floors in which there was very good drainage. Two doors provided an air lock at the entrance. At Elmdon its position in relation to the Hall and the lake provided an ideal situation.

# THE ELMDON ESTATE

The Ice house for The Hall, 1990.

At the onset of winter and with the lake now frozen over, the head gardener, Mr. Charles Haynes, (Denny to those who worked under him), initiated the cleaning out and replenishment of the ice in the ice house. A gang of estate workers were assembled with saws, picks, shovels, a horse and cart and many hessian sacks. The cart was filled with clean hay and positioned near the boat house. The ice cutting began during which Denny had to be very vigilant to ensure there was no foreign matter in the blocks of ice, as its presence would reduce the efficacy of the ice and reduce the storage time. At the end of the day, if he was satisfied, Denny summoned all the workers up to the stables where they were plied with hot, warming drinks. Often a tankard of beer was spiked with a red hot poker from the fire in tack or saddle rooms.

Early in the 18th century the "Pleasure Grounds", were established a short distance from the Hall. They contained three specific areas "The New Orchard", "The Fish Pool", and "The New Garden". It was customary for owners of large estates then to enjoy such adjuncts to their properties. They provided much sought status and personal aggrandisement.

Two gates, one an impressive five barbed one and an ornamental clap gate opposite the South Lawn, led down a wide drive into the Grounds. The main drive led straight to a large pair of tall, dark green double doors in the south wall of a walled garden. Half way down, a path led off to the boiler house, two small doors gave access to the back of the garden, a sluice gate at the rear of The Fish Pool, and finally it terminated at a "Bothy", in front of which was a lily pond and sun dial.

The New Orchard contained trees and shrubs of many different varieties and species. Its purpose was not solely for its visual effect, it also served as a screen for the garden against the north and east winds. One of the shrubs, planted in profusion, were Rhododendrons in many colours and flowering seasons. At that time they had recently been discovered in China and were soon being grown in all the large estates. They served a very important need in providing ground cover for pheasants, game birds that had been introduced on those estates in large numbers. At Elmdon the Rhodies were planted round the Fish Pool to provide a delightful background to it. Despite the long neglect since the dissolution of the Estate, they still serve that same purpose in early summer.

The Fish Pool, a large pool of approximately half an acre, was enclosed by decorative iron railings. An island in the middle of it, also had railings around it and on it were flowering shrubs. Around the pool were many tall yew trees making the whole a very attractive feature of the estate.

The New Garden was the pièce de resistance: a walled enclosure of two acres with paths around the periphery and one in a cruciform, the centre of which was a fresh

The author pollarding Willows in The New Garden, 1988.

water well. On the south wall were many "stoves", (commonly known as greenhouses ). There were also some on the inside of the south face of the north wall.

The walled garden is now but a shadow of its former self. Gone are the stoves, the bothy, boiler house, potting, store and tool sheds. The well in the centre that provided all the water for the garden is now derelict. The south facing walls still bear evidence of the turning gear which once controlled the ventilation in the stoves. There are still vestiges of whitewash on the walls, liberally applied to increase the light in them. All the walls have strands of rusty wire and nails which once supported the many fruit trees that grew on them. As young men my father and cousin Jims' father spent many hours covering the fruit trees when they were in blossom if there was a threat of frost. They used wattles, bracken, straw and yew branches and each morning all had to be removed. On the walls, a wide range of fruit was grown. The choice of wall depended upon the conditions favoured by each fruit. On the north facing wall there were Morello Cherries, for cooking, Conference and Josephine de Magines Pears and Czar Plums. On the East wall were Beurre Hardy, Conference and a cooking variety of pear. On the hot south wall grew many subtropical fruit, peaches, apricots, nectarines and figs were the almost the exclusive crop. On the west there were plums, variety not known, damsons, and Pitmaston Dutchess pears. On the outside of the south wall there are still very mature Doyen de Comice, William and a cooking pear, together with two varieties of cherry trees that crop heavily depending upon seasonal weather.

To transport water from the well to the various plots, a water cart was wheeled around by a journeyman gardener who also did the watering. An unusual feature at Elmdon was in addition to the conventional method, a small water-cart, hauled by a dog was also pressed into service when the need arose. The employment of animals in the large gardens was common. Cats were tethered in rows of soft fruit bushes to deter the birds, they also kept the mice population under control.

The "bothy" which I have referred to, was a number of bed-sit rooms and attendant facilities for washing and cooking. They were provided for single men employed on the estate. The system was well entrenched and even my father and Uncle Harry, whose home was a short distance from the hall, went to live in it when they started work. My father, Joe Beavan and George Blizzard were apprentice gardeners in the walled garden. Mr Cook, the head game keeper, cousin Jims grandfather Uncle Harry, an under-keeper, our great Aunt Lizzy Drinkwater, Bill, (Ginty), Street, and Alice, his wife, together with several other members of our families were all employed by Squire Alston, either as domestic servants in the Hall or on the estate. These are excellent examples of the close relationship of families, workforce and community and their reliance upon the big estates to provide the means of livelihood for them. A lad or lass was given excellent training and experience and they were expected to repay that effort by devotion to a life of dedicated hard work on the estate, in most cases was achieved to the benefit of all concerned.

The working day began at 7 o'clock sharp! It came to an end when all the allotted tasks for the day had been completed. The wages were low by today's standards, but if one considers the advantage of rent free accommodation, food and many other perks, they were much better than those of the people who worked in the grime, smoke and soot in nearby Birmingham. For example, Denny Haynes, the head gardener, could expect to receive about £50 a year. That, however, was supplemented by sales and services he provided to the Squires' friends and associates. The gardeners got about 30 shillings, (£1.50p), the improver, 15 shillings, (75p), and the apprentices, five shillings, (25p), a week. Denny and his family lived in the small, single story lodge by the main gates on the Coventry Road. A drive led from there up to the rectory, hall and terrace. The condition of it today requires urgent need of repair. I remember very well how both it and the other drive from Damson Lane to the Hamlet were always in a sad state. In the latter case it is now well maintained as it provides access to a public park.

When my father left the Dames school and went to work in the garden it had reached its zenith in variety and productivity. As well as all the fruit from the walls and the wide variety of vegetables from the garden itself, the stoves provided an exotic range of subtropical fruit, vegetables and flowers. Vines in profusion with their black and green fruit. Bunches of grapes which were picked with a long stalk at the end of the fruiting season and placed in special vases. These had an elongated neck into which the long stalk was inserted, its end entering water at the bottom of the vase. Grapes could be kept in a cool store in the vases for many months. Melons, mushrooms, tomatoes and for added interest, one stove, was used to exhibit Tortoise. There were Cucumbers both in the stoves and outside in pits specially designed for the purpose,

One stove was devoted to exotic flowers and was the one in which my father found his greatest interest. On one occasion when we were looking at tropical flowers at a flower show he pointed out to me a display of *plumbago serenthis*, its delicate blue flowers on their long stems made a great impression on me. He explained to me the difficulties in growing such plants and the care needed for them to thrive. They had been one of his responsibilities when he had worked in the flower stove at Elmdon.

The Victorian Squire demanded a grand style to be maintained in his domain throughout the year, both in his country retreat and also in his London apartments. The head gardener had to provide all the fruit, vegetable, game and flowers required for day to day use and in addition, the many banquets that were held frequently at both abodes. Good husbandry in farm, garden and game covert and a well maintained ice house met the requirement. It was not unusual for there to be food of every description in perfect condition twelve months after it had been gathered, harvested or shot! A testament indeed to the dedication and success of the

Elmdon Terrace with the Dame's school in fore-ground.

highly skilled men and women who worked on estates like Elmdon in their heigheday.

A path led from the front of the hall to a small gate opposite the door of the church. The main entrance to the church was through a pair of iron gates opposite the stables. If one looks closely at those gates, one will see the letter's "W" and "H", wrought into them. They are the initials of Canon Hayter, The Rector of Elmdon who served our community for many years before World War II.

The stables, coach house, grooms and stable lads' quarters and the tack, store, boot house, Bake and Brew house and gun rooms formed a three sided square round a cobbled yard. A large clock tower in the roof of the stables housed the clock which chimed the hours for most of the inhabitants of Elmdon and its environs. In front of the double doors which gave access into the stable yard was a shallow, brick built depression with sloping access at each end. It was known as a "wash", and was provided to wash down the horses, coaches, wagons and harnesses. In the '30's, when our families attended the graves of our loved ones, we always used the wash to clean the vases and to replenish them with water from it. Now, in the '90's, there is not even a tap anywhere in the vicinity of the church for that purpose! It was rumoured that an underground tunnel linked the Hall and both church and stable block. It must have been a figment of someone's imagination because despite exhaustive searches we never found evidence of one.

The drive from Damson Lane to the Hall also served a row of terraced cottages and the Dames school. The butler, game keeper, school mistress and our great aunt, Lizzy Drinkwater lived in them. The school was small but of sufficient size to meet the needs of local families, most of whom worked on the estate. Near the school gate, a five barbed one led along a path to the head keepers house and was occupied by Jim's grandfather, Mr Cook. He was a very important man in the staff hierarchy. Another gate and style led across Elmdon Park, down the hill and to a small wooden bridge over the brook and to Lode Lane near Olton Hall.

Retracing one's steps past the terrace, one arrived at a crossroads. An ornamental gate on the right guarded the front drive and entrance to the Hall. The drive was lined with a variety of tall rhododendrons, an avenue of intense colour each summer. To the left, a drive led first to the Rectory and its many outbuildings and home for Canon Hayter and his wife. From there the drive meandered down to the small lodge and the main gate on the Coventry Road.

The Canon was of the old school of church elders, recognising his responsibilities and demanding respect for his status in the community. In return he required a devout commitment to the church by his parishioners. He regularly visited all of them, especially the old and the sick. On those visits he rode in a black coach which was drawn by a black horse and a coachman dressed in black. He dressed in true Victorian fashion for a high churchman. A long top coat and jacket, breeches and soft gaiters buttoned down to soft sided boots. The severe appearance was

Head game keepers house in Elmdon Park, c1920.

Elmdon Rectory, 1990.

accentuated by the white wing collar, pince-nez perched on a thin nose in an ashen face below a round black hat.

   At the sight of his coach, everyone turned to face him, the men and boys doffed their caps, the women and girls gave a small curtsy. He was "HIS" plenipotentiary and let none of the plebeianise forget it! Our secret thoughts while genuflecting were for those unfortunates on that days calling list. We knew their fear of his admonishment if he, or his wife, had not seen them in church last Sunday. His visits gave scant relief from a latent fear of authority so common in those days.

   At the bottom of the Rectory drive was the Lodge. It served both the Hall and Rectory and was occupied by Denny Haynes and his family. My father often regaled us on a winters' evening with tales about him. Of his high standards regarding the work on the estate and also of his consideration for the people who worked for him. That is not to say that the young lads from the bothy did not play pranks on him. His high pitched voice added zest to the occasion when he chastised them. On one occasion they dressed themselves in large white sheets and lay in wait for him one Saturday night as he returned from his usual visit to the Anchor pub at Elmdon Heath. They positioned themselves at the clap gate where the path across the Church Field joined the Church drive. As he approached they jumped out emitting blood curdling screeches and "Too, Whoo's". Despite his "happy" condition, he was not fooled by them and was quick to berate them. My father took great delight in recounting Denny's "I know who you are, you young so and so's"! Father's inability to reach the high notes did not diminish the enjoyment for his listeners.

My father soon found good reason to refrain from those activities because he began to spend most of his free time with Denny's daughter, Ruth. One of their pursuits, an unusual one at that time, was to ride a tandem round the local lanes. Father always claimed they were the first to do so. A couple of decades later, they were a common sight. Ruth was a member of the church choir and its principle singer. She had a fine contralto voice which gave a cadence to what would otherwise have been a mundane sound. In our day, the choir sang from the gallery which gave it a celestial presence. She remains as one of the main reasons why my early church going remains so vividly in my memory.

The lodge at the entrance to Elmdon Park, 1990.

## Chapter 10
# A Keepers Year

The dawning of a new year was witness to the Head Keeper, his under keepers and many estate workers making their preparations for the hopefully successful game season. When the men who ploughed, harrowed, rolled and drilled the fields they often saw evidence of pheasant runs, partridge "jug's" and which pool was most favoured by mallard and geese. They would become the nucleus of that years' source of eggs.

February and March were the months when potential breeding stock was "caught up", and put into what were known as rearing cages; these were areas of woodland that had been carefully netted to protect the incumbents from their many predators. By carrying out that annual exercise, the keepers were able to increase the numbers of eggs laid by each hen bird.

Once in lay, after a number of eggs had been laid, each subsequent egg was removed from the nest and put under a broody hen. When the keepers considered that sufficient number of eggs had been gathered the caged birds were released back into the wild to begin the process for themselves, and obviously would add to the eventual total of birds in the shoots. The method also ensured greater control over quality and health rather than buying eggs in from a egg farm. Jim and I often took part in the "catching-up" exercise simply because we formed part of a keepering community. Most country folk liked eggs from many wild birds, pheasants, partridge and plover, "PEE-WIT". They were very rich, with red yolks, and became available at a time when the back yard hens had not started to lay.

Meanwhile, other men were setting up rows of hen coops along chosen rides, in the rearing field. A hut or other mobile caravan was also sited near to the coops. The keepers lived in them until the young poults were moved into the release pens.

The broody hens most often used were Light Sussex or Rhode Island Reds. They were heavy birds and prone to become broody as soon as the weather became warm in Spring. A dozen pheasants eggs were put under a hen and the same number of partridge eggs under a bantam, although in the wild it was common to find up to 18 in a partridge's nest. The coops housing the sitting birds required protection, which was achieved by fitting vertical bars on the front, two of which could easily be taken out. They were so spaced that the chicks could roam at will. A further protection was a solid piece of wood which was let down over the front of the coop at night to prevent weasels and rats getting at the valuable contents.

Uncle Harry, game keeper on The Elmdon Estate.

Keepers always carry their guns as they patrol their shoots. Predators were shot at every opportunity and in the rearing season were used to acquire protein for inclusion in the food for the young poults. Rabbits formed a large part of the countrymans bill of fare. My memories of holidays spent with Uncle Harry and Aunt Ethel was the food. An unending diet of rabbit in various menus with loads of potatoes and cabbage. The puddings were invariably a huge pile of boiled rice and currants. A cheap and well tried means of feeding a hungry family of three boys and four girls and me.

When the poults were about 11 weeks old they were removed from the coops and put into the release pens. These were similar to the cages which had housed the adult breeding birds caught up early in the year. They were used to protect the young birds until they had learnt to roost and were no longer potential victims of their predators.

Here in Elmdon a ride ran along the edge of Bill's Moor wood and the nearby field. The keepers hut stood in a corner close to a barn and a large pond. The pond was an adjunct to the estate lake and was used as a duck trap. A long funnel net had once led from the lake to end in a small enclosure from which the ducks could be taken. My father and I spent many hours fishing the pond for roach and perch. On one occasion a roach on the end of father's line was taken by a voracious pike. Not only did it take the fish, it also took the line and the end of his rod! Near the hut, Fred Smith, the keeper, had set up an alarm gun and asked me if I knew how to set it up. My answer was in the negative, but as a seven or eight year old, I had visions of following Fred and Uncle Harry into the profession. Later, the economics of the '30's and firm advice from both of them encouraged me to make other arrangements for my future. I still enjoyed learning how to set the gun though.

Cousin Jim and I recently recalled how the sounds of pheasants, the whistle and voice of Fred as he fed his birds in the early evening, and the song of nightingales, with the "crex-crex", of the corncrakes wafted across the silent hay meadows and assailed our ears. With many more such sounds they served as a lullaby as we slowly succumbed to the "dust in our eyes", and surrendered at the end of another long day. If one stands at the junction of Damson Lane and Walsgrave Drive on a summer evening now, the roar of traffic along the road, the scream of jets lifting up from the airport, and the constant background "hum", emanating from the Land Rover works now sound the knell of those once calm, peaceful times. This is progress?

The period from June through to August was perhaps the hardest of the keepers year. The young birds and their surrogate mums had to be fed morning and evening. The cops moved their own distance every 3 days where the grass was greener. Each day rabbits were shot and skinned and formed one of the ingredients in the young poults food.

A fire was lit beneath a boiler in which there was sufficient water to cook a range of groats, wheat, corn and such like. The dismembered rabbits and a special remedy were also thrown into the bubbling cauldron. The rabbits provided much needed protein, the remedy was to prevent the dreaded "gapes". It is a condition which results in the young birds rapidly losing weight and quickly dying. It manifested itself by the birds standing listlessly at the edge of the ride and gaping continually, hence the name. Every keeper takes precautions to avoid that dreaded disease.

The contents of the boiler, when cooked, resembled a large pudding good enough to eat. A hurdin feed bag was slung over the shoulder, filled with the product of the boiler and off we went. As one approached a ride, the only sign of life was an odd poult wandering around and one or two necks stretching out from the coops as their occupants searched for an odd tit-bit. At that point, every keeper I ever knew began to whistle in a particular way and with an occasional "kooks, kooks", to put both hens and poults at their ease. A slow walk down the ride and as we walked, the food was thrown to each side. Suddenly, the ride was alive with frantic birds, running around haphazardly, all looking for the best and tastiest morsels. After walking down one side and returning along the other, Uncle Harry always turned and viewed the spectacle of what seemed to be hundreds of scurrying red-brown birds. Where there had been green grass was now a carpet of glorious colour. A delightful scene for an onlooker, for the keeper, a celebration, if not a boast, of a dedication to his skill and devotion over the past months. Alas! I believe those days have now gone and efficiency is now the name of the game, but a much less picturesque one.

By mid-August the poults were ready to go into the release cages. To prevent the birds from flying out of them before they could take care of themselves, the primary feathers on one wing were shortened so preventing them from getting airborne. After two or three weeks, the birds had learnt the art of roosting and the primaries had grown so they were now comparatively safe to be released. The coops in the rearing field were now collected, repaired and painted and stored ready for the next season.

It was now the concern of the head keeper to keep the losses of his birds to a minimum. Each shoot was carefully combed for hides or tracks which spelt danger. Any, and all, animals and birds were seen as a threat to the safety of the young birds. All the predators were kept down in a war of attrition by gun, trap and poison.

On each shoot, the keeper kept a vermin line. A length of wire strung between two trees or posts on which he hung all the kills, weasels, stoats, sparrow and kestrel hawks, all the members of the corvid family, rooks, carrion crows, jays, magpies, jackdaws and of course owls. The brushes of foxes that had eluded the hunt but had met their fate at the hands of the keeper were all proudly displayed on the line. The lines were not merely for the self-satisfaction of an individual keeper, they made a definite statement as to his ability as a good one. At every visit to his game reserves, the Lord of the Manor paid particular attention to the lines. It was woe betide the keeper whose line was not full. His job would be in jeopardy if it was not full on the next visit.

The Elmdon Estate was hunted over by The South Warwickshire Hunt whose Master was Lord Willoughby de Brooke, and we always turned out on Boxing Day to watch as it tried to find a fox.

The constant threat of poachers was now a major concern and every effort was made to combat their activities. Meadows used for grazing cattle were now also likely to be used by partridge coveys. They were "Englishmen", as opposed to the now common "Frenchmen". The difference being, the former were our native common or grey partridge, and until a generation ago, a main quarry as a game bird. Alas! it is now quite rare because it is less able to adapt to the new farming practices

Red-Leg's, or Frenchmen, are now the common bird in the shoots. They have an affinity with pheasants and are able to take advantage of the provision for them.

Irrespective of origin, coveys, the family of adult partridges and young of a brood remain together until the following mating season. To ascertain their favourite sites, the keepers, farm workers and in our case, Jim and I, spent many happy hours scouring the fields looking for their droppings, these formed rings denoting signs of "jugging". This is the term used to identify the resting place of a covey for a night. The birds do not roost in trees, but gather in a tight circle in the middle of a field. They continue to do so until the covey breaks up, the parent birds, who often mate for life, start a new family and the young cocks entice females away to start their own brood.

Poachers and gypsies main concern was to support their families. The poachers were quite often workers on the estate. The gypsies, the true Romanies, roamed the countryside selling clothes pegs made from hazel twigs, or skewers made from alder twigs. They would hawk an area, the women folk telling the future to the housewives if their palms were crossed with a silver coin, usually a sixpence. Both of these habitues of the countryside had more nefarious activities to supplement their meagre incomes, — poaching eggs, game, rabbits and anything else that appeared valuable that could be sold or used. The gypsies caught hedgehogs which they roasted over their camp fires and which they always declared as one of their delicacies.

To prevent loss of partridge and rabbits to these people the keepers collected young hawthorn plants, (quicks), and planted them at random intervals across the meadows favoured by the quarry. The method used to catch the game was to drag a "long net", of some 100 feet in length, and about three feet in width, vertically across a field at night. This was quite legitimate when used to catch rabbits for the land owner, but not for partridge.

The modus operandi, was to choose the right conditions. A quiet night with little wind, broken cloud cover and threequarter moon. Two men stealthily unrolled the net and with one at 100 yards across the chosen field, they walked slowly from one end to the other. It may have taken two trips to cover a field. At the end of the operation up to 40 birds may have been caught. In addition there may be a hare or two and several rabbits. A nights work which reaped high rewards when sold to local hotels and shops. More often than not, the keeper had forestalled their activities with his timely planting of the quicks. The end of the night would have resulted in torn nets and the odd hawthorn bush. I used to help plant the quicks replacing those caught in the nets. Uncle Harry often approached a known poacher to ask "Did you sleep well last night so and so?" The riposte was often a black scowl which was reward enough for efforts taken early in the season.

The period between late summer and the following February was the busiest and crucial for the head keeper and his men. On the 1st August, wild fowl, snipe and woodcock came into season. On the 1st of September, partridge, and then pheasant came in on the 1st of October. All of these birds became protected again on the last day of February, at least, legally, but the poachers and gypsies still took them given the opportunity.

At the start of the shooting season, Squire Alston issued his many invitations to friends and acquaintances for shooting days or weekends. Together with the Packington Estate, many influential dignitaries attended the parties. Edward the VII, The Prince of Wales, was a frequent visitor on these occasions, his enthusiasm for the sport was well known and his presence eagerly sought.

In consultation with the Squire, Bill Cook, devised a full programme of shooting for the specific days. How many? Which were to be pheasant only, those partridge only, those when both were fair game, and then at the end of the season, a day for cocks only and finally, a day was set aside for the farmers and keepers. The final day was always the 31st of January and the first day was usually one in mid November. The definitive start dates were not used because rarely does the climate in England match the statutory breeding seasons.

Many additional workers were recruited for the shooting days, beaters, pickers up, and general helpers. The butler and cook at the Hall were provided with the programme as there would be need for many hot drinks and meals on those days. Many of the local population were keen to play a part, especially we lads. There was a small remuneration for our efforts but more importantly, there would also be a brace of birds. For the lads it was an exciting time charging through the undergrowth in a line, shouting and thwacking sticks against trees to get the birds into the air over the guns. So often had we stealthily crept through the same woods trying to avoid the keepers when we were bird nesting. On shooting days it usually rained, or there had been a hard frost the night before or there was about six inches of snow on the ground and so the going was hard underfoot. To add to the discomfort we were regularly peppered with shot from the guns, by those ignorant of shooting standards and etiquette.

Before setting out on those sorties I remember Gran tucking brown paper around my legs, under the long stockings, and wrapping newspapers around me as she did up my top coat. All of that to protect me from the cold, the rain and the wet undergrowth; needless to say, all the effort was not completely successful, but at least they did help and I very much appreciated her concern for my comfort.

In the early part of this century the weapons commonly in use were a wry mixture. The variety created much interest. There were 12, 16, 20 bores, most with exposed hammers and the odd muzzle-loader. As the years passed the hammerless version became the one most used. The muzzle-loaders were considered too dangerous for the lads to handle in the heat of the moment. We often stood in for an absent loader. Anything to do with guns appealed to Jim and I so we jumped at the chance of handling some of the expensive and exotic weaponry. When the birds were flighting well, dogs barking, beaters shouting and whistles blowing over the shoot, it was very exhilarating, difficult, but rewarding, to keep ones particular pair of guns loaded so that the "gun", did not lose a shot at an offered bird. Had he not been able to take the shot his loader was castigated, but more importantly, both he and the loaders abilities among the shooting fraternity suffered, which neither could afford.

At the end of the day the head keeper blew a long, loud blast on his whistle to warn everyone that the days sport should cease. Assured that all was well, he instructed the beaters and pickers-up to go out and make a search for birds that may have been wounded but had escaped both dogs and earlier searches. It is an unwritten law that all quarry must be accounted for and put down humanely. There were usually two drives in the morning and one in the afternoon. Many of the ladies shot in the afternoon as it was shorter in length and over easier ground.

The days bag was loaded into a horse drawn cart and taken up to the stable block. Meanwhile, the Squire escorted his guests to the Hall for refreshment and to prepare for the nights entertainment. At the stables the bag was sorted and apportioned to everyone who had taken part in the days activity. The birds with plumper breasts and less obvious damage were reserved for the Squire. His guests, the farmers, loaders, beaters and pickers-up were also rewarded in some measure.

Wet through, tired, cold and exhausted, I strutted home to the ever welcome roaring fire and affectionate grandmother. Proudly I threw a brace of pheasants onto the table and collapsed into the nearest chair to the fire. Very soon the days events were being recounted with some exaggerated gestures and boasts. They were oft repeated on long winter evenings by the light of the oil lamp and bright fire. After hanging for a week, the birds were plucked and we enjoyed them for Sunday dinner. Oh happy days!

## Chapter 11
# The Farming Year

The long hot days of summer and the cold, icy days of winter, spoken of by the older generation with some nostalgia, are not figments of their imagination as some "experts", would have us believe. Generations of crop growing, sports and children's games related to, and were dependent upon, well established climatic conditions. The realization that the previous status quo can no longer be assured make many of my generation yearn for the comparative harmless but severe conditions we endured before World War Two.

Examples of our reliance on the seasons can be seen from my own knowledge of winters in Elmdon and Elmdon Heath. Almost every family that I knew possessed at least one pair of ice skates, but more often several pairs. They were put to good use every year between December and February. Up at the Hall, Squire Alston and his predecessors stored produce from their estate in an ice house which required large quantities of ice to maintain it for 12 months. We all lived by the natural order of things. Oh! that it was so today!

After the Christmas holiday, which meant just Christmas Day and Boxing Day, everyone busily returned to their labours. Elmdon and its Heath were rural communities, farmers, game keepers and gardeners were impatient to start the years programmes and seasonal tasks. The hard frosts prevented cattle, horses and sheep from grazing in the fields so they were kept in pens, stables and cover by the farmyard. They were fed with crops still in the fields, kale and roots, supplemented with bran, oats and other meal bought in from Napiers shop in the High Street in Solihull who were the local chandlers and seed merchants.

It is debatable which work on the farm was the most disliked, harvesting foodstuffs from the fields in the harshest of winter weather, or the long hard days threshing corn in the Autumn. As a lad who spent many hours on Les Nock's farm, my own aversion was the former and especially cutting kale and lifting and carrying roots. Both of those jobs required a high degree of stamina because of the conditions at the time they were gathered. A man, horse and cart was drawn up near to the first row of the crop. When I took part, the man cut the kale and I threw it up onto the cart with a pitch fork. When the roots were harvested we both did the same job. Each of us was armed with a short, sharp-bladed sickle. There was an art to that job. A root was prised from the frozen earth, held by the green top and the root portion was sliced off with a single swing of the sickle. The turnip, beet or swede was then thrown into the air and as it fell the green top was also sliced off. The root was stabbed with the sharp point of the sickle and with a deft movement, thrown up on to the cart. A great deal of care was exercised when carrying out that manoeuvre to avoid harm to ones fingers and shins. The swedes, mangels and beet were heavy and bulky and so the cart quickly filled, much to my relief.

Back at the farm, the roots were tipped into a barn where a hand turned cutter was situated; when the need arose, the roots were put through it and fed to the cattle. The kale was fed to the animals as it came from the fields without further treatment. Both of these crops provided excellent cover for game and we always kept a sharp eye open for them when gathering the crop. We always told the keeper where we had seen them so they could be protected and subsequently caught up, at the start of the next breeding season.

The short, cold, wet and frosty days of winter gave way to pale sun and lengthening days. Their warmth soon triggered a whole range of changes to the countryside. The drying soil allowed ploughing to begin on fields from which the winter forage had been harvested. The fields from which the corn had been harvested had been manured and ploughed in the Autumn to allow Jack Frost to help the farmer by breaking up the turned soil. It was now a period of sustained effort when plough, horse and man worked long hours with little rest except when the weather stopped work in the fields. After harrowing the ploughed fields those that required it were spread with lime. Its application was to accelerate the beneficial effects of the previously spread manure. It was also essential to provide a friable surface to the heavy clay in this part of Warwickshire.

One pictures the farm of sixty years ago as an idyllic way of life. The plough drawn by a couple of Shire horses and the ploughman striding behind with not a care in the world. On the odd occasion, that may have been the case. The reality was much different. The work by its very nature was the first to be attempted when the ground was considered to be in the right condition for horse and plough. No work could be contemplated when frozen, or worse still, sodden. Imagine what would happen if two Shires or Clydesdales, each weighing nearly a ton apiece, plus the plough, tried to work on water-logged or frozen land!

Before we children left home to go to school, the sounds of horses hooves were heard as George Peachy, Les Nock's wagoner, sitting side saddle on one of them, brought them to Jack Cotton's smithy on the Common. After being shod they were taken to the field to be worked that day. They would be harrowing, rolling or drilling. On meadows left fallow a chain harrow may have been used to scarify the sward to remove old and dead grasses, and to spread manure if it had been spread on earlier.

With the major tasks completed, it did not mean that there was time to stand and stare. Hedges required repair to contain animals, and ditches dug and cleared. The sheep were now lambing and the heifers bought earlier at the cattle market behind the Engine public house at Hampton-in-Arden at the Michaelmas sale had begun to calf. No respectors of Sunday dinner or the darkest hour, the new generation were born and their mothers often needed help, otherwise there would be expensive and unnecessary deaths or injuries.

In late spring the poultry houses and pig sties were cleaned out and repainted with whitewash in readiness for their new occupants. The hens were bought on the point of lay and chicks from the previous year came into lay about June. Piglets were set up in both farm and cottage sties ready to be fattened for the coming Autumn. The fowl and their eggs were the womans domain. The proceeds went into the housekeeping or the odd trinket for herself.

The times of which I write were very different to those of today. It was especially so of farming methods and also of man's attitude toward his environment. There was very little use of chemicals in the growing of crops or the husbandry on the farm. Manure from the farm animals, with an occasional dressing of lime, was all that was put on the land. A routine exercise in weeding from both field and garden, was carried out by bent backs, strong fingers and hand-held hoes. The land was recognised as the life blood of us all and as such, was accorded the respect it deserved then and unfortunately, lacks now. As children we were taught and positively encouraged to respect it, other people's property, and the wild life that we were in daily contact with. We were made to realise that all of these elements were very important and required our constant protection. As a consequence of that tutelage, the countryside was a very pleasant place in which to live and work, and our heritage was assured.

Apart from man's historic necessity to hunt and kill for food and the activity of their predators, animals, birds and insects were in no danger. The use by farmers, water and local authorities, and even the gardener, of harmful chemicals such as pesticides, herbicides and artificial fertilizers, put humans, animals and the ecology at risk. In the 1950's many of our wild birds, especially the hawks and owls were decimated by the use of such chemicals. If one examines the containers in which chemicals are stored and delivered, the warning notices on them read, "Wear protective clothing. Do not use near domestic animals, fish or human populations. Do not overspray buildings or unprotected individuals. Immediately remove any spilt liquid from exposed skin and wash thoroughly. Wash hands after use."! What of the wild life, how do they know that they are at risk?

The countryside in general and Elmdon and its Heath in particular were very quiet places, sounds travelled a long way. In the summer the Grammar School cadet force practised their drill on the playing fields near Broomfields, accompanied by the shouted orders of their N.C.O.'s and officers, also notes from the instruments of the cadet buglers as they practised. The bell ringers in St Alphege's church in Solihull were clearly heard as we stood by our garden gates. Our elders also told us that when the sound of trains steaming through Solihull station were heard, then rain was not far away, they were generally right too. On other summer evenings at dusk, the whistles and screech of bats could be clearly heard as they left their roosts in the cottages to begin their search for food. Their searches were around the tops of the tall walnut trees and we spent many happy hours just watching as they weaved their unerring way among the foliage. On other such evenings we watched enthralled as "sheet lightening", and occasionally, the more threatening forked variety, played in the Hampton Copse trees. Now, Walnut Tree Cottages, the trees that gave them their name, but also too the bats and even the lightening are no more. Familiar sights and sounds now lost forever.

Lady Day and the Summer Solstice heralded an air of expectation on the local farms. May and June saw the many coloured hay and clover fields, cut, carried and made into ricks, either in the corner of the fields or in the rick yard at the farm. The corn crops, long in stem, yellow ears bulging and God willing, would soon also fall to the binder.

To assess the yield from the crops, the farmer was seen frequently walking the fields, picking a stalk of grass here, tasting it, nodding in approval and moving on. Conversely, he spat out the offending ear and tried in another area of the crop to find an acceptable taste. If his search found the crop to be at its optimum condition, the business of harvesting began. Hay and clover to feed his animals throughout the coming winter. The intense yellow rape so often seen today had yet to put in an appearance in our fields.

The horses, with Martingales clinking, ambled down the Lane to be harnessed to the mower in the first field. A clear area round the crop was made by driving the mower round twice. That produced a open area in which the mower could turn at the end of each row without causing damage to a still standing crop. I realize that age plays tricks with memory, but I only remember fine weather as each field fell to the mower in those halcyon days. High winds sometimes beat down the tall corn crops and made life difficult.

I spent many happy hours and days walking behind George Peachy as he cut the various crops. He sat up on the mower, reins in hand, twigs of elder in his cap and the horses bridles to ward off the flies. Constant encouragement to his team, "Walk on Major. Cum, cum, steady theear Baron, " and so on through the long, hot summer days. There were not many breaks in the steady work. An occasional drink from the cider flagon for us and water from a bucket for the horses. The mornings wore on with the sound of hooves striking exposed stones, a rhythmic beat of mower knives, gears and wheels as they inexorably cut the standing crop to leave regimented lines of green hay or clover. At mid-day, the welcome sound of a church clock or quite often, a factory "maroon", announcing the time for a break for refreshment for horse and man. With sweat poring from every pore of both man and beast, we retreated to the shade of a tree to escape the heat, light and dust of the field. After a repast of home cured bacon, home made bread and pudding of jam tart

Billy Markham hay making on Whar Hall Farm.

with more cider to wash it down, we were ready to return to the fray.

At the end of the day's work, the horses were unhitched from the mower shafts and with George on one of them, and me on the other, we rode them back to the farm. They were well aware that the days work was done and they needed no encouragement to get home. Their harnesses removed, they were led into the stables, hay was already in the manger and a bucket of cold water by the door was waiting for their return they took great gulps from the buckets and pulled long strands from the iron mangers we groomed them to make them comfortable and relaxed for the night. It is always the recognised practice that, "man's best friend" is attended to before one's own comfort is considered. After they were settled, we made our weary way home, knowing that there was yet at least another half a field to do on the morrow. Apart from my aching limbs, hot, tired and hungry, and the soles of my boots slipping with each step from the effect of the grass on them, I was nevertheless looking forward to another day following the mower if the weather held.

It was very unusual for a field to be cut in a single day unless it was a very small one. The average size was about four to six acres. From experience that was the optimum size which could sustain the number of animals on the farm and one which could be worked most efficiently.

The man up on the mower or binder, kept a sharp eye open for the wild life which frequently lay in their path. That was especially so in the hay and clover fields because it was the time when most were nesting or rearing their young. Pheasants were not a problem as their nests were in the bottom of the hedgerows and if one was caught out in the field it could easily outstrip the speed of the mowers. The birds most at risk were the partridge, corncrake, plover and skylark.

Young rabbits and occasionally a leveret, (a young hare), was found in its form. Like the deer, the female hare leaves her single offspring in a form, while she goes off foraging for food. The leveret is safe so long as it remains perfectly still, no matter what the temptation to move. It is well camouflaged and odourless so their predators are unaware of their whereabouts except by sight, not an easy task for the chap on a farm machine.

George, — it was always he who I found myself following — would shout, "Whoa, whoa up there", and pulling on the reins, brought the team to a halt. If we had been in the field for some time he got down to stretch himself; otherwise, he shouted, "There's a nest, eggs, or young something in front", and with knarled finger, pointed in the direction of the find. Then, "Have a look and see what you can do". After removing the endangered eggs or lives out of harms way, the horses were encouraged to, "Gid up there. Move on there Captain", and the work continued remorselessly until a narrow strip of the crop was left standing.

At that stage, Les Nock would have arranged for a few friends to position themselves at strategic positions at each corner of the strip with their guns at the ready. The time had come to rid the farm of some of the many rabbits that infested it. Those that escaped the knives of the mower had run into the surrounding hedgerows, or had foolishly moved further into the centre of the crop. As the last few rows of hay or clover fell to the knives of the mower, there was a mad dash by the remaining bunnies to get back to their burrows. Alas, in most cases, their time had come. At the end of the day there was often a good crop of rabbits as well as hay or clover. Their meat was a staple diet for country folk and the skins were sold to the itinerant rag and bone man for a few pence.

The crop was left for a couple of days to dry one side then a turner was driven over the field to turn the rows of partially dried crops so that it would dry out almost completely, or at least dry enough to carry. For that, all the hands on the farm were mustered. A horse drawn rake was driven at right angles across the rows to form larger ones, but fewer of them, so making it easier for it to be gathered. That done, the hay carts and wains were brought into the field. The haywains, long picturesque carts portrayed so accurately by Constable in his painting of that name, announced to we children that it was time to play in the hay as it was stacked. It provided an excellent medium in which the girls made houses and the boys made castles. After a day playing in the fields our parents were quick to stop us on the doorstep to make us shake most of the hay from our hair and clothes before we set foot indoors, no matter how thirsty or hungry we were.

## THE FARMING YEAR

After the hay or clover had been gathered and made into ricks, either in the corner of the field or in the farm's rick-yard, there was a pause in the harvesting calendar until the corn was deemed ready, usually in August and early September. Almost every day when the barley, oats or wheat were expected to be ready, the farmers walked the fields taking many samples of the crop to ascertain its condition. Experience played a major role in that procedure. An ear of grain was plucked some distance into the field. It was examined closely then cupped in the palm of one hand. One knarled fist rubbed the ear in the palm of the other to separate the grain from the chaff, which was blown away. A careful check to look for signs of mould or decease, if all was well one or two grains were then sampled by being slowly chewed. This critical test established taste, texture and that certain something that provided the basis for a decision on whether to cut or not. Those days have long gone. Condition and quality of the crop are now assessed by scientific means. I think that all the chemicals sprayed on the crop at various times during its growth also makes the "taste test" dangerous to the taster nowadays.

If all the tests were good and the weather appeared to be set fair, the work of harvesting the corn crop began. Barley was the first, then oats and finally wheat. The binder was overhauled, the horses re-shod and several spare knives were sharpened—all was now ready. A tripod was set up in the corner of the first field to hold the knives when they were resharpened during the work in the field. In the same corner, the food and drink for both man and animals was stored in the shade of a tree, usually a stately elm. Unlike hay making, the task of cutting the corn demanded far more effort. The binder was a large, heavy machine cutting a swath of the crop which it processed before ejecting it as a sheaf. Horses were worked harder and they were changed at least twice during the long day. Stacking the sheaves as they were thrown out of the binder required many hands, men, women and children were often recruited for the job.

As with the hay field, a strip was cut around the periphery of the field to allow the horses and binder to turn at the end of each row without causing unnecessary damage to the standing crop. The strip was cut the previous day or two by men with scythes. With a sack on the seat to provide a minimum of comfort, the driver of the binder would be sitting on it for about a month or more, from dawn to dusk, so it was essential that he enjoyed some comfort throughout that period. A few twigs of elder placed in the halters of the horses and one in the brim of the driver's cap, warded off the many flies that pestered everyone who worked the land with animals.

The clocks on the stables at the Hall and Solihull church would be striking five o'clock as the horses were led out of the farm gate and down the Lane to the field to be cut. Work began and continued without stopping, apart from breaks for food and drink, and the occasional rescue of wild life, until the sun set. A steady stream of men and horses then set off back to the farm. George and I rode back. Throwing a leg over wide, sweating haunches and grabbing a handful of withers, we were off home. "Major", "Captain" or "Lady" knew that the days work was done and a comfortable stable awaited them. Clean hay, a huge, trough of cool water and so they invariably broke into a canter to reach that haven. As a mere lad of 8 or 9, riding without a saddle, it is not difficult to imagine my efforts to stay on the bucking, heaving back under me!

When work halted at midday, the team were taken out of the shafts and attended to. Buckets of water first, then on went their nose bags full of sweet hay and bran to give them energy. The workers settled in the gentle shade to enjoy their dinner, cold tea, cider or home made lemonade. The food was usually bread, the top of a cottage loaf, mouse trap cheese, (very mature), a hunk of fat, home cured bacon or ham. To top it all, a "Tittyovy", or cold rice pudding. After half an hour of shut eye, the driver would get up and sharpen a knife or two before rousing everyone else for many more hours until the light began to fade and work ceased for the day.

The food we ate would now be considered health threatening. Poly-unsaturated fats, salt and sugar free terminology were unknown to those men and their families. "God's little acre", Elmdon churchyard, testifies that despite their ignorance of supposedly, "healthy eating", they still attained the biblical three score years and ten, and in many cases, many more. These were the families who had worked the local farms throughout the 18th and 19th centuries. My grandparents were well over 70 years old when they died.

As the binder worked its way round the field, an army of workers with pitch forks and long-handled wooden rakes, sweated throughout the long day gathering up the sheaves as they were flung from the binder. They were stacked in stucks of 8 sheaves to each stuck: the result at the end of the day was an area of the field full of small tents of golden corn. After a few days drying in the sun, another army of men, horses and hay carts, moved in, lifted and carried the harvest back to the rick-yard to be built into large ricks, and the overflow stored in barns.

In October, the barns and rick-yards bulged with the results of the years work. Questions as to whether the respective crops had been dry enough when they were carried and stacked now exercised the farmers minds. Had there been a shower of rain before all the crop was safely gathered in? The harvest could be in jeopardy and precautions had to be taken to prevent an expensive disaster. Everyone who worked on a farm kept a sharp eye on the barns and ricks in case spontaneous combustion occurred and a fire was about to destroy a particular store. The early mornings provided the right conditions to note any change in the state of the stores. If excessive heat had built up in one there may be a hint of steam wafting along its sides. At that stage a device was employed which gave an good indication of what was happening in the centre of the rick or barn. The term "A pin in the hay stack", came from the use by farmers of a rod of iron which was poked into the suspect store. It was inserted at different levels and positions. After it had been in for a few minutes it was withdrawn and with bated breath, the end was felt to assess if it was

# THE FARMING YEAR

excessively hot. If it was, the store of hay or corn was hurriedly broken open and scattered to allow it to dry out further before it was rebuilt.

The closing months of the year, then as now, was the time when the efforts of farmer and cottager came to fruition. The hay, clover and corn had been harvested. The live-stock, hopefully, had all produced offspring which would be the seed stock for the coming year and the surplus was sold at the local market. The wives had bought all the isinglass from Winfields and Jasper Halls, the chemists in Solihull, to make up preserving liquid in which surplus eggs were "laid down" for use during the winter when the hens didn't lay. County folk were busy carrying out all the seasonal tasks their forebears had done for many generations. In the days before refrigerators, deep freezers, super and hypermarkets, and micro-wave ovens, the preservation of all produce grown locally required the knowledge and ingenuity of the housewife and bread winner, if their families were to be kept warm and well fed until the next harvest time.

To illustrate the economy of effort and planning I recount my own participation in the process. On many sunny days in late summer I often spent happy afternoons with my grandmother gleaning corn ears after the crop had been carried. That bounty, metaphorically from Les Nock's table, was used as fodder for both fowls and the pig. An ancient and profitable activity which most farmers encouraged. Beech-mast, acorns and crab-apples were also harvested for the same purpose.

Unlike the cottager, the farmer could not count all of his blessings until the threshing had been carried out and the corn sold. A major operation which entailed all the local farmers and many of their workers. Liaison between each farmer was imperative if they were all to get their stores of grain threshed during the relative quite period in the autumn and winter months. A local contractor was employed. At the agreed time he drove his large steam traction engine, towing behind it, a caravan and the threshing machine into the first farmyard. On the days that Les Nocks, Billy Markhams, Dunstans and The Home Farm were going to thresh we heard the familiar sounds of the traction engine, "chuff, chuffing" along Damson Lane.

The farm hands from the contract farms were all assembled and waiting. The engine hauled the threshing machine into position and then took up a position a short distance in front of it. The caravan was manoeuvred into a site at the back of the yard to be used as living accommodation during the threshing season.

A long leather belt was attached on the pulleys of the traction engine and the threshing machine. The men were allocated to their particular tasks, some on top of the thresher to feed the sheaves of corn into the bowls of the machine. Others prepared to hold sacks onto the funnel from which the ears of grain fell after being threshed from the chaff. Other men, usually the strongest, were assigned to the job of carrying the full sacks of corn into the barn where they were stored until sold. That was to Woolaston's in this area. They were flour millers whose mill was at Shirley. They also had large grain hoppers at Avonmouth from where their contents

Whar Hall Farm, c1910.

were exported all over the world. The sacks were collected from the farms in Foden steam wagons. They used to stop at a Sandels Pit in Damson Lane to replenish their water tanks before starting their journey back to Shirley.

The first rick to be threshed slowly vanished under the swinging pitchforks of the men on top. We lads who had gathered, were ready for some sport. As the last few sheaves were moved there was an explosion of rats and mice as they tried to escape from the sudden daylight. With air-guns, sticks, catapults and the odd Jack Russell terrier, we killed as many of the rodents as we could. The activity continued until all the ricks and barns had been threshed. Large quantities of beer and strong tea was consumed as were the large meals of stew and dumplings before the final sheaf was safely dealt with. The circus of engine, threshing machine and caravan with their attendant operators then moved on to the next customer.

When all was safely gathered in most of the local community paid tribute by attending The Harvest Festival in Elmdon church. An event which was looked forward to with enthusiasm and a feeling of thanksgiving which we children could recognise.

My mother made sure that I had washed behind my ears and my boots were well polished and my tie was straight before we set off up Damson Lane. By the time we reached Foredrove Farm gate, the church bells were ringing their two note call to prayer. As we walked across the Churchfield and past The Fish Pool, they changed to just one note; the warning that there was only a short time left to settle ourselves in our pew. We always sat on the right-hand side about half-way down the aisle. The front pew on that side and the first seat was reserved for Canon Hayters wife who kept a sharp eye on the laggards. They would be taken to task later in the week! On those occasions, the altar was loaded with produce, all of it natural and locally grown. The large ornamental loaves were made from corn threshed on Billy Markhams farm and made by his wife. They also provided a great deal of the other produce for the service. The service was always enjoyed by those who attended it in spite of the regular long-winded sermon by the Canon. It was magical to sit beneath the tall candelabrums, each with six candles at the end of every other pew. With the large ones on the altar, a shadowy music-drama, especially when the choir joined the chorus played on the walls. It could only have been achieved in the small, cosy, blessed church of yesteryear. After the service we departed to make our way home in gathering darkness which enhanced the occasion for us all.

# Chapter 12

# Off to School

In November, 1925, I became five years old and in January, 1926 I started school at Park Road Infants School. No more riding to Birmingham on open topped buses with my mother when she went shopping. I had enjoyed those trips even if it was very chilly in the winter months.

So it was with considerable enthusiasm that immediately after Christmas, 1925, we set off to the new adventure. I was looking forward to the new experience although my mother was no doubt sad, the first tentative untying of the apron strings. My new school clothes felt itchy and a little uncomfortable. The mode of dress for many years varied only between winter and summer. To keep me warm in the winter my clothing consisted of a thick, grey, woollen shirt and a tie, the latter with coloured horizontal bars, and thick, serge, short, lined trousers held up with bracers, plus a grey, "gansey", (a sort of jersey). Underneath those was a common garment then but one rarely heard of today, a pair of combinations, long, warm and woolly. To complete the picture, a strong, blue macintosh at least two sizes too large, but it accommodated a fast growing lad. On my head, either a flat, peaked cap like my fathers', or a black Southwester, and on my feet, strong boots with long stockings up to my knees. In the summer, the combinations were discarded in favour of a vest and pants, the rest of my clothing remained the same except my footwear. Instead of boots, I wore sandals. All of my clothes were bought from Gamages by mail order or from Fosters, either from their shop in The Bull Ring or the shop in the High Street in Solihull.

Appropriately fitted out, a heavy satchel on my back, off we went. Until the age of ten I walked to school with my contemporaries. In the early days I was taken by my mother but as soon as I moved to Mill Lane at the age of seven she thought it best that I should make my own way in the company of my friends.

The route didn't seem far, over the Common, up Beechnut Lane to Hampton Lane and along to Maids Cross on the Warwick Road. From there it was up New Road to the Church of England school in Park Road where Miss Bragg was headmistress. She is still remembered with deep affection by all who were privileged to have been taught by her.

A civic event which occurred there still remains a highlight of my time at the school. All the schoolchildren from the schools in Solihull were assembled in Malvern Park together with many other organizations. A brass band played as

Miss Bragg and class in Park Road, 1926.

elegantly dressed and important personages sat listening on a raised platform. After a while, the band stopped playing and a very dignified official rose and made an announcement. I forget what the occasion was but I believe it was a facility in the park being officially opened. That ceremonial was not what grabbed my attention, but what followed. A lady came forward from those on the platform and stood in the front and centre of the stage. The band began to play and she sang, "Land of Hope and Glory". Her voice was a deep, clear and a strong contralto which echoed across the park and stilled all sound other than the sound of a pin falling. She made a great impression upon me and all those present. Everyone stood or sat, transfixed, and at the end of her performance there was tumultuous applause. That scene still evokes very strong and emotive memories for me. I have failed to establish the singers' identity but because of her outstanding performance I have no doubt that we were all privileged to a moment of sublime pleasure in the company of Dame Nellie Melba.

After two years at the infants school, boys moved to Mill Lane school and the girls moved to classrooms at the back of the infants school. I joined my cousin Jim and other boys whom I knew and played with at home in Elmdon Heath.

Mill Lane School stood about half way along Mill Lane on the left hand side as one walked up from the Warwick Road. It was surrounded by a brick wall and topped with iron railings, (taken and used to make armaments in World War II).

There was a good playground on one side, bordered by the school gardens. On the other side of the building was an earth playground. A row of outside lavatories stood at the back. These stood against the boundary wall, on the other side of which was Touchwood Hall. They were over-hung by a locust tree, the long, dark beans were eaten as sweets. Along the back wall was the cycle shed. Our tuck shop was run by Mrs. Biddle in a small shop next to the school. I am sure she gave us preferential treatment because her son attended the school. Another shop on the other side of the lane also sold sweets and such like but was not used as much as Ma Biddles. A shop in the lane sold sports equipment. My father bought my cricket bat and football from it. The bat was made by Quaffe & Lilly and was signed by the Warwickshire team of 1930. The football was also signed by all the Birmingham City players of the same year. They both gave excellent service over many years.

Our journeys to and from school formed a large part of our playtime. At school we spent all of our time in the company of our fellows, whereas, as we sauntered along the paths, girls joined with us and teased us. We considered ourselves superior to them, both in sport and intellect, however it slowly dawned upon us that such assumptions were unjust. The period of which I write was one in which it was assumed that boys would become the bread winners and the girls would find unimportant jobs to sustain them until they married and ceased to be part of the

Mill Lane school football team, c1930.

work force. The same assumptions resulted in lower standards of education for them. Between 1939 and 1945 those assumptions were proved entirely wrong and without their expertise, our efforts then may not have been enough to save us.

Of the teachers who taught me at Mill Lane, Mr Peppit was the one from whom I consider I learnt the most. He was recognised by all of us as the best one at the school. He also took a great deal of interest in our spare time activities. He also acted as Deputy Head Master in the absence of the Mr Orritt. Both of these teachers moved with the elder boys to Sharmans Cross Road School when it opened in 1932.

My time at Mill Lane at the age of 12 came to an abrupt end as I looked forward to moving up into Form 6. The whole school assembled in the hall and Mr. Orrett announced that from the 1st. of January, 1932, the older boys and many of the teachers would be moving to a new school which had been built in Sharmans Cross Road. It had been purposely built so that each subject would have its own room and teacher, a far cry from Mill Lane. The subjects were to be at a higher standard and far greater range. As far as we lads were concerned, the most immediate effect was that it would be a mixed school with separate playgrounds and washrooms but the classes shared by both sexes. In my first year, the top of the class was taken by a girl. I however, was pleased to take second place.

At the announcement of the change, our main concern was "How do we get there"? We were told that that had been recognised as a problem and buses would be laid on for those children who lived two and a half miles or more from the new school. We at Elmdon Heath were provided with a bus. We collected on The Pound outside Roger's paper shop where the coach picked us up and took us to school. After the first two or three journeys we all found a favourite to sit by. I found myself sitting by a girl who lived in a small cottage on the corner of Yew Tree Lane and Beechnut Lane, her maiden name was Mildred, I have no idea what her surname was. She always said that she was an American, and she did speak with an American accent, how she came to be living in Elmdon Heath at that time I also do not know. I believe her father worked at G. Lines Dairy which later became Wathes, Cattel and Gurden. The dairy had been developed from the farm which used to occupy the site. It is now operated by Crest Dairies.

A couple of years before our move to Sharmans Cross School I had acquired a second hand bike which I used to get to Mill Lane school. My father must have known that it would not have been suitable for the longer journey so as my Christmas present in 1931 he bought me a new Hercules with a three speed, chain case and all the accessories. After a short time travelling on the bus I began to use my new cycle. Several other lads also preferred home cooking and hurried home for lunch. Jim Goodall was one of those and as we were already good friends we rode home and back each day for the rest of our time at Sharmans Cross.

Had circumstances not prevented it, I may not have gone to that school. I had sat the examination for entry to Solihull Grammar School and was successful in passing it. Unfortunately, my mother who, unknown to me, had been suffering with a terminal illness, died. My father had made every effort to avoid such a catastrophe and in so doing, had spent all their savings in trying to find a cure. Despite the scholarship, provision of uniform, sports equipment and other essential requirements to the school standards were beyond my father's reduced circumstances. That being the case, he had no option other than to continue to send me to a church school. At the time I was naturally disappointed, I did not comprehend the reasons why I was denied the opportunities for which I had worked. In later years I understood the agonising decision he had to make.

## Chapter 13
# Hobbies and Sports

The games, sports and interests of children who lived in villages like Elmdon Heath in the early part of this century were related and in a sense, complemented by, the definitive climatic conditions that prevailed at the time. The inventiveness and enthusiasm each of us could muster from our resources also played an important role. The absence of continuous "laid on" amusements, and the cost of those that did exist, encouraged us to develop our own.

During the cold, icy conditions of winter we donned the warmest clothing and made slides on the frosty footpaths and ponds and toboganed down the hills in the Park. We skated on the lake or Fish Pool in Elmdon Park or on the canal. The latter was not a favourite because its surface was often lumpy after the passage of the ice breaking boat. When the sun became stronger and the cold, wet conditions gave way to dry, marbles, cigarette cards and "tip-cat", for the boys, and skipping for the girls was the order of the day. Football and cricket at school and in the field behind the cottages were also much enjoyed. As winter gave way to Spring, cousin Jim and I returned to our favourite pastime, that of bird-nesting. We spent long, happy days and evenings searching the hedgerows, banks, ponds and trees for any nest which appeared to be a "this years"!

In the long, hot days of summer, it was helping in the fields with the hay and later, the corn harvests. As children, the hay fields provided excellent playgrounds in which to fulfil our imaginations by making houses, usually built by the girls, and castles by the boys. Cricket now took over from the muddy game of football. With the onset of the golden, fruitful days of Autumn it became time to search the fields and hedgerows for the abundant harvest of nature waiting to be collected. The shorter days and longer nights of winter, wetter and colder journeys to and from school heralded dew drops on our noses and a rush to hug the fire when we got inside the warm, inviting kitchens.

When opportunities presented themselves, either after school or at weekends, the skates were taken from the hook in the shed, cleaned and checked, and then we were off to find ice that would bear our weight. The canal was not much used by us as the ice could not be trusted, it often cracked and was thin because of the over-hanging trees. There were years when it was so cold that it did freeze so hard that all canal traffic was halted. On those occasions it was necessary for ice-breaker boats to be used to break the ice so that the barges could get through. That operation was an

The Fish Pool in Elmdon Park in winter.

exciting and interesting spectacle. A special boat was employed which was long and narrow with a steel prow, hauled by at least five or six horses. In the boat were eight men wearing thick warm waterproof clothing. Another man, sometimes two, were on the towpath to drive the team of horses. The chanting of the men in the boat and the shouts of encouragement from the lead man to his horse echoed up from the steep sides of the canal and they could be heard for some considerable distance. The iron bridge soon became lined with excited children and some adults watching the action. As the teamster and his charges appeared around the corner from the gas works, this was the scene. The man at the head drove the team as hard as he could and the men in the boat, accompanied by a steady chant, rocked it violently as it progressed slowly forward. The violent side to side motion of the boat broke the ice and made an open channel through it. The forward movement was halted at times by the thickness of the ice as it built up in front of the boat. The teamster then needed to exercise all his skills to control the team as they were brought to an abrupt halt. If one horse shied, they would all have fallen onto the ice and through it with disastrous consequences for both horses and men. The team and boat slowly made its way with the encouragement of all of us on the bridge.

Our favourite skating venue was The Mill Pool in Lode Lane or The Fish Pool in Elmdon Park. We often spent all day on the ice, oblivious of hunger pangs or admonishment from concerned parents. As dusk began to fall and our limbs refused to react to the needs of balance, we sat on the sluice gates. By the light of stable lamps we sat and relaxed and enjoyed the picturesque scene. Hoar frost hung from the branches of the surrounding trees. The blades of the skaters who still had the energy to circle and gyrate flashed in the subdued light of the lamps and the rising moon. Those still on the ice were wreathed in a fine mist from their breath as they hissed and whirled around. It was certainly an unforgettable scene which is now but a memory.

Winter gave way to Spring. As children we are told that "At the end of the rainbow there is a pot of gold". The fields 60 years ago could be said to encapsulate all that was golden. The view from Damson Lane as one looked over the gates of the "Hill Field", (now known as Row-wood Drive) or, "The Water Meadow", (now the test track for Land Rover), and many others, were all the colours of that elusive arch. It was as if there had been as many rainbows as fields and each had alighted on a green carpet where they exploded and became lakes of glorious colour. Not only were they so vivid, the scents and sounds also added to the overall impression of colour and gaiety. A silence pervaded only by bats as they wheeled around the roof tops. The call of a calf and its reply, or the screech of swifts as they circled or the shriek of a sparrow hawk or kestrel as they sought their prey, was all that could be heard. A truly magical environment in which to grow up. Is it any wonder that country folk such as I yearn for those fragrant galaxies that have been lost for ever, certainly in the once quiet corner of Elmdon and its Heath?

Across such a countryside, cousin Jim and I set out to search those same fields and hedgerows for the first elusive bird's nests and their contents. We found it a very fascinating hobby and spent long, happy days in our quests. Jim's egg collection was kept in a good set of wooden drawers. Mine were in a couple of shoe boxes, but nevertheless, they were just as valuable to me. After we had got them home, they were blown, identified and then a small label was stuck on each one to show which bird had laid it.

Many of the birds and their nesting locations which we knew so well can no longer be found in this area. Corncrakes, turtle doves, barn owls, snipe, plovers, (pee-wits), spotted flycatchers were encountered frequently and nested in and around our homes. One of the locations was a wood known as Bills Moor, it is now a shadow of its former size and forms part of the Land Rover complex. My father and I often fished its pool. Pheasants were reared along its boundary. on one occasion, it was midsummer and we had just started for home when we heard the sound of an engine, not from a nearby field, but from the sky! Slowly, it got louder until we saw a small biplane aircraft attempting to land in the field next to the wood. The pilot made one pass before he landed and pulled up close to the corner of the wood near to the keepers hut. After he dismounted, he told us that he had run out of fuel. The unusual sound had attracted a number of our friends and some of them soon sped off to get some petrol so that he could resume his journey. After he had replenished his machine he restarted the engine and took off with a noisy roar and clouds of dust. His departure caused a great deal of disturbance to the young pheasant poults which were about to be put into the release cages in the wood. Fred Smith, the game keeper mouthed several choice words when he later found most of them scattered over the nearby fields.

The habitats of birds that we sought were found within a square mile of our homes and especially around Walnut Tree Cottages. Our herons eggs came from the heronry in the tall beech trees which stood on high ground in Hampton Copse. Our plovers, snipe, and swallows came from nests in the marshy ground and barn by the Gossies. It was also in those bushes that our linnets and long tailed tits eggs were found. The Linnets were trapped from there to be put into the cages that hung by the cottage doors. The house, tree and hedge sparrows, blackbirds, thrushes, (throsles), swifts, robins and starlings eggs were all collected from the cottage buildings and their gardens.

The eggs were safely carried from the nests to our homes by one of two methods. Jim took a couple of small cylindrical cardboard tubes stuffed with cotton wool. I used to employ the same method as my father when he was a lad. Neither were foolproof in the face of authority. Jim's tubes were simply confiscated, but alas, in my case it was a little more hazardous. I used to carefully stow them in the peak of a flat cap which were common then. It was very successful until one was apprehended by George Pilenger, the local bobby, or one of the game keepers. If one could not convince them that one did not have any eggs they often carried out a simple test, suddenly reaching forward, and a hand firmly tapped the bulging peak. A warning was then given not to disturb the game or to trespass in future and with a flick of the bobby's cape or a smart kick from the game keepers boot on a tender spot, we made a hasty retreat. There were no red faces, but there was always a very yellow, sticky one! Even in those circumstances, it was still de rigueur, that no more eggs were taken from the nests from which the originals had been taken.

Throughout the summer months the shouts and calls of we children as we played along the canal bank or roamed the fields, gave our parents the knowledge that we were safe. The canal banks were the haunts of Redskins, who had to be fought and beaten. Those of us who were chosen to pretend to be them had first to plead with our mothers for pieces of corrugated paper and a selection of pheasant, pigeon and duck feathers with which to make our head-dresses. Our bows and arrows were made from hazel and sycamore off the bank. The cowboy, the goodies, ran home to collect the big, silver six shooters, complete with rolls of caps.

At other times we persuaded our mothers to make up a picnic to take to Ravenshaw. Our chosen spot there was by a relatively deep hole in which we used to swim. It was a couple of hundred yards along on the left from the Ford. It was not large enough in which to swim properly, our most popular bathing hole was in the

"The bathing hole", in the canal near The Gossie's, c1955.

canal near to the Gossies. The bottom there was sand which was washed out of the stream that ran across Lugtrout Lane by Cox's farm.

The condition of the water in the canal was very good with very little pollution. The regular passage of the barges did, however, disturb our activities somewhat. We also used to go to the outdoor pool in Park Avenue in Solihull but there we had to pay. It was very pleasant and we did not object to the small cost.

Unlike today, children were allowed, and in fact, encouraged to go out to play in the lane, across the fields or along the canal banks by our parents. There were no restrictions other than those of safety to our peripatetic boundaries. The one difficulty was when they needed to get us back home. My father solved that problem. During his army career he found one sure way of making himself known to the working gangs of Arabs in Egypt and Palestine was to use a police whistle. With different blasts various predetermined instructions could be relayed. He

Weston-Super-Mare, c1926.    Weston-Super-Mare, c1927.

adopted the same procedure to attract my attention when he wanted me to return home. It proved to be a solution which all our parents enjoyed.

When the weather prevented me from playing outside I was fortunate in that I had many toys and games to play with. There was not a great deal of space in our home at 59 Damson Lane for a busy mother and a tall, energetic lad. When the need arose I was reluctantly allowed to play in the front room. My large railway layout and a film projector were the only reason for the concession to an otherwise complete ban on play in the sanctuary which was the front room. In my confinement to the small kitchen I was fortunate to have many more choices.

From the age of eight I had a Number 3 Meccano Set and each Christmas or birthday saw an Accessory Set added to it as presents. Eventually I was the proud owner of a Number 5 Set, with a Gear Set, and a clockwork motor. In addition I was given a vertical model steam engine with which I used to drive the models I made from the Meccano. We also had a small billiard table which my father and I enjoyed despite the cramped conditions. A popular game which we all played was the game of Rings. A board in the form of a diamond, about 18 inches tall by 15 inches wide had a number of hooks at discrete distances from each other and numbered. There were five rubber rings, about two inches round which one threw from a given distance at the board. The object was to ring as many of the high score hooks as possible. We spent many happy hours playing it in the long winter evenings.

To further my education I was given a chemistry set and a gyroscope, both of which provided me with many informative hours of pleasure. The former was also the cause of some concern and a stern warning from my father. I attempted an experiment which went sadly wrong, the result was a yellow stain on a wall above father's favourite chair. I thought it would be the end of that hobby, but no, he saw the funny side of the episode and after a mild scolding we had a good laugh at my misfortune.

My father was fortunate to have a secure job and he was able to provide for his family very well indeed. We never went without anything and in fact, unusually for a working class family in that period, he took us each year on holiday to Weston-Super-Mare for a week each August. We quite often met up with the Pratley family there and that made for a very enjoyable time for us all. We always went by train whereas they went on Fred's motor-cycle combination.

Several weeks before the end of the year, preparations were made for the coming festive season, some of them in secret. Mother carefully looked through her store in the pantry to note which extra items she needed to make all the traditional food we liked so much. As she did so a question was put to my father "Do you know if Harry will send us the birds as usual, Joe?" Dad's reply was invariably, "Yes, of course he will. I hope they don't spend as long in the post as they did last year though. Do you remember, they were a bit high weren't they!" With the main item of the Christmas dinner taken care of, she was able to concentrate on the rest of the meals.

The catering requirements for the "big day", took her about six weeks. She made the Christmas Puddings first. Four white, crock basins were filled with a glutinous mass of fruit, suet, spirits of several varieties and several "joey's", the very small three'penny piece's which were common currency then and also an essential item in the puddings. The basins were put into a large oval pot on the fire and boiled for at least five hours. The kitchen then filled with all the delightful odours and promise of good times to come.

With the puddings safely stored, it was the cake next to receive attention. Made with a similar mixture to the puddings except with less alcohol. After cooking, the cake was put on one side to mature until about a fortnight before it would become the centre piece of the festive table. At that time, a layer of marzipan was put on it before the final icing and decorations. Of those it was the small pearl ones that I liked most.

The night before Christmas Day I hung a pillow case on the bottom of the bed. In the morning I awoke to find the case had mysteriously been filled with most of the toys I had secretly hoped for. Quickly dressing, I would collect all the presents from the bed and, skipping over the cold linoleum, I rushed down the stairs into the warm, inviting kitchen. My father would be smoking a cigarette while seated in his tall chair by the door. Mother meanwhile was busy cooking the breakfast. Bacon, eggs, sausage and fried bread. Not a special meal but one eaten by many people each morning before World War II. The sound concept then was, "A man couldn't be sent out to work without a full belly, could he?!" There were many more men who were manual workers than today, so the belief then held was a sound one. After breakfast and many grateful "Thank You's", I retired to the front room. That was a special treat in itself, because, like so many of my contemporaries, the room was reserved for special occasions; other than those, it was forbidden territory, although I must acknowledge that I was often allowed to play in our front room with my large railway layout.

On Christmas Day the room was put to good use. I would have hung the decorations, with help from Dad, and he would have lit the fire early that morning so that it was bright and cheerful and the room was warm and inviting. The scene was of dancing flames reflected in the large landscape pictures which hung on each side of the chimney breast. They were originals, and copies by the same artist who had painted the several large panels on the walls of the new Picture House in Solihull. The artist had painted them as a favour for my father when they were both employed in building the new cinema. I wonder where, and if, they still exist?

My father and a lad who lived in one of the small cottages which stood on the corner of Damson Lane and The Coventry Road had been pals from their school days in Elmdon. His name was Fred Pratley. They lost contact with each other during World War I. Fred went to France and my father to the Middle East. After the war their friendship was renewed and frequent weekends were spent at one another's homes.

They lived at Hockley Heath in "The White House", which stands on the Stratford Road a short way along on the right from where Box Trees lane joins the main road. They used to pay frequent visits to us, more often than we to them, the reason was Fred owned a motor-cycle combination. It was a Sunbeam and considered to be one of the best makes of motor cycles of their day. The large side-car held the two girls while their mother rode on the pillion; a draughty position in the winter but a very good one in the warm sunny months of summer. We always knew when they had arrived. Looking up from his paper, Father would announce "Listen! That's Fred and family. Doesn't that sound lovely! Listen to that engine!" There was a hint of envy in that comment.

Virtually all internal combustion engines used in cars, lorries and motor-cycles from their introduction in the latter part of the 19th century until the 1930's were slow revving, long stroke engines. That design meant they produced a very smooth, steady, distinct resonance from their exhausts. To anyone who had trained as an engineer, that sound was instantly recognised and remains the epitome of an exemplary standards and practice. It still inspires people like cousin Jim and I when we happen to hear one of those old machines whispering past us. We both owned motor cycles using that type of engine and we also competed on them in the '30's and therefore we become very nostalgic in their presence. Where is the great motor industry which British engineers built up between the turn of the century and the 1950's?

The two days of Christmas signalled the years end, The church bells at Elmdon pealed out to bid farewell to the old and to herald in the new. Those families who had enjoyed good health, not easy then, and full employment over the past year, looked forward to the same good fortune in the new.

## Chapter 14

# The Pound

In Elmdon Heath, the only street light was provided by a single gas lamp which stood against the hedge between Jack Cotton's forge and Lugtrout Lane. We children gathered under it to play in the early evenings until called in for bed. A dark and comforting mantle was soon to be replaced with roads whose gas lighting, on the streets and in the houses, would for ever replace the splendid isolation that we had taken for granted. At home, the only light in the evenings were oil lamps, candles or the fire. We no doubt developed an ability to see in subdued light, unlike today when nowhere escapes the glare of incandescent, fluorescent or yellow sodium arch lighting.

The Ash, Cinder or Dark Lane, apt descriptions all, was very dark at night and tricky to negotiate, especially for those who had imbibed a little too freely in The Golden Lion or Malt Shovel. Where is that very popular, inviting alehouse of our youth? Apart from those unfortunates, most of its users experienced no difficulty in finding their way along it. It could be an exciting experience but not a frightening or hazardous one. We always recognised who it was that approached and a cheery greeting helped each of us on our way.

The first changes to our surroundings occurred in 1925 when the tall hawthorn hedge which stood between the houses at the bottom of Beechnut Lane and those in Cornyx Lane was torn down and replaced with a row of shops. As we passed the building activity on our way to the village, I plied my father with many questions. "What's that for Dad?" and so on. One of the operations that intrigued me was a large pit which had been dug on the site. A white powder appeared in it and then large quantities of water in barrels. Meanwhile, a metal sieve in a wooden frame had been set up at one end of the pit. My father took great pains to show me the contents of the pit, which to my surprise was a very hot, white mud. He gave me a strict warning, "That is a lime pit. It is very dangerous and even when it has cooled down, the mud will burn you badly if you get it on your skin". He explained that it was being "cured", for it to be mixed with sand and horse hair to make plaster which would then be used to cover the inner walls.

Very soon two blocks of shops formed a gentle curve where the hedge had once been. Everyone wondered what sort of shops they would be. Would they compete with my Aunt Lottie's small shop or with Swinglers? In the event, they simply filled a gap in the demand for a wider choice of goods.

Aunt Lottie's shop on The Common.

The first occupants in the shops, from Beechnut Lane end, were Rutters, the green-grocers. I think cousin Jim went to work there when he left school as a delivery boy. Next were the Misses Lillies, the sub-post office and wool shop, next was Mr Rogers, a very brusque individual who with his wife kept the newsagents and lending library. It was from him that we bought our fire-works and comics. The last in that block of four was Clews, a grocers. A service passage led between the two blocks. The first shop in the next block was Harris's. His was the ironmongers and hardware and it still provides that valuable service. The shop served to displace a regular, itinerant hardware man whose name was Draisy. Jovial and cheeky, he was well liked and before Harris arrived he enjoyed a good living from his business. I can remember him with his horsedrawn shop, later to be replaced by the ubiquitous motor driven lorry. The shop was a veritable wonderland for inquisitive children. Each Saturday afternoon he would arrive at Gran's gate with cheerful shouts of "Who wants, oil, soap, paraffin, tins or plates?" Rolling up the, green tarpaulin which hung down each side of the shop that kept the goods safe from the elements, he was in business. My memories are of the strong smell of paraffin and the many other strong smelling aids for the cleaning of houses, fire-grates and bodies, Sunlight Soap, Zebo grate polish, Robin Starch and many others. As he drove away, the pans and saucepans often needed to replace those we had (in use) as they sprang leaks from constant drawing across the hobs and fire grates, rattled as they swung on their hooks.

Items that we children were always in need of, Draisy didn't sell. As very young children we went fishing with small nets, then as we got older the need for more comprehensive tackle was essential. Our inept methods meant constant snagging of the lines in the over-hanging tree branches. All of these we bought from Harris's. The tackle came already made up. A length of silk line on which was a large float, several weights and a hook, the whole was then wound onto a short length of bamboo which had been cut in half to provide a shallow holder. Tied to the end of a stick and a worm impaled on the hook, off we went to Henwood Mill to catch minnows.

Next to the ironmongers was the chemist, a Miss Jackson by name. The large Mahogany counter behind which she dispensed the many evil concoctions filled one end of the shop. Adolescence brought with it the need for the boys to smarten up in our pursuit of the opposite sex. To do that it was necessary to buy from Miss Jackson's cache of many of the pomades and items with which to groom ourselves.

We bought Californian Poppy hair-dressing in blue, oval tins and later, jars of Brylcreme, which had recently been launched from a small factory in Shirley. That particular dressing was soon to become very well known when members of the Royal Air Force were given the identity of "The Brylcreme Boys". I am happy to confess to being one of them!

The shop next to Miss Jackson's was opened by a chap named Paul Harrat as a cycle shop. His main line of business was the repair and sale of second-hand bikes, and accessories for them. My father knew him well and I recall the first visit we paid to the shop. Outside, on a small slabbed area was a hand wound petrol pump. They were all operated by hand in those days. Standing by the pump was a B.S.A. round tank, 2¼ HP, belt driven, pedal assisted motorcycle. It had acetylene lighting and was one of the few motorised vehicles to be seen in Elmdon Heath. The machine was Paul's means of transport. That machine sealed a lifetime's interest in things mechanical, especially internal combustion engines.

The shop was a wonderland to a lad whose interest had been captured by science. The door was always open with Paul carrying out much needed repairs. The need to provide illumination to our bikes resulted in frequent visits to the shop. In the 1920's, acetylene lamps were common on most of the vehicles. An explosive gas mixture of carbide and water, under control, was the source of illumination; it was very good too. There were several problems with the lamps, a major one was the hazard of explosion if care was not taken, also, after a period of time, the water eventually ran out and required replenishment, although there were plenty of full ditches, horse troughs, or village pumps, available. If the light slowly faded when one was out in the country, it was often a case of "When the Devil drives, the needs must!" and if one had recently refreshed oneself at a hostelry there was an obvious

*An acetylene lamp of the type in common use for many years.*

solution! Soon, acetylene was replaced by oil. Much safer, easier to maintain and much less costly to buy and refill. The lamps, almost exclusively made by Lucas, were attached to the front bracket of the bike by a spring loaded device. Then in the early 1930's, oil gave way to electricity. The new lamps used flat batteries and small glass bulbs. Despite the obvious convenience of them, we quickly found that the batteries went "flat" very quickly, especially if the lamp was left switched on for too long. Moreover, if the flat battery was not removed it swelled up and discharged a clear liquid which rapidly turned all the metal parts of the lamp green and useless.

Yet another change introduced small dynamos to replace the battery lamp and they were driven by either the front or rear wheels. So many changes in the space of just a few years. The last shop in the row was opened as a butchers by a Mr. Smith. My mother did not make use of the shop as our butcher was Ravens in Solihull and later, she used Leo Herraty when he opened his shop in Elmdon Heath.

Later, several houses were built on The Pound, some opposite the shops in Yew Tree Lane. The proprietor of Lines, The Well Sinkers, whose yard used to stand behind the surgery on the corner of Lode Lane and The Warwick Road, came to live in one of them. The Greswold pub was built and more houses were built in Cornyx Lane almost opposite the entrance to The Ash Path. We enjoyed the company of two special personalities in the early '30's. One was Bill Lines. As well as running the well sinking business, he was also a water diviner, and a good one at that. The other was a lady named Miss Raven. A dignified celebrity who moved from Wherretts Well lane into one of the new houses. She dealt in second hand clothing, that however, was not what she was well known for. She always dressed in black, often had a parrot perched on her shoulder and possessed a mystic aura. My parents knew her very well indeed and I often visited her with my mother, both in her old home and her new one. She was well known also for her uncanny ability to read tea leaves and one's palm. Her implied powers and mode of dress often resulted in the suggestion of witchcraft as one of her hidden powers. That was not so. She helped many of those in need.

## Chapter 15
# Solihull Gas Works-The Wharf

The village of Solihull and its environs in the early part of this century was entirely an agricultural economy and community. There was one exception, Solihull Gas Company, which was established in the 19th century. Despite the recent introduction of the railway to the village, its original proprietors chose to site it on the canal which passed nearby.

A new lane was cut from the junction of Cornyx Lane and Hermitage Road down to the canal, and there a wharf, retort house, coal yard, gas holders, weigh bridge, public house and stables were built. The raw material for the production of gas was unloaded onto the wharf from longboats or barges. By-products from the process were reloaded for transport to factories in the nearby Black Country. The Anchor pub provided rest and refreshment for both bargees and workers from the gas works. The stables and stores provided for the horses used to haul the barges and carts.

The heart of the complex was a tall, brick built retort house. As the name implies, in it were 24 long, horizontal retorts, or ovens. Around the building were many smaller ones essential in the production of gas. A narrow foot bridge spanned the canal providing access from the towpath. There was a boiler house with its tall chimney, and inside, a large steam boiler. Next to the building was a coal yard where the gas coal was stored until required as fuel for the retorts. An extension to the main building provided a rest room for the workers and next door was an engine house in which there was a powerful gas engine. Further up the site was an area where the spent coal, in the form of coke, was cooled, graded and stored before sale. Beyond were several low brick built beds, each about 20 feet long by ten feet wide and four feet high. These were purifier beds in which the raw gas from the retorts was cleaned before it was fed into tall gas holders where it was stored until required on demand. Along the high wall which enclosed the whole complex were several low buildings which had become workshops and stores.

In a yard near to the two smaller gas holders stood the original manager's house. A larger holder and a new house had been built across Wharf Lane opposite the top entrance gate.

Down on the wharf were stables, a weighbridge and The Anchor pub. A gate led into a meadow at the rear of the pub. Jack Raven was the popular landlord of the pub. The hostelry was very important to the workers in the gas works as well as

Aerial view of Solibull Gas Works, c1935.

The Anchor public house on the wharf.

being a natural, stopping off point for the many bargees who worked the narrow boats. It was also a very popular local pub for the inhabitants of Elmdon Heath. The game keepers, farm workers, and woodsmen regularly availed themselves of its hospitality.

As a family we frequently walked along the tow-path on a Sunday evening in the summer months to The Anchor. Behind it was a small paddock and orchard under which were tables and benches. My father would get a shandy for my mother, a lemonade and packet of crisps for me and a pint of Ansells Walnut Brown ale for himself and we sat beneath the trees and enjoyed the short break from the daily routine. Many of the local fathers sent their children with "little brown jugs", each Sunday dinner time an an accomplement to the meal..

Uncle Harry used the pub regularly when carrying out his keepers tasks in Bills Moor Wood. A short walk over the small hump backed bridge which originally carried Lode Lane, or over the foot bridge. He became famous or infamous, depending upon one's point of view, when he took action one winter's evening. A bitter night outside, a roaring fire in the snug, all looked very inviting. Unfortunately, the chimney had not been swept for some time and it was smoking very badly. As this had been so for some time Harry's temper at last got the better of him. To add to the gloom, the glass chimney of the oil lamp was black and there were locals puffing hard on twist filled pipes! One may possibly imagine the scene, although it could be difficult in today's affluent society.

Harry could be quite irascible, especially if he had lost sleep chasing poachers the night before. On this occasion he declared "I didn't come here to be smoked like a kipper and I'm going to do something about it". Without further ado he took his gun, put two cartridges in it, walked solemnly to the offending fireplace and releasing the safety catch, pressed both triggers. There was a resounding bang, and everyone's ears rang in the small room. Jack Raven came rushing in to be met by a dense cloud of soot, dust and smell of black powder. Harry, needless to say, had made a hasty retreat together with all the other customers. Jack was not pleased and was issuing loud threats of what he would do to Harry Beavan. Some of the customers were also a little grieved at the loss of drinking time, especially those from the shift in the works. I believe it cost Uncle Harry many drinks all round from that night's work, but knowing him he would have turned it to his advantage at the retelling.

The pub stood with its front facing onto the wharf. A wall about four feet high and ten feet long was built out from the front along the edge of the canal to act as a guard against anyone falling into it. Despite that, many a man went home soaking wet through with a sorry story of how he missed his footing. The womenfolk knew it was the beer that caused the drenching.

The production of gas, the laying of the large iron pipes across the district, the installation in various premises and the provision of the different appliances were

Back row, centre: Bill Beavan. 2nd from right: Frank Lander.
Front row, 2nd from left: Arthur Coton, Arthur Smitten, Charley Butler,
George Butler, the remainder escape my memory.

originally based at the works on the wharf. However, when my father joined the company in 1921 the administration, commercial and installation functions had been transferred to offices, workshops and a shop in Mill Lane in Solihull. The shop stood just below the rear of Davis, the bakers. The current West Midlands Gas shop stands virtually on the same spot. It was there that he would eventually spend much of his working life, but initially he was employed at the works on the wharf.

His first job was helping to lay mains around the district. It involved digging trenches by hand, laying the pipes, jointing them and refilling the trenches. Hard manual labour and often very hazardous when gas was already flowing partway through the main when connections had to be made to them. He often described how he nearly passed out when making a connection. The most dangerous situation was of course when he had to mend a break or repair an escape. Although he thought that job was hard and hazardous, he found his next job to be even more so.

He had not known many of the men with whom he had worked on laying the mains, he was now about to work with many of his family. His elder brother Bill Bevan, Bill, (Ginty), Street and George, Charley and Stan Butler were but a few. There were others who he knew very well. Frank Lander, Arthur Smitten, Archie Maynard and Frank Lander.

The method of making gas in the early years was primitive, but it worked and because of its simplicity, was cost effective. Those methods were retained until the late 1920's at Solihull. My father often took me with him to watch a shift at work.

The process was relatively simple. Fires were lit below a row of retorts and continued to be kept in until the fire-bricks in the retorts required replacement. It was then "Ginty" Street with several other brickies, and their labourers, had the thankless task of entering the still unbearably hot retorts to carry out the work. On each shift, a batch of retorts was recharged, the shift being of about eight hours duration. Gas coal had to be carried from a large heap by the boiler house across the yard and made up into a long heap some distance from the front of the bank of retorts. The scene was now set for the process to commence.

The shift stepped into a dark, brooding cavern. The top of the rear wall of the retort house had openings in it to provide daylight on the scene, they also dispersed the heat, smoke and fumes. At night, illumination came from gas lamps set high in the roof and also from the open mouths of the retorts. A couple of men stationed themselves in front of the first retort to be recharged. They had long handled tools made up in the form of rams.

The doors at each end of the first retort were opened. A blast of searing heat hit everyone in its path. The men with the rams approached the blinding white cauldron and slowly began the Herculean task of extruding the burnt residue by hard, laborious effort. At the other end of the retort, other men were similarly engaged with long handled rakes, hauling the red hot embers into heaps on the floor. Yet more men doused the embers with water from buckets to cool them. When cold enough, it was loaded into barrows with shovels and taken to the coke yard. When cold it was graded into different sizes ready for sale.

The retort now empty, the men who had pushed out the burnt coke, now commenced the equally hard task of recharging it. With large shovels, working like well oiled machines, they rhythmically reduced the long heap of fresh coal as it was thrown with consummate accuracy through the open door of the empty retort. As they worked, other men pushed the new fuel along to ensure that the retort was fully charged. The doors at each end were shut and firmly secured with strong screw fasteners. The process continued until a given bank of retorts had been recharged and was in full production.

The task was a seven days a week, 365 day a year commitment. A measure of each shifts achievement was the height of each gas holder. As they filled up with gas their tops rose from ground level up to a considerable height, say 40 feet! Not a difficult task to keep them full in warm, summer days, a different matter in the cold days of winter. A shift coming on who saw a low holder knew that they would be working full out for many hours in an effort to recover the situation.

In the late '20's, the antiquated procedure could not sustain the requirements of the enormous increase in demand as Solihull expanded. The old system was replaced by a modern, mechanised one. The slave-like conditions of yesteryear with men wielding hand held rams, rakes and shovels, working almost beyond the limits of endurance, were replaced by huge electrically operated machines.

The gas works at that time was the epitome of the "Dark Satanic Mill", and the Industrial Revolution of which of course it formed an essential part. To capture the scene it was necessary to see it in the murky darkness of night when the whole area was a sea of blazing and winking lights. Ear shattering noise and frenetic activity. Imagine standing by the opening into the yawning cavern of the retort house! The long banks of black, dirty retorts with a huge ram and coal hoppers standing mute and in repose. The opening of a retort door released a shaft of intense orange light and flame which lit up the whole area. Dark shapes and figures danced and jigged like puppets as if on unseen wires. Suddenly the ram moved forward and thrust its inexorable way through the incandescence beam, accompanied by an ear shattering screeching, tearing rattle. It then slowly withdrew and was lost in renewed gloom. The puppets then began shouting and blowing whistles to position a coal hopper in front of the now empty retort. With more shouts and noise the new fuel was fed into the red hot oven. Frequently, the coal dust exploded into sheets of flame, billowing out and licking up into the roof. The poor light from the slots in the wall was lost and the scene became even more Satanic.

On the other side of the retort house, more puppets were dancing in the glow of red hot cokes and spraying them with water, and at the same time, desperately trying to escape the scalding steam which blotted out the whole area. Uncle Bill then came along in a overhead crane and collected the cooling coke and took it to a long, sloping, steel cylinder in which there were different sized holes. The slowly revolving cylinder tipped the cold coke into separate stalls graded ready for sale. Dramatic, grandiose and in a sense, picturesque scenes never to be witnessed again on the wharf.

The men who worked, slaved, sweated and strained in those conditions paid little attention, or even appreciated, the fantastic beauty or dangers in which they passed their working lives.

In the early days, the concept of industry providing adequate welfare facilities was virtually unknown. Showers, changing and drying rooms, comfortable dining and rest rooms were non existent. Neither were special diets or additional fluids provided. Workers provided all their food, drink, clothes and transport from their own resources. Transport was often on foot, no matter the distance or weather. After World War 1, cheap transport systems such as trams and trains were introduced, but in the countryside only "Shanks's Pony", or the bike which was now becoming readily available at reasonable prices.

At the gas works the men worked in extremes of temperatures and discomfort. The retort house, boiler house and coke yard were most affected. The clothes they wore reflected the conditions in which they toiled. Fierce heat alternating with icy cold draughts which whipped through the work areas. Thick woollen vests and long-johns were essential to soak up the sweat, but also gave protection from the icy blast. They also wore thick woollen shirts, no collars and sleeves rolled up to the elbow and thick serge trousers supported by bracers and a wide, thick leather belt. These were worn by all the men who worked on the land or on heavy tasks. They were considered essential to protect a man's kidneys. Hob nailed boots were worn, and on their heads, a flat cap, it's peak encrusted with black sweat from constant re-arrangement trying to protect the eyes from the glare and heat of open retorts. To complete the ensemble, a muffler, similar to a scarf but narrow in width along its length. It was worn by draping it round one's neck with the ends tucked loosely under each side of the exposed bracers. The ends were used constantly mopping the sweat from face, brow and neck. Sometimes it formed part of the one's accessories when one walked out in the evening to the pub or shops! Then the ends were tied in a bow on the chest either above or below the obligatory waistcoat, or "wes-cut". In one pocket of the wescut, was a thick, silver, Turnip watch. From it, an equally thick, silver chain ran across the chest, through a button-hole and into another pocket on the other side, at the end of which was a golden sovereign or half sovereign.

The health of those men required extra dietary needs, the most essential being liquids to prevent dehydration and heat exhaustion. They drank copious amounts of beer, tea, water and milk, the latter usually straight from the cow. All of these were partaken at every opportunity during a shift and at the meal break in the middle of a shift. Also at the end of a shift, most of them went straight over to the Anchor to further slake the thirst but in more congenial surroundings.

There were many other jobs carried out at each recharge, two of the most important was the provision of steam power and the starting up and running of the gas engine to provide electrical power. To establish if steam pressure was being maintained, two glass gauges mounted on the front of the boiler were checked and the pressure recorded. The accepted procedure was that someone on each shift took it upon himself to make the checks when he arrived for work, he also paid regular visits across the yard during the shift.

On one of the first occasions when my father took me to watch a shift at work, he was responsible for carrying out the checks. "Come on lad, I've got something to show you!" was his invitation, and with that we walked across to the boiler house. The slight escape of steam from odd spots on the large, black boiler did not disturb me. It reminded me of a kettle hissing on the hob or Uncle Harry quietly hissing through his teeth as we walked the rides. Little did I suspect any violent change. Father started his checks, a satisfied grunt meant that the fire was burning well. As he opened the fire door, the heat and glare had already caused me to move back a little. He closed the door and looking across to me said, "Now I am going to test the pressure in the boiler. There will be a loud noise and some steam, but don't be frightened, it will be all right". Without further ado he opened the valve on the steam gauge. Despite the warning I was quite unprepared for the ear splitting shriek accompanied by a fierce jet of steam, the most frightening, which kicked up the ash below the fire door. My reaction was immediate. I clapped hands to ears and cringed, shivering against the wall near to the entrance. Father closed the valve and with a wry smile turned and looked in my direction. His instant reaction was to rush to my side when he realised how alarmed I was. He led me out of the now quiet house repeating how sorry he was to have caused me such distress. He promised never to do so again and subsequently took great care to warn me of the possibility of unusual sounds or noise.

One of my favourite places in the works was the engine house. The men who worked in the complex held the engine which stood inside with great affection and reverence. My invitation to the holy of holies took place one evening in summer. Beckoning me with the words, "Come on, I will show you how to start the engine. There won't be anything to frighten you this time"! and with no knowledge of what I would see I eagerly followed him through the green doors into the engine room. We passed from the noise, grime and smoke into a chapel of tranquillity. An electric light was switched on as we entered. That in itself was unusual, for until that moment, candle, oil and gas light was the only light I was aware of. The sight which met my gaze was of a clean, colourful room in the centre of which was the object of the adulation felt by those who had access to it.

The engine house had a tall ceiling from which a bare electric bulb hung. The green varnished walls contrasted with the highly polished red tiled floor. In the centre of the room, behind black iron railings, lay a majestic, horizontal gas engine. The engine, its vintage unknown, but I would estimate it to be circa 1900, was most impressive. Its enormous fly-wheel made the greatest impression upon me. A shallow depression at one end of the engine accommodated part of the huge wheel. It had a diameter of approximately eight feet with the lower third of it suspended in the depression. The colour scheme of the room was repeated on the engine, the fly-wheel of green with the wide edge of its rim in black contrasting with the large red cylinder, black frame work and shining bright steel connecting rods to piston and valve gear. A benevolent giant waiting to unleash the power for which it was installed.

On subsequent occasions I was given many opportunities to watch as the engine was brought into life. The operator walked slowly round it inspecting each oil, reservoir and replenishing them where necessary. As the hand which held the oil can was withdrawn, the other religiously wiped and polished all the gleaming metal until it shone in the dim light from above.

The preliminaries over, a tap was opened on the cylinder head to allow gas to flow into the cylinder. The thick rim of the fly-wheel had holes at approximately every two feet around its periphery. Inserting a short steel rod into one of them, the man put pressure on it and slowly the wheel began to move. Slowly at first, then as it gathered speed, the rod was quickly and deftly transferred from one hole to another to maintain momentum. When the wheel had reached a critical speed, a switch on a magneto was thrown which provided the essential spark. The gas in the cylinder was ignited and the once still giant crept into silent and impressive life.

The speed was controlled by a governor situated on the top of the main frame and it was operated by two brass balls connected to the gas input to the cylinder. As the engine gathered speed the centrifugal force exerted on the balls made them move out to a pre-determined point at which the gas was cut off. The engine speed then fell allowing the gas to once again flow, and so on. It seems that to produce an equivalent power or momentum today it is necessary for the machines and engines to work at extremely high speeds with fuels that create many unknown problems. A situation not envisaged by James Watt, Mathew Boulton and their like. I believe they did not intend that subsequent developments to their original designs would put the world's population at risk.

The production of gas by cooking coal resulted in many desirable and undesirable by-products. The former such as tar, ammonia and others were syphoned off. The coke, an extremely important product was stored and sold to industry and domestic consumers. The unwanted products were taken out by the purifiers. These were the long brick beds in the yard above the retort house. At six monthly intervals, the filtering material in the purifiers had to be replaced. In so doing, the nauseous and putrid residues were also disposed of. It was at that time that the whole of the surrounding area braced itself for a most unpleasant experience. A cloud of sulphuretted hydrogen and other obnoxious gasses were released when the purifier beds were opened. The stench persisted for many days and at home we lived with it for much longer. When my father was involved in that job, his clothes were left to hang outside for some considerable time before they were eventually hung in the shed. Even then every time the door was opened we were reminded of what would happen six months hence!

To sustain the engineering and manufacturing industries in the Midlands, much of the coke produced at the works was transported to those factories and the steel foundries. The location of the gas works on the canal lent itself to that operation. Coke was loaded onto the barges and longboats which had brought the gas coal which initiated the whole process. From there it was delivered along the canal network to the many foundries and factories in Birmingham and the Black Country. The steel produced was then used in the manufacture of the thousand and one items which established the area as the engineering base of the colonies, dominions and some would say, the world. The finished articles were then loaded onto the barges and were shipped worldwide. One of our eminent poets, John Masefield, paid tribute to our industry in his poem "Cargoes".

"Cargoes"

"Dirty British coaster
With a salt caked smoke stack,
Dipping through the Channel in the mad March days
With a cargo of Tyne coal, road-rail, pig iron,
Firewood, *iron-ware and cheap tin trays.*"

The men who worked in those conditions did not receive a high wage. As with farm workers, game keepers and other manual workers, their wage did not reflect the skill, knowledge or dedication which they applied in their particular fields. The average pay was about 28 shillings, (£1-40 pence) a week for a labourer, an extra two shillings, (10p), was paid to those who had spent several years learning a trade. There were no unsociable hours, productivity agreements or such like operating then. Considerable overtime had to be worked if a family was to enjoy any small extras to an otherwise low living standard. Nevertheless, I am sure that many of "we long in the tooth", consider that we found much to make our lives then very worthwhile and enjoyable. Why else do we feel so nostalgic for times past!

## Chapter 16
# Solihull Gas Works — Mill Lane

When my father joined the Gas Company in 1921, a Mr. R. Ainsworth was the Manager. Shortly, Mr. Ainsworth found it necessary to retire because of ill-health and a Mr. S. Sadler was appointed to the post and remained in that position until the company became part of the West Midlands Gas conglomerate.

Perhaps because my father and Mr. Stan Sadler arrived at Mill Lane at the same time, a rapport was established that was sustained both at work and in their private lives until my father's death in 1961. Despite that common ground, they frequently crossed swords and had differences of opinion. I well recall during tea, my father would relate a certain instance and his comment "I could see the back of his neck getting redder and redder, but I made my point"! There always seemed to be an element of challenge between them. Nevertheless, they got along very well and over the years Father was happy to do many odd jobs for him.

The seat of power in the company had moved from Wharf Lane to the more salubrious premises in Mill Lane. Here there were offices, workshops, stores and a shop. The shop stood almost exactly where the present gas showrooms now stand. Above the shop were the offices and behind these, up a long wide yard, were the workshops and stores. There, a Mr. George Kennard reigned supreme as foreman. He was a well travelled man who had spent many years in South Africa. He provided a paternal guidance and control for all those employed in the workshops. Because of his concern for their well being he was held in very high regard by them all.

My father and he also enjoyed a very good working relationship. There were a number of fitters and a store keeper under his control. Of those, the only name that comes readily to mind is one Tom Colman. He is remembered because he always joked with me and pulled my leg when Dad took me with him to the yard.

My father's experience in the gas industry up to that time was laying the large iron gas mains across the district which the company served and as a stoker in the works. A departure from those tasks was now in prospect if he could master the skills of a gas fitter. On reflection, I am sure that the prospect held no terrors for him as he was a man who willingly accepted a challenge. After a period under the guidance of George Kennard, he was recognised as a fully fledged fitter. Trained and experienced as a driver of many types of vehicle during the Great War, when the gas company acquired a small motor driven van, he was given the job of van

My father with the first Solihull Gas Company motor vehicle, c1923.

driver. At the works on the wharf and on his move to the yard, he retained that function. The progressive expansion of Solihull in the aftermath of the recent war resulted in a great deal of work for all the men employed in the gas industry. Because of the work load my father found himself to be very busy indeed.

It was a very lucrative period in the companies history. The inclusion of gas as a means of heat, light and power in the new houses was eagerly sought by those buying and renting them. Small portable fires that could be taken from room to room, flat irons without need of an open fire to heat them and cookers with a degree of heat control undreamt of by the users of open fire hobs and ovens.

The method of payment for this revolutionary amenity was by a meter situated in a convenient position in the house. Two different types were available. The first sort was a quarterly, which was read at three monthly intervals and the resultant reading in therms was presented as a bill to be paid by the user. The other type was a coin in the slot type, and were known as slot meters. The quarterly type was usually fitted in the larger house and the slot meter in the many smaller houses that were being built at the time. Initially, the slot version was designed to accept an old penny, later they were adjusted to accept both pennies and the old shilling, (5p). The rise in the cost of gas, the availability of the correct coin at awkward moments, and the large number of customers presented formidable problems in the collection of the coins. The old penny was heavy and after only a relatively small number of meters had been emptied, the collector had a considerable weight to carry and deal

## SOLIHULL GAS WORKS — MILL LANE

Solihull Gas meter inspectors. From left—Joe Beavan, Erik Pike, Archie Maynard, Earny Berry and Cyril Ward, c1952.

with. In addition there was an increasing security risk when more shillings were collected.

Initially it was the practice for the fitters to read meters and collect the cash as well as fitting out new houses or making extensions to installations. The escalation of new properties, which was to enable Solihull to become an urban, rather than a rural, community, required a revised method of collecting the monies. To meet the requirement, my father was offered the job of meter inspector. His function was to read all the meters and collect all the monies. After some thought, he accepted his new job. He was given a free hand to organize and programme the routine as he found fit. He continued to carry out that task from its inception in 1930 until he retired in 1958. Over that period he claimed to have visited every property served with gas produced by Solihull Gas Company. Originally he found little difficulty in meeting the requirement, the villages of Solihull and Shirley were not very large. However, on retirement, the district covered Earlswood, Hampton-in-Arden, Henley-in-Arden and many other areas which had been added over the years. My father became very well known and a familiar figure as he rode round the district, firstly on his own bike and then subsequently on a carrier bike supplied by the firm.

When he retired the task had expanded enormously and there were five men employed on the job.

On occasions, when counting the coins from the meter coin box, an unusual size, weight or appearance was detected which meant that it was a foreign coin. Irish, French, and strangely, Straights Settlements items were the ones commonly found. The deception was rarely successful. My father used to deduct the equivalent value of the odd coin from the rebate which at that time was paid. He then put the offending item back into the cash box before replacing it back in the meter. That effectively removed the temptation of it being used again and he could not be accused of taking the coin.

In the early days my father still found time to drive the small lorry delivering items for the fitters or the mains layers. A routine which he had carried out for many years was the lighting of the street lamps which had not been fitted with time clocks. It was with great delight I often accompanied him on that job. Most of the lamps to be lit were in the Shirley area, Danford Lane, Marshall Lake Road and Hasluks Green/Bills Lane. Most of the lamps in Solihull had been converted. At each lamp, he took a long wooden pole from tha back of the vehicle which had a small hook on one end. The pole provided him with the means of using the small hook to turn on the gas tap on the lamp. A small pilot light in the lamp then ignited the gas and slowly the flame developed into a bright, yellowish, warm glow. When a lane had been lit there were pools of light at each lamp with a dark area between each. The whole made a pleasing pattern as one walked along. Of all the lamps, the ones lining the High Street were the best. The one outside the Post Office stood out as being special.

When visiting either The Wharf or Mill Lane with my father, I was always given a very warm welcome. As I neared the time when I was to leave school and start work my father had expressed the wish that I follow him into the gas industry. "You are not going to take a dead end job. If you take a skilled job after an apprenticeship, you will then be able to command a good wage." If he were alive today and could see the loss of so many of our traditional skills, I wonder what his reaction would be?

As I cogitated my future, he and George Kennard were devising a small occasion which they hoped would influence my ultimate decision. With the stated motive of doing some shopping, he and I cycled to the village and as usual dismounted and walked up the yard in Mill Lane, ostensibly to park our bikes there. I was surprised when one of the fitters approached me and asked me to go into the workshop with him. I did not think we were going there on a working visit. Inside the workshop all the fitters were assembled and George Kennard was also there. Urging me into the centre of the group, George told me that they wanted to give me a school leaving present. I thought that unusual but did not refuse the offer. He then took up a fitter's canvas tool bag in which there were several items.

## SOLIHULL GAS WORKS — MILL LANE

There was an eight oz soldering iron, a stick of Grade A solder, a tin of flux, a pair of gas pliers and tin cutters, and another item was a tin of metal rivets, why those I never resolved? Not a complete kit, but very acceptable to a young lad just starting out. With a flourish and in his usual familiar but formal manner, George offered the bag to me with the words," Stanley, we would like you to accept this as a gift and we hope that you will join us in the industry and make use of it here at Solihull when you leave school". I thanked them very much indeed, rather self-consciously, but added that I had not yet made up my mind which job I would choose.

The following day, Arthur Street, my cousin, who lived next door came round and asked me if I would like to work with him. He told me, "You will serve your apprenticeship with me while working for a Mr. Tommy Gibbs. He owns an electrical business at Hampton-in-Arden. Would you like that"? The offer appealed to me and I accepted it on the spot.

I considered that the gas industry did not have a secure future. In the '30's, the young, rapidly expanding electrical industry appeared to be the source of energy of the future. Who had heard of a gas motor vehicle, wireless set, or a gas Hoover? To those fortunate enough to have used one, how much easier to switch on a light when one entered a dark room rather than scrabbling for a match to light the gas lamp! There was also the kudos of working with a medium so few could comprehend and which was looked upon with considerable mysticism. The small hut from which Tommy Gibbs operated his business appeared to be an old ticket office which stood next to the railway station at Hampton. A car park now stands on the site.

I began work with Arthur two days after Christmas 1934/35.

The tool bag gave me excellent service in my chosen profession for many years. I did go to the workshops at Mill Lane after I had made my decision to inform them that they had lost out to the new form of power. Naturally I was chided and told that gas would never be replaced in the home. How right they were!

# Chapter 17

# I Spread my Wings

At the age of ten I realised that my horizons could be widened if I became mobile like some of my friends. I stress that not all of them were fortunate to have the wherewithal to be so. My initial overtures to the man with the money, Father, met with some resistance. Undeterred, I persisted until he agreed to buy at least a second-hand bike. In his words, "I want to be certain that you will look after it and be able to ride it properly. I've seen how some lads treat theirs and I am not going to let you do the same with a new one". I was happy to accept the conditions just so long as I could join those tear-a-ways.

Together we found what we wanted in Paul's shop on the Pound. It was just big enough for me. Even at the age of ten I was five feet ten inches tall. It was in good condition and had a unique form of brake which operated on the rear wheel only. To apply it one had to put the pedals into reverse very quickly which locked the rear wheel. Except in icy conditions, it worked very well indeed. Little did my father realise that when he brought that type of machine it was just right for the "antics", of which he so much disapproved of.

To learn to ride was the first step. Cousin Jim already had a bike and was quick to encourage me to learn. The lane outside sloped gently down from Walnut Tree Cottages to the Iron Bridge and it was the ideal situation. With trepidation I mounted for the first time and after a brief explanation of what might happen, we set off. I put both feet on the pedals but made no attempt to use them. Jim took hold of the back of the saddle and we made slow progress down the hill were I fell off. Back up the hill for another go and so on until no doubt Jim got fed up with the slow progress. He now told me to make one more go and we set off, only on that occasion he let go soon after we moved off. I quickly realised that there was no hand steadying the wobble and so I took control and completed the first successful ride. From that moment I was one of the mobile lads.

It was not long before I was in trouble with Father for cavorting and skidding in the road as if I was on a dirt track. My bike was ideal as by slamming the pedals rapidly into reverse and at the same time throwing the bike into a low turn; dirt, dust and stones were scattered everywhere and often the rider followed. Invariably, after a short time our parents came out to put a stop to the noise and, subdued, we retired only to try again another day.

The treatment which we meted out to our cycles was in great contrast to that of our parents and their velocipedes. My father possessed a Sunbeam cycle which he bought in 1920 and apart from the odd puncture, it continued to give excellent service both to him and to me until after World War II.

My earliest memories of my parents riding cycles was when we attended a British Legion fete held in a field adjoining the Manor at Hampton-in-Arden in 1924. The Sunbeam was a prestigious company whose products were known for their excellence. Apart from push bikes they also manufactured very high class cars and motor cycles. They also held the land speed record on land with their Sunbeam racing car. My father's cycle came fitted with a fully enclosed chain case, in the top of which, near to the chain wheel, was a 2 speed device. A carrier, acetylene lighting and superior black and gold paint, gave it a very impressive finish. My mother's was also a Sunbeam ladies model with all the same features, plus, the addition of dress guards which covered half of the rear wheel. They consisted of fine elasticed cords which were attached to the wheel nuts at one end and to a row of holes along half of the periphery of the rear mudguard.

It must be remembered that the introduction of the cycle was the first alternative means of mobility other than by foot or horse. To mount a sturdy steed it was usual to climb up onto a small mounting block, these were often brick built attached to the side of the stables, Manor, or hostelry. One such was to be seen by the front door of the old Cock Inn on the Coventry Road at Elmdon. It was there for use by the local people who used a horse. They were frequently used by the coachmen who operated the stage coaches which used the Inn as one of the relief stages between Birmingham and London. The other form of block was a wooden version which could be carried from stable to horse or carried on board a coach or commercial vehicle.

From the top of the block, one put one's foot into a stirrup and then swung the other leg over the saddle and placed it in the other stirrup. One was then mounted. The change from horse to cycle still retained the requirement to mount the new form of transport; why not employ the well established method? In the early part of this century, most men who possessed a cycle used that method of getting on, and off, their machines. My father always used that method although he later adopted the now accepted method of throwing one's leg over as one moved off. The cycle manufacturers of the day recognised the need to make it possible to use the old method and so most men's cycles were fitted with a step which replaced one of the retaining nuts on the rear wheel. It was an elongated nut, about one and a half inches long and the outer inch had a diamond pattern etched into it to provide added grip between boot and metal.

To get on a cycle, one stood behind the rear wheel, both hands on the handlebars and one foot on the step. Kicking out with the foot which was still on the ground a reasonable speed was reached so that it was safe to move the foot from step to pedal and other other one onto the other pedal. Hey-presto!—one was then mounted and

# I SPREAD MY WINGS

mobile. The ladies did not use that method. Their machines cross bar was in the form of a low slung curve from saddle to head, that allowed them to step through the frame, sit on the saddle and they were able to peddle themselves off.

The new form of transport brought drastic changes to the fashions of both men and women. The men adopted breeks, long stockings, Norfolk jackets and a flat cap. The ladies still wore their voluminous dresses with a large head scarf over their hats to prevent them from being blown away at the high speeds! Later, those fashions were also adopted by the motoring fraternity for use when travelling in the many open topped cars which were a feature of the time.

At the age of ten I realised that I needed to spend money on my bike if I was to join my pals on their Sunday afternoon forays to the countryside or to use it to deliver papers, which I now considered as a way of obtaining more pocket money. My first attempt to find a job as paper boy was at Rotherhams, the main newsagents in Solihull at their shop in the High Street where the current paper ship stands next to the Nationwide and Anglia Building Society. I was unlucky as they did not need a boy at that time. Mrs Rotherham was a large, stately lady who ran the shop with her husband. She was undoubtedly the power behind the throne. They had two sons, John, the eldest and Brian. He was my age and we got along very well both at school and at play.

My disappointment at not getting the job I wanted was soon dispelled when my father asked me if I would like to work for Les Nock in his dairy. I naturally jumped at the chance. That evening I shot up to the farm to find out all about the job. I knew that the farm was half arable and half dairy. The increasing development of Solihull and the consequent population explosion meant that Les was encouraged to sell his surplus milk around the area. This involved selling it, on the doorstep, rather than, as he had done in the past, to other farmers who were selling it to the public. To do so he bought a Ford van and recruited Fred Smith, the game keeper who was now redundant because the shooting syndicate who had taken over Elmdon when Squire Alston sold the Hall, had ceased to function. Les told me that I would be helping Fred to deliver milk and dairy products each morning, including Sunday's, and also I was to assist in the dairy. When I asked how much I was to be paid he offered me 5/- shillings, (25p) a week if he found that I could do the job. I accepted on the spot.

When I got home after landing the job, Father was very pleased for me. After a moment he began to chuckle. "What are you smiling at Dad?" said I. "You realise what time the milk is delivered don't you!", he said. That comment reduced my enthusiasm somewhat when it dawned upon me that I had forgotten to establish what time I was to start work each morning. After some discussion, Father told me that he had discussed the start time with Les and they had agreed that I should get to the farm at 6 o'clock. That meant I would have to be up at 5.30. Horrors! Like most active youngsters I liked to stay in bed until the last moment, nevertheless, I accepted the situation and soon became accustomed to the early rise.

My first morning was in early January. I found myself standing in the farmyard looking for Fred and his van. A voice from a barn led me to where he was inspecting the van for levels of water, oil and petrol and tyre pressures. The tyres were checked every day for cuts and nails because the rubber from which they were made was not as good as it is today. More significantly, the road surfaces left much to be desired, nails, flints and sharp edges on stones and rock were common because of the many trenches being dug to extend the gas, electrical and sewer services round the area. On the first morning Les joined us from his job milking the cows. "Do're reckon Stan can do the job Fred?" Fred's answer was "We'll be alright won't we Stan!". He then reminded Les that we had worked together many times feeding the birds, by Bills Moor. We then loaded the van with milk, eggs, (mostly white ones, brown were less common then), cream and butter and off we chugged.

The milk was bottled the night before. Mrs Nock had also skimmed the cream and put it into tubs and had patted the butter into half pound blocks and they were wrapped in grease proof paper. She also gathered the eggs and put them in an old orange box, lined with straw. A white crock basin was left by the house wife with the number required. If they were bought in a shop they were sold in white paper bags and then placed very carefully on top of the groceries, there were no egg boxes then.

Our round began from the farm and our first customer was in Beechnut Lane. We then served others along Hampton Lane, Brueton Avenue and Park Lane. The houses between there and New Road were only half built. Then down New Road and Churchill and up Homer Road to Streetsbrook. Because I had to get back to the farm for my bike before going to school, Fred turned round after we had delivered to one of the small cottages which stood by the brook in the old lane. When we arrived back at the junction of Hermitage Road and Wharf Lane I jumped out of the van, bid a happy, "Cheerio", to Fred, and sped off down Wharf Lane, over the footbridge and across the fields to the farm. A race down Damson lane to Gran's where she was waiting with a steaming cup of tea and a large bowl of hot porridge. I have many fond memories of her taking each frozen hand in hers and rubbing them briskly to restore the circulation and warmth. After satisfying herself that I was well fed and warm she helped me on with gloves, scarf and cap from near the fire. With a grateful, "Thanks Gran", I was out of the door and off down the lane to school.

Ice cold bottles, basins of eggs and tubs of cream became routine, however, conditions then and now were very different. No warm cab on the float. All the items on the van for sale had to be handled, none were ready packed for easy handling or hygiene. The road conditions caused the greatest problems. The surfaces on many caused a great deal of damage to the tyres of vehicles and pushbikes. Punctures were common and imagine changing a wheel in icy conditions on a very uneven surface, or worse, repairing a puncture in those conditions! Out with the John Bull puncture outfit, find a puddle in which to test the inner tube to find the hole. Repair the puncture, back in the puddle to ensure that there was no leakage of air, dry off the tube, dust it with French chalk and replace in the tyre. Oh happy days!

At the weekends, after returning to the farm at the end of the round there was work to do in the dairy. As we did not get back before half past twelve we left the unloading of the van to the afternoon and went home for dinner. On my return it was cleaning the churns, the metal measuring jugs, the buckets and all the other items involved in the bottling process. I very often landed the job of cooling the milk as it came from the cows. A cooler had been installed near to the dairy by a low path along which the churns were moved. To take them from the cooler to the cold room they were stood on the bottom edge and "spun", or twisted. The motion enabled full churns, which were very heavy, to be handled easily. The cooler consisted of a thin tank, — each of its vertical sides were corrugated. The tank was fed with cold water which flowed through its sides. Along the top of the tank was a channel into which the warm milk was poured. Along the bottom another similar channel collected the cooled milk from where it was poured into waiting churns. As the milk flowed slowly over the external sides of the tank, it was cooled before collection and storage in the cold room. Other jobs were to feed bottles through the washing and sterilising machine. Also I arranged the cardboard tops, with their centre hole, ready for them to be fitted on the bottles after filling. At the end of the day we collected all the utensils and scrubbed them with boiling water, as were the floors of all the working areas. The milking parlour was also cleaned thoroughly before each milking session. It was a thankless job but we knew that the good name of the farm depended upon a very high standard of hygiene.

My grandmother and I often sat by her fire, just talking of days gone-by. Often though we were busy doing one of the many jobs that the housewife then accepted as routine. Maybe we were plucking a fowl for Sunday dinner, or during the winter months it was plucking pheasants, partridges or the odd turkey, some of them as favours for either Les, Nock or Billy Markham. During some of those nostalgic moments she often told me of her pleasure when she was able to acquire the very rich milk given by a cow immediately after it had calved, which was known as "beastings". She often licked her lips in remembrance of times past. My first opportunity to taste it came when I began work in the dairy. The first time one of the cows calved I asked the cow-man if I could have some of the beastings, for my grandmother. The request was met with a knowing wink and the comment, "She knows what's good doesn't she!". He gave me a jug full of the thick, creamy milk and I hurried home. "Look what I have got for you Gran". When she saw the jug she obviously guessed what it contained and it gave me immense pleasure to see the delighted anticipation in her eyes. She asked, "Have you tried some?" I said, "No, but I think I may". She took a small drinking glass into which she poured the still warm liquid. She offered the glass with a warning "You might find it too rich so only take a sip first". The sip confirmed her warning, it was much too cloying for my young taste buds. I passed the glass to her and she drank the remainder with an appreciative smile saying, "It's been a fair while since I have enjoyed some of that. Lovely!". That day she made me a rice pudding which I liked very much indeed, it was very rich and very satisfying. After the first tasting I always sought a source of the liquid gold. What happens to it now? No doubt the E.E.C. have decreed that it is unhealthy and unsuitable for human consumption and it is washed down the nearest drain. If that is so, why is it not made available to children's hospitals? It never did us any harm.

Six months after I became a milk delivery boy, Les Nock told us that he was going to cease running the dairy. His decision was not because he was unable to make a profit, on the contrary, the infant business was very successful. The reason related to recently introduced Government legislation. The new policy related to the abysmal standards common on farms at that time. Until 1930 most farmers could sell their milk and dairy products to whoever, and what is more, however they liked, regardless of hygienic standards or the lack of them on their premises. The laissez-faire attitude meant there were many things wrong.

I have already paid tribute to the standards which were imposed at Foredrove Farm. Unlike the herds on that farm, many were affected with T.B. and other preventable deceases all of which were the result of poor husbandry and management. In the cow sheds and milking parlours, conditions were those that existed centuries before. The attitude was "This is a farm, what else do you expect?". Utensils, cowmens and milk-maids clothes, their personal cleanliness, the storage and movement of milk and its products left much to be desired. A common practice was to dilute the milk with water, itself of unknown quality. By so doing a handsome profit could be made. I very well remember both my mother and grandmother inspecting the measures used by the milkman as he ladled the milk from pail into jug on the doorstep.

They were looking for signs of blood, insects, foreign bodies and especially the colour of it. The addition of water gave it a blue tinge. An example of the care taken by housewives and cooks is shown in my mother's receipt book. Where milk is required it stipulates "New milk", A reference to the scrutiny paid to its condition.

The problems were recognised by the Government and to ensure that the whole rickety system did not collapse they set up The Milk Marketing Board.

The stringent measures introduced by the Board quickly resulted in the demise of many local milkmen because the small farmers were unable to meet the new standards, either because of the cost or circumstance. To overcome the problems, farmers began to cooperate with each other to form a much improved industry. In Elmdon Heath a member of the Lines family, well known and respected in several local businesses, set up a dairy in Yew Tree Farm and founded the first local milk round under the new regime. After some time his business was taken over by three local farmers who set up a company known by their own names — Waifs, Catell and Gurden. They prospered as they were all well known in the community. A few years later the farmers were taken over by another well known local company, The Midland Counties Dairy. The company had built up a strong name with its sale of a very good ice cream. They were the local competitor to Eldorado, of the "Stop Me and Buy One" fame. The United Dairies replaced them and they in turn have recently become Dairy Crest.

After my short sojourn at Foredrove Farm as a milk boy I found a paper round with a Mr. Bramwell whose shop stood on the Warwick Road almost next to Horrobins, the clock repairers and it was opposite the Grenville Mens Club. Another well-known Solihull business, Rogers Garage, was also nearby. The shop sold all the usual items associated with a newsagents, papers, sweets and tobacco, but Mr. Bramwell was also well-known in the village as a piano tuner and tutor.

Initially I did just one morning round which encompassed The Warwick Road from the shop along to Manor Road, then Ashleigh and Broadoaks Roads and the three or four new houses in the new road which became Heaton Road. After a while I was given the opportunity to do an evening round. That one took in The Warwick Road to George Road, Park and Brueton Avenues and New Road. On Sundays I combined both of the rounds with the addition of Churchill, Homer and Herbert Roads. I also collected the money on that day and consequently I rarely finished it before mid-day.

I was now about 12 years old and one of my favourite pastimes was train spotting. After tea I would race up to Streetsbrook Road bridge where I went down the footpath which led down from the road to the station. There was a good vantage point where I often stood, sometimes with my pal, Norman Pardoe.

There were four tracks through Solihull then; the two inner ones were used by expresses and fast goods and the two outer tracks were used by local trains. The greatest thrill was to watch as the expresses came thundering through on the centre lines between Paddington, High Wycombe, Didcot, Oxford, Leamington Spa and Birmingham. The trains were hauled by the cream of the Great Western Railway, the G.W.R. or to put it more succinctly, "Gods Wonderful Railway". The engines were all known by their "class", either, Halls, Castles or Kings. The latter were undoubtedly the most illustrious. Their names were evocative of Great Britain's past, King Edward IV, VI, & VII, James I & II, Charles I & II and Georges I, II, III, IV & V. The latter was considered the greatest of them all and it was that engine which toured the U.S.A. in the '30's, making a lasting impression upon the American public. On its return to England it sported a silver bell on its front, below the fire box. It still excels in providing immense pleasure to everyone fortunate to see it hauling special trains around the country.

With the new bike I became one of a group of five lads who used to spend most

Sunday afternoons cycling round our part of Warwickshire. One occasion still brings amusing memories flooding back. We had ridden to Meriden and on toward Nuneaton. The tall pit heads of Keresley Colliery gave us something to talk about and to tell our parents when we got back home. As we retraced our route we found it necessary to attend the call of nature. A thicket of willows looked just the spot. At a most inopportune moment an angry voice came from an adjoining field "Get out of them thier Osier beds!". With a mad rush, adjusting our dress as we did so, we complied. In those days, gamekeepers, and other land-owners did not hesitate to blast off a shot gun if trespassers were slow in their response. Cousin Jim and I still recall that episode with some amusement.

## Chapter 18
# Family Leisure in The '20's & '30's

In the third decade of this century, my father, like the majority of his contemporaries, worked an eight and a half hour day for five days and for four and a half hours on Saturday mornings. That pattern of work was accepted as the norm by most breadwinners. However, shop workers endured much longer hours, their day did not end until about eight o'clock each weekday and not until nine on Saturdays. The effect of those long hours, prior to the war, was that Solihull's High Street remained a brightly lit and an active shopping market. It's attraction was the rendezvous for young people where they could promenade and enjoy themselves.

As Friday was usually pay day, bills were paid and what was left was spent on entertainment. Friday evening was when I held out my hand for my weekly sixpence, (two and a half pence), which I found more than adequate. My father's wage of two pounds and ten shillings, (two pounds and fifty pence) a week, not a large sum, but average for the time, remained so for many years, as did my pocket money. An important aspect of the monetary system then was its stability. The Pound was worth 240 old pennies, whereas, it is now worth only 100. The difference in the cost of everything between then and now is reflected in the ever escalating prices one pays for essentials. We were once able to enjoy a good standard of living on what now appears to be very low wages. To give an example of the stable conditions, a seat in Solihull Picture House was either 3d, 6d, or 9d, depending upon where one sat. Those prices remained constant throughout the period.

An event in our calendar which required an increase in our pocket money was the arrival of the travelling shows. There were three major ones, Sir John Sangers Circus, Bostock and Wombwells Menagery, and Solihull Carnival and Fair.

The circus always set up in a field next to the gas works in Wharf Lane. As soon as I heard unusual sounds coming from that direction I made off to see what was going on. After standing just inside the gate for a short while, one of the men erecting the Big-Top would ask me if I wanted to help, they were always looking for additional hands to hang onto the ropes as it was raised into position. Time had no meaning for me, I became so engrossed in all the sights, sounds and smells until one of the men would ask me, "Do you know what time it is?" Someone else would shout, "It's one o'clock," and with that they ceased what they were doing and made their way down to The Anchor for their dinner. I realised that I was in trouble and hurried home as fast as I could. My disreputable appearance as I stumbled through the door was met with the order "Get yourself cleaned up or there will be no dinner for you, and what have you done to your clothes?" I could ignore the scolding as in my pocket were tickets for all of us for Saturday afternoon's show. It gave me a great thrill when we walked across the invariably muddy ground to show my parents which poles I had helped to raise, or which ropes I had helped secure. Settled in our seats the show began. Were there ever trapeze artists who could perform so many somersaults? How well trained the animals were and how we laughed at the clown's antics. The large elephants that were paraded round the ring had that morning been used to spread straw over the muddy entrance and to slowly walk back and forth to make a firm footing for the many people who attended the shows. All too soon it was time for it to move on and I always made sure that I helped with the dismantling of the big tent. The sounds and smells of the performing acts and also the areas round the Big-Top will remain as one of the highlights of my childhood.

Bostock and Wombwells Menagery always set up in a small field in Union Road beside the old chapel which was used as a Sunday School. The location was opposite "The Spike", or Workhouse or Union from which the lane was named. There were large overhanging Horse Chestnut trees from which we children used to collect our conkers. There was always an air of mystery and a sense of being exploited. We always thought that the entrance fee was expensive. It was 6d, (two and a half pence),—then one had to pay to enter most of the side-shows and exhibits. Some could be a little frightening for a young child and we often dared each other to go in to look at them. Each small tent had a rogue in front of it extolling the "amazing exhibition within! Things never to be seen again anywhere in the world are behind me!" I recall a few of those sensational spectacles, "Rats as big as cats from the sewers of Liverpool", The most hairy woman in the world", "A two-headed lamb born on a local farm" were just some. Although we easily saw through the subterfuge and cheating we still paid to see them as they formed part of our annual high spots in the calendar.

The event which attracted us far more than any other was Solihull Carnival and Fair. There was so much to see and do. It was great fun to stand on the corner of Mill Lane and The High Street in front of Davis's the bakers, pushing and shoving as everyone tried to get the best view of the passing tableaux and bands. There were "whoo's" and "aaah's" when the girls in their smart uniforms strutted by playing their gazzutters. In 1932 my father and I took part. Mr. Sadler, the manager of the gas company, was also a member of the Chamber of Commerce and in that year offered his car to the carnival committee. For some reason they decided that it should form part of the parade and so we found ourselves in the midst of brightly coloured floats and performers. The car was a Rover Big Nine, one of the pre-eminent marks of private cars. We joined the procession in George Road, where is that pleasant lane now? From there we wound our way along The Warwick Road,

# FAMILY LEISURE IN THE '20'S & '30'S

Solihull Carnival 1932.

New Road, the High Street and Station Road to Ashleigh Road where we turned down to rejoin the Warwick Road and returned to our start point. On return to school I was chided and revered by those who had seen me in the car.

Rover "Big 9" the coachbuilt saloon model

After the excitement of the procession we gradually made our way down Park Road to Malvern Park. The very large fair used to occupy the field on the left near the entrance to the park. Its entrance was often muddy and strewn with straw like the circus. The need to jump and skip over the mud only added to the joviality of the occasion. It was rare for the fair to be set up in fine weather, yet, if memory serves me right, the day of the Carnival was usually, fine and pleasant. Once inside, we, my pals and I, made for the shooting ranges. It was well known that the stall holders took certain measures to ensure that not too many of their prizes were going to be won. In our case, after only a shot or two, we knew that either the gun sights, the darts or the shot had been tampered with to reduce accurate shots. Because of those measures, we invariably got involved in an argument with the stall holders when the targets refused to fall and we did not win a prize.

Our shooting activities throughout the rest of the year, and especially between September and January, ensured that we were well practised in the art and few, if any, of our quarry escaped our aim. Why did the targets as presented elude us? Despite our protestations we rarely found a weapon that shot accurately. I must have been lucky on one occasion though. Standing on a shelf in a bedroom is a small Chinese vase which I won. I would like to think that it was my expertise that enabled me to, but it is more likely that it was just a fluke, the odds were always stacked agin us!

One year my father took me to watch the boxing bouts in a large tent in which a ring had been erected. Outside on a small platform, a barker was boasting of the virtues and prowess of his boxers and challenging anyone to go three rounds with their weight equivalent. If they were still standing at the end they would receive a percentage of the purse, he didn't say what that percentage would be! Some of the light and fly weight contests were exciting, but the heavy-weight bouts were not pleasant and merely bloody mauling matches. Father told me that some of the challengers were part of the show and were there to encourage the men in the audience to try their hand.

The razzle-dazzle and glitter of the fairground paled into insignificance as far as I was concerned when I located the very heart of all that glitter; the very grand steam show engines where they stood at the back of the sideshows, their restless motion providing the electric power for the whole fair. They had a duel role, to haul the large caravans and trailers in which the many stalls and shows and their owners were stored and transported. Their other function was to provide all the power for the dodg'ems, carousels and hundreds of lights. The tents, living quarters, sideshows and stalls formed a formidable, slow moving convoy as it made its way from town to town. The approximate four miles an hour was not an undue problem then, it was after all the speed of a man or horse walking; but it became unacceptable in modern traffic conditions.

It was a magical sound, the chuff, chuff, of the engines, the shouting men as they slowly guided the mighty machines along the narrow lanes to their temporary destination. As soon as we children heard the sounds the word quickly passed round and we raced to watch their progress. The entrance to the show ground in Malvern Park was through a large five barred gate in New Road where the large ornamental ones now stand. The ground is low lying at that point and unless it was a very fine summer, it was a wet area. With traffic halted, whistles blowing and many orders and counter orders being passed, the drivers of those magnificent machines slowly inched their charges across the road and into the field. All of that accompanied by black smoke, white steam, racing flywheels and the scream and screech of iron rimmed wheels as they made what appeared impossible manoeuvres into the field.

There were similar difficulties when the circus came to Wharf Lane. The gate there was also low lying and created many problems for men and machine. The entrance in Union Road used by the Menagery was narrow but at least it was usually dry and firm.

For a week each year the short length of Park Road became a happy, shoving, jostling crowd of revellers. Some of them were making their way toward the noisy, musical entertainment at its end, others were coming away sporting decorative and gaudy jewellery and toys they had won. As with the shooting ranges, there were several opportunities to reduce the chances of winning a prize. The coconuts were often forced into their holders so making it very difficult, if not impossible, to knock them out. Even when one of the coverted nuts had been won and a hole knocked into it so one could take a drink of milk,one was invariably disappointed. The milk had been drained from it and replaced with an evil smelling looking liquid of unknown quality.

On occasion, the park itself was taken over for large and exciting displays by various organisations. Solihull Fire Brigade demonstrated their abilities in putting out a fire in small wooden house built for the occasion. They also shinned up and over a tall tower and provided enormous fun for the crowd with a display of water from their powerful hoses. Their big, red Dennis fire engine with its gleaming brass,silver bell and large ladder added to the scenario. Further down the park, an area had been roped off to form another display area. We made our way there after the fire-fighting display to see what was going on. Suddenly, there was the sound of bugles calling, horses snorting and straining at their bridles as they galloped into the centre of a ring. On the horses were soldiers dressed in their full dress uniforms and carrying long wooden lances. I tried to take in the scene as my father pointed out a number of wooden pegs, set at an angle in the ground and some distance from each other. A contingent of an army cavalry unit were lined up at one side of the field. An officer using a megaphone, — no loud hailers then — announced to the large crowd which had now gathered,that his men would demonstrate the art of "pig sticking". The "pigs" on this occasion were the pegs which I had been shown. He went on to announce that "This forms an important part of our training when we are stationed in India and other far away places. The object is for each man to ride furiously from one side of the field to the other, and on the way to impale a peg on his lance. Later we will have a competition with the Birmingham City mounted police who have challenged us".

A call on a bugle and the display began. A cavalry charge took place across the field, and as each rider passed a peg, it was successfully speared. The pegs were removed from the lances, replaced in the ground and a repeat performance took place. With the crowd now enjoying the spectacle, a team of police riders entered the arena. The cavalry officer encouraged the crowd to enter into the tournament by cheering on one side or the other. Another bugle call and off they galloped. On the first pass, the cavalry stuck all their pegs, the police missed two. On the second run, the score was reversed, I now suspect that that was an agreed outcome by the competitors beforehand just to heighten the crowd's excitement. The crowd demanded a "sudden death" run off, which was accepted by both sides. The final result was of course the cavalry with all pegs stuck and the police leaving three still in the ground at the end. The cavalry proudly rode off with their trophies held high on the point of the lances. The officer then announced that "This training enabled his men to equip themselves very well in war". For those present who had not been involved in conflict,the statement did not fully explain itself, for the others, the object was all to obvious. My father was later to tell me that when the army trained in earnest they used pigs heads as they were roughly the same size and weight of the human head and therefore represented that of the enemy!

In 1935 the Silver Jubilee of King George the V's coronation was celebrated. The whole country enjoyed a day of carnival and rejoicing. Here in Elmdon the festivities were held in The Hall and on its grounds. In the afternoon a tea party was held on the South Lawn for all the old employees and their families of the estate. The long tables were laid out on what is now the green area between the trees behind the church and the lake. In the evening the large entrance and lounge in The Hall was decorated, tables had been set up from where drinks were served and a few musicians provided music for singing and dancing. Anyone who could perform were encouraged to do so. In our group,Ron Topping was only too pleased to play his harmonica and to recite a couple of monologues. His "Albert and the Lion", and "Sam, Pick up your Musket", which were recited in a Lancashire dialect, was an excellent imitation of Stanley Holloway. The revelry continued until late into the night and everyone had a marvellous time.

The cinema in the '20's and '30's was our major source of entertainment. When I was a small boy we saw our first film shows in the tin hut in Catney. The wooden seats did not detract from the joy of watching figures moving across the silver screen. Felix the Cat, Micky Mouse and Our Gang all made us shout and scream at their antics. Later, when we were older, we learnt to dance the valeta, gay gordons, waltz and other popular dances in the Youth club which was also held in the tin hut.

Family gathering to celebrate King George V's and Queen Mary's Silver Jubilee in Elmdon Park, 1935.

My parents and I regularly went to the pictures every Saturday evening. The prelude to those outings carry my thoughts back to the kitchen in 59 Damson Lane as we prepared for the outing.

Mother stirred the fire under the large black kettle murmuring on it. Father filled an enamel bowl from it and also his shaving mug. After washing he began the serious business of shaving. A well worn strop was hung on a hook by the fireplace. A piece of paper, about six inches square, was torn from an old newspaper. After well lathering his face, and making a cautionary warning for me to stay away from him, he began to carefully draw the very sharp blade of an open razor across his cheeks and up and down his neck. He was always careful as he negotiated his adams apple. When I asked as a small boy what it was, his answer was sufficient to curb further enquiry. "That's a bucket which helps the drink to go down!" The excess soap on the blade of the razor was wiped off on the square of paper. All of this was accompanied by a well modulated voice from the loudspeaker on top of the wireless announcing the football results. These provided the points for the recently introduced Football Pool; Father then disappeared upstairs, meanwhile, my mother inspected me to make sure that I was up to her standard. At last we were ready for the evening's entertainment.

More often than not, we walked to Solihull along Dark Lane, and as we passed the gas offices, father invariably looked up the yard to ascertain that everything was alright. Round the corner into High Street and outside the cinema a group of young children would plead to accompany us in if the film was an "Adults Only". Father always refused their pleas because he considered that it was their parents responsibility.

Once inside we always sat on the right hand side in the rear seats about six rows down from the back. Once settled, Dad reached into his pocket for the packet of sweets which he always made sure were there. They were always a mixture, with large, square, pink ones tasting like soap.

As Solihull increased in size, bus services gradually increased to provide adequate transport for the additional people, eventually there were very good services throughout the region. In the 1920's and '30's, there was a frantic rush by various entrepeneurs to be the first to build a cinema in village and town. We were fortunate that most of the new ones were in easy reach of Elmdon Heath with the extended bus service. Those cinemas which come readily to mind are:

"The Mermaid" in Sparkbrook.
"The Olton" at Olton.
"The Warwick" at Acocks Green.
"The Odeon" at Shirley.
"The Sheldon" at Sheldon.
"The Gaumont" New Street, Birmingham.
"The Alexander" Station Street, Birmingham.
and many more in the city.

There used to be a small cinema in Knowle, in Station Road, which is now occupied by a garage.

On arrival at our chosen picture house I rushed up the steps and stood hopping from one foot to the other as my parents made their leisurely way behind me. Father would have remonstrated with me "What's the hurry? You'll see everything all in good time". My father was noted for his laid back approach, often to the exasperation of the rest of the family. With tickets in hand we passed from light to inviting dark. As we followed the attendant and the searching beam from her torch, the many odours from tobacco smoke, dusty carpets, sweet papers, sweaty bodies and on cold, wet evenings, the musty smell of wet woollen clothes. There were no man-made fibre materials in clothes then.

Led to our seats by the searching beam, we settled in them and began to enjoy the additional entertainment of music. In the early days at Solihull it was provided by the pianist who accompanied the action of the films. Later on when the Odeons and other large cinemas established themselves, they provided entertainment by a cinema organist. During intervals between programmes, the lights came up to their full brilliance and somewhere from the depths of the orchestra pit floated the signature tune of the resident organist. Slowly, he appeared sitting at the instrument which was itself brilliantly lit with lights of many colours. Strains of familiar and popular tunes helped the audience to relax. The most often played were, "The Lincolnshire Poacher", "The Whistler and His Dog", "The Skaters Waltz", and others that slip my memory. One local organist, Reginald New at The Mermaid, also joined with Dudley Savage, Sandy MacPherson, Reginald Fortt and Florence de Jong, playing regularly on the wireless. The popularity of cinema organ music on the wireless was also accompanied by that of the more classical church organ. The latter found esteem with a wide listening audience at that time. As a lad I enjoyed listening to George Thorben Ball playing Bach's "Toccata and Fugue" or some other classical piece as I ate my dinner in our small kitchen. In later years I met Oscar Deutch, a Birmingham entrepreneur who was the driving force behind the Odeon chain of cinemas which eventually was to cover the whole country. It was as a young apprentice electrical engineer that I met him at a hotel that he was refurbishing at Portway on the Alcester Road.

After the death of my mother, my father realised that he still needed to take me out and to provide my entertainment. After a period of time we began to go to the pictures again. He now encouraged me to invite Cousin Jim to come with us which made our outings that much happier.

I remember we saw "Sanders of the River" in The Gaumont and went to a pantomime at the Alexander which was "Babes in the Wood".

In 1933, when I was 12 years old, I, together with my contemporaries of similar ages, was refused admission to Solihull Picture House to see the film "King Kong". Our curiosities were aroused, only to be unfilled, as the film had received a considerable amount of adverse reportage by the critics. The press debated whether it was suitable to be viewed by the young. The film was at last given a new category, "X", which excluded everyone below the age of 18. Considerable disgust was voiced by many of the younger picture goers, all to no avail. When at last we were old enough to see it we could not understand why we had been denied the pleasure earlier. Methinks, we have come a very long way since those innocent days!

Our leisure activities then were far less sophisticated than those of today. For instance, we drew great pleasure from the sight of my grandmother going shopping with a small piglet trotting along behind her. Every year about March, she bought a piglet from the local butcher to replace the one slaughtered in the previous Autumn. Usually a Large White or Gloucestershire Old Spot about four weeks old. For two or three months the small pink animal became a member of her household. A wooden orange box lined with a piece of old blanket was set near the fire. She quickly house trained it and unlike the more prosaic pets, it did not create havoc with the furniture or fortunately for it, my grandfather's slippers.

Each one provided immense pleasure because of their skittish natures and the mad dashes made around the room whenever a visitor to the house arrived. Fed on a baby's bottle, after a month they were weaned off it and by May had grown from an affectionate small pet to a large formidable animal which was then banished to the sty at the end of the garden. There they grew fat and sometimes, unpredictable. An adult sow is heavy, has very strong jaws and large teeth, all of which are used with considerable ferocity when disturbed or angered. Their end was always the same, in October the local butcher came and the once small household pet became hams, bacon, sausages and many other succulent cuts of meat hanging in the larder or up the chimney.

On warm summer Sunday evenings Father would suggest that we take our usual stroll and drink somewhere. "Where shall we go, Lass?" My mother's response came as no surprise, it was almost always, "Let's have a look at the Park and then The Anchor, aye?" On the way up Damson Lane either she or Father nipped into my Gran's to tell her where we were going. It was a very enjoyable experience to walk up the lane. The quiet and calm scene broken only by the lowing of cattle recently returned to the fields after milking, or the call of a kestrel or sparrow hawk as the former hovered in search of an unsuspecting vole, the latter quartering a hedgerow for finch or linnet. In late summer as we made our way across the Church Field we picked mushrooms for breakfast next morning and sweet chestnuts from a tree that stood close to the clap gate where the path entered the Church Drive. Stepping over pot-holes and ruts we arrived at the church and paid our weekly visit to the graves of many of our family. By the main gate to the church Father invariably looked carefully at the coach-wash and stables to ensure that there was no damage to them. Although the estate had been sold and the Squire had gone, the old employees still took a keen interest in the place. A housekeeper was still in residence in The Hall and she took care of the interior. Until after the last war there had been no vandalism or damage to the property or land.

We walked along the front drive of the Hall between the row of purple Rhododendrons, to emerge at the crossroads where the lanes led off to the Rectory and the Terrace. We always took the latter as it led past my great Aunt Lizzie Drinkwater's cottage. A short stop there to pass the time of day and ask after Annie's — her daughter's — health before we continued past the school and down the path to the wooden bridge over the brook. One evening as the sun was slowly sinking below the ice house by the lake. I recall my mother telling me that she and Father used to pay frequent visits to the bridge when they were courting before the war, — she of course referred to The Great War. She also told me that they were often joined there by Uncle Harry and Aunt Ethel. There had been immense pleasure in those meetings as my mother and Aunt Ethel were cousins. She told me that the popular colour for ladies' dresses then was powder blue. The popular song, "Two Little Girls in Blue", was then an apt portrayal of their own relationship.

In recent times there has been another graphic description of Elmdon Park, the path across it, the bridge over the brook and the many other attractions of the place

The Gossie's

in Edith Holden's book, "Diary of an Edwardian Lady". Her reference in it to a conversation with a game keeper could have been either with cousin Jim's grandfather, William Cook, the head keeper, or it could have been with my uncle Harry who was an under-keeper at the time.

After a mild scolding for getting my boots wet from paddling in the brook we would continue on our way along the path beside the fields of oats and wheat to the gate which led out onto Lode Lane near Olton Hall and opposite a farmhouse. Before we emerged from the path, Father would draw my attention to the view over the lake in front of a large house which lay back from the path. It was now a short way to the old canal bridge where we descended onto the tow-path below. With the warning "Watch your step!" I ran off in front anxious to make sure that we changed direction to saunter over the small, hump-backed bridge between Bills Moor Wood and the meadow behind The Anchor. Seated at a table at the back of the pub, Mother and I chatted while Father bought his pint of mild, Mother's shandy and my lemonade and packet of crisps. The latter were Smiths in a greaseproof bag with a small, blue twist of paper containing the salt. After about an hour we would leave for home. Making our way across the wharf and over the foot-bridge, as we approached the tow-path I used to enjoy running my fingers over the smooth blue bricks which formed the wall of the bridge. Sometimes we walked along the towpath to the iron bridge on Damson Lane and then home, or we climbed through the fence and made our way home along the top of the canal bank.

The Gossies were another regular walk to Catney and The Boat. The original inn had recently burnt down where it stood a short way down a rutted drive by the side of the canal. After our usual refreshment it was decision time – were we going to walk back along the canal or via Lugtrout Lane? If we took the latter we invariably stopped at George Duttons place. He was an old friend of my fathers' he had been one of the gamekeepers up at The Hall. While our parents passed the time of day, their son, Leslie and I raced round the small paddock by the house. All too soon I was called to leave for home.

On the odd occasion we took a route along Lode Lane to see the swans on the Mill Pool and then along to the Wheat Sheaf on the Coventry Road. Refreshed, our route took us along The Coventry Road, past Tigers Island and on to the Lodge and impressive gates into the Park. Sometimes, on other occasions, we carried on up to The Cock Inn if it was a warm evening so that we could take more refreshment before we strolled down Damson Lane and home.

My father was not of a high academic standard – after all, like many of his contemporaries, he left the little school in Elmdon at the age of 12. Despite the paucity of his education, he possessed a high intellect and was always eager to face a challenge. On joining the army he was able to exploit those talents by successfully training as a mechanical engineer and to fulfil his ambition to improve his knowledge.

He was also a visionary and his view was that for each year of war, there was a corresponding period, at least of ten years, in advancement in science and engineering techniques. Such perception gave him considerable advantage over his fellows. He continued throughout his life to seek new information in his fields of interests and encouraged me to do the same. In the '30's a very important and large industrial fair known as The British Industries Fair was held. I do not remember its periodicity, but it was something like every five years. There were two venues, one in London, the other here at Castle Bromwich. The B.I.F. as it was known, comprised two sections. The London one was devoted to our commercial expertise, here it was devoted to the thousand and one trades in which we demonstrated our supremacy. The fair was also designed to enable us to sell our wares to the many countries who were equipping themselves to the best standards of engineering.

The Fair at Castle Bromwich was held in a very large hangar type building. A short time later it became a factory producing Spitfire aircraft during World War 2.

The Fair was the focus of British engineering talents where they were displayed for the world's approbation. Items which "the city of a thousand trades", proudly displayed were pins, buttons, and jewellery right through the gamut to chains of every size and description to the many makes of vehicle that were produced here then. One special incident remains vivid in my memory. It was when I was invited onto one of the stands which was showing a highly polished steel disc at least 15 feet in diameter and about six inches thick. A shaft extended each side from its centre.

# FAMILY LEISURE IN THE '20'S & '30'S 145

The whole was mounted on two large roller bearings which in turn were themselves mounted on large wooden blocks.

I was dwarfed by its size. A demonstrator ushered me up to the intimidating object, he positioned me at the leading edge of it and taking my hand instructed me to turn the disc with my forefinger! With some trepidation I put my finger in one the holes which ran round its periphery and pressed. To my astonishment the large disc began to spin easily on its bearings and continued for a considerable time under its own volition. The demonstrator then informed all those watching my efforts that the disc was the base on which fan blades would be attached and its ultimate destination was the ventilation shaft in the soon to be commissioned Liverpool Mersey Tunnel.

Father and I visited the fair at least twice and always spent most of the day looking at all the exhibits. Before we left for home we made our way across the access road to the airfield fence. Beyond the fence we could see the pride of our air force, Hawker Harts and Furies. Both were bi-planes in silver livery with R.A.F. roundels painted on their wings and tails. They were aircraft operated by 605 Squadron which was the County of Warwick Auxiliary Squadron. On one occasion we were entertained to a very proficient aerobatic display. It was only a short period before those exercises would be put to a very different purpose in defending us from the attention of the German airforce. Nor did I realize that I would be a member of the R.A.F in their endeavours.

Yet another opportunity occurred for us to enjoy the antics of flying machines, however, rather different to the modern ones which were picketed round Castle Bromwich aerodrome. These were of a much earlier vintage, one in which they had joined combat with the best of that same German airforce. They were mostly Avro 504's which had fought in the skies over France in The Great War. Sir Alan Cobham, a pilot who had survived the war, realised that it would be in our countries' interest to familiarize the general public to the potential of the aeroplane in our future. To do that he set up what became known as an aerobatic circus with which he toured the country. The public were encouraged to attend the shows, watch the displays by experienced pilots and to fly in the same aircraft which they saw being thrown across the sky. This a mere 25 years after The Wright brothers first flight!

A field between Smiths Lane and Wydney Road with its entrance off Wydney Manor Road was the local venue for the circus when it visited Solihull. The aircraft were thrown all over the sky, sometimes making it appear that they would crash into the ground. It was always a very good display at the end of which the crowd were encouraged to take a trip. The fare was 5/-, (twenty-five pence) for a short flight around the airfield. For those who could afford 10/-, (fifty pence), one was taken on a flight over the surrounding countryside and an aerial view of Solihull village.

Alan Cobham was a visionary, ahead of his time. It was his desire to persuade the government of the day to establish worldwide air routes for mail and passengers to serve our far flung Empire. Sea routes to the Far East took at least a month, whereas, by air the same distance could be flown in a week. By attracting the general public, and especially the young people like myself, he ensured that the message got across.

His enthusiasm percolated through the corridors of power and the Royal Air Force began to establish air-mail routes across the globe. They also established record breaking times between many destinations. They were the first to fly over Mount Everest in Hawker Audaxes! Very soon many other countries entered into the spirit of the competition and soon the skies in the 1930's were full of small aircraft attempting one record or another. It was a very exciting time for we earthbound folk. I made a point of going each time when the circus came to Solihull. Once again the effect was to encourage me to join the Royal Air Force at the outbreak of war in 1939.

## Chapter 19
# The Wireless Arrives in Elmdon Heath

Until the turn of the century, the general public found their relaxation in the 'pub, in sport and the Music Hall. With few exceptions the latter was enjoyed by both sexes, as also were Ladies Shoots. When each baronial hall held the annual shoot, time and effort was made available for a Ladies shoot.

In the Music Hall, the artists, especially the vocal acts, were much admired and their songs and tunes were sung, whistled and played at home by many. The errand boys in those days heralded their arrival by their cheerful whistling as they walked up the front path or rode their carrier bikes down the lanes. The Victorian and Edwardian drawing rooms became miniature theatres on each Saturday and Sunday evening; families and friends stood round the piano and sung their hearts out from song sheets. The early 1800's saw the emergence of the great engineers, Mathew Boulton, James Watt, Thomas Telford and Isambard Kingdom Brunel to name but a few. Their work resulted in the Industrial Revolution which began in Britain and consequently gave us a dominant position in world trade and influence. Later, the 19th century became the province of the physicists, Alexander Graham Bell, Flemming, Faraday, le Clanc, Marconi and Eddison. The need for reliable and efficient communications, world wide, had long been recognised but had not been available.

Eddison was the first scientist to bring the voices of the popular entertainers of the period into the home. He did it by inventing the barrel phonograph, many of which were eagerly bought when they appeared in the shops. The quality of reproduction on them left much to be desired, nevertheless, the die was cast. The recording was made on a cylinder of aluminium with a metal horn similar to those used as megaphones. The reproduction was made by rotating the cylinder while a metal needle transferred the information from it through a metal horn like the one used during the recording. Other companies quickly began to make great efforts to improve upon the primitive machine.

His Masters Voice were the first to achieve that and they quickly patented their instrument and its associated material. Their machine was of course what became known as the humble hand wound gramophone. In 1910 my father bought one for my grandparents, a Christmas present together with a record of Peter Dawson singing "The Road to Mandalay". The singer was recognized as one of the world's best barotones and he was enjoyed by many. However, they did not include my

Grandfatber. He was unable to understand from whence the music and voices came, never accepted it or was happy when anyone played it in his presence. Twenty years later, he strongly objected when as a lad of ten I played, "Red Sails in the Sunset". The gramophone brought a very good standard of entertainment into the home and it would be many years before a better choice was available .

At the outset of The Great War, even the common telephone was looked upon as somewhat of an oddity. By the time of the Armistice in 1918, it, together with the wireless, had proved themselves in the worse possible conditions. Fred Pratley, my father's pal of their younger days, was employed by the Post Office before the war. After he was demobbed, he returned to his old job with them. During the war he had worked with both telephone and wireless for the army and after it he retained his new found love of the wireless.

On his return he began to build small wireless sets as a hobby from designs now being published. Components also had now become readily available at reasonable cost. A common design was known as a "crystal set". It consisted of a coil of wire, a crystal, steel needle and assorted terminals, which one purchased from shops selling them. When they were assembled to a published design it became a primitive wireless set. To make it work, the needle was delicately moved along the crystal until a signal was received, either music or voice. The various signals, what there was of them, could be heard with a pair of earphones, not very loudly, but it was a means of entertainment. To operate one could be very frustrating and tiring, the signal was often very weak and the needle and crystal often wore out and had to be replaced. To save money they were often replaced from the operators own resources. The needle as a thorn from the nearest Hawthorn bush, as were gramophone needles, the crystal by a piece of coal from the cellar.

At that time a great deal of work was being carried out by the government and industry to provide a national wireless service. Industry and commerce were building transmitters and receivers for their own use. These were quite sophisticated, and slowly the equipment in the shops used by the amateur also met the new standards. Names of some of the manufacturers who became synonymous with the industry were His Masters Voice, (H.M.V.), Marconi—, the inventor of the science—, Cossor, Pye and Celeston who were the prime suppliers of the components. Later, other companies also became household names, Ferguson, Pilot, Invictor, Echo, Vidor and Beethoven. With Pye, the latter two catered for the portable market.

A new, basic set now became very popular with the home constructor. It had three valves, two large dials on a black front panel together with several switches, and there was also a row of terminals along the back; all of which was assembled in a strong, highly polished wooden box the top of which formed a lid giving access to the components and brightly glowing valves. The row of terminals provided the means of connecting the various power supplies, aerial and earth, and the earphones or loudspeaker.

Initially a large, 'wet', battery, a square, glass container in which there was a quantity of sulphuric acid and two plates connected to two terminals on the top of the battery. It provided two volts which lit the valves like small lamps. Another row of 'wet', batteries provided 120 volts as a high tension power to the valves. Two more of the terminals were used to connect earphones or loudspeaker to the set, and two more were used for the aerial and earth. Unlike today, those were very essential components in the wireless installation.

The aerial consisted of 50 feet of wire suspended between two insulators, from a pole at the bottom of the garden to a point on the roof above a suitable window which gave access into the house. An aerial switch attached to the window frame provided a supposed safety feature. The aerial was connected to it, as was the earth, before they were connected to the set. The earth consisted of a wire which led to either a convenient water pipe or a rod driven into the ground below the window. In the latter case, in a hot summer, the user had to water the pipe to ensure a good performance from the set! The purpose of the aerial switch was to isolate the aerial from the set and to divert it down to earth.

The object was considered imperative during a thunder storm to safe-guard the set and house from being struck by lightning. When a storm was imminent the house-holder religiously earthed the aerial with the switch. When one considers the enormous power expended by a flash of lightning, the operation was fruitless. Nevertheless, they remained in use for many years and I removed many after World War Two.

Our first wireless set was made by Fred Pratley in about 1926, a three valve version with a pair of headphones. The set sat on a small table between the pantry and the bathroom with the batteries on the lower self. More accurately, the batteries were accumulators which required regular recharging by shops with the equipment to do so. The two volt version needed recharging each week, therefore at least two were held, one in use and one on charge. The high tension versions did not consume so much power and therefore only required recharging at monthly intervals. The two volt acc's. were charged locally, however, the high tension ones were collected and taken to a shop opposite the Mermaid at Sparkbrook. I believe the name of the proprietors was Bagnalls. The pole to which our aerial was attached was formed by several lengths of old gas pipe obtained by my father from the gas works.

The row of terminals along the back of our set nearly caused a serious incident. I had a Hobbies Fretwork Set and a new spare set of saw blades had been placed on the top of the set behind the loudspeaker. One evening a loud cadenza in an organ recital caused one of the steel blades to fall down the back of the set onto the battery terminals. There was a loud bang, a flash and a smell of very hot metal.

My father leapt to his feet, shot over to the source of the eruption and tore the red hot, semi-molten blade from the terminals with burnt fingers and strong words. The offending item was thrown into the fire and a very salutary lesson had been learnt.

In the early days, earphones were the most common form of converting radio signals into audible sound. They suffered from two critical deficiencies. One, the reproduction was very weak and could not easily be heard. Second, only one person at any one time could listen to the chosen programme. To overcome those problems an early solution was found. The earphones were placed in a crock basin on a table in the centre of the room, that effectively converted them into a form of loudspeaker and the whole family was able to enjoy the programme. My father quickly became disenchanted with that arrangement each time we wanted to listen to the wireless. He obtained from Fred Pratley a black, swan-necked horn speaker in the base of which was a small lever which provided a coarse type of volume control; rarely used as the signals at that time were quite weak at source. That set up served us for many years until I provided a modern set run from the mains.

Wireless broadcasting became official in Britain when Station 2LO was established at Savoy Hill in London on the 15th November, 1922. It quickly achieved popularity but the British Broadcasting Company did not attain Corporation status for some time. Expansion of the service meant that the Midlands were selected as the second region to enjoy its own station which was erected at Daventry. It began broadcasting in 1925 with 5XX as its call-sign. Because of its innovative concept and certain misgivings in high places, limitations were imposed on programme content and material. Cost no doubt was also another factor. Transmissions were restricted to the evenings between five and eleven o'clock, Mondays to Saturdays. The spiritual and moral needs of the listeners was considered of paramount importance, in consequence religious programmes featured prominently on the sabbath, therefore, Sunday enjoyed a full day of programmes. Subjects which were known to enjoy wide appeal and were not controversial, formed the basis of all programmes. Light operettas, shows and popular music, sport, news, religious and children's programmes formed the bulk of most schedules.

Like many other homes, routine changed dramatically when the wireless entered our home. Chores that the womenfolk had silently done before the fire in the evening, were now enlivened by what came from the loudspeaker. One of these was darning socks and gloves, which were often "More Holy than Righteous", as there was no man made fibre then to reinforce them. The work in the gardens also now often suffered as the breadwinner sat and listened to his favourite programme. A task which he found less of a chore while listening to a programme was cobbling our footwear. It was a common practice for the breadwinner to repair all the families footwear as well as all the other tasks he tackled after his days work. An "iron", a device consisting of a cast iron object with three short legs, the ends of each one terminating in three different size foot shapes, one small for a child, a larger one for the womenfolk and finally a large one which could accommodate the hob nailed boots of the man of the house. It was on that all the repairs were carried out.

Before this could be done certain preparations were essential. A piece of suitable leather was purchased from the cobblers and — soaked for a considerable time in hot water to make it supple so that it could be worked. Sprigs, nails, and toe and heel "taps" were also bought from the same source. My father would settle himself on the floor with a soft leather square, the iron, hammer, curved knife, and the assortment of fixing nails and sprigs. The first job was to tear off the worn sole or heel. That done, the piece of leather was placed on the boot being repaired and with the knife it was cut exactly to the shape of heel or sole and then nailed firmly into place. It was usual for him to tackle several boots at one time so the whole exercise took most of an evening. As he tapped away he often did it to the rhythm of the music coming from the speaker on the table above him.

The set also had a considerable effect upon me. Instead of grabbing a well-buttered top half of a cottage loaf or a succulent Tittiovy and dashing off to join my pals, I now sat sedately at the table and ate my tea as I listened to Children's Hour. A favourite of mine was Commander Stephen King-Hall. He invariably captured my attention with his reporting of current affairs made in such a way that we youngsters could easily understand what was happening in the world. He also often recounted his adventures of daring-do as a naval officer.

On the 7th of November each year I imposed a complete silence on my parents as I listened avidly to Uncle Mac wishing me "Many Happy Returns of the Day, Stanley Beavan". A unique privilege and something which made me very proud. I enjoyed the greeting as I was a member of the Children's Club which I joined as soon as it was formed when the Birmingham studio began broadcasting. I also proudly wore a badge in my buttonhole proclaiming my membership.

As now, the six o'clock news was the programme which most folk listened to. Read by the doyen of news readers, Stewart Hibbert, in a well modulated Oxford accent, with suitable inflection when the portent was either happy or dire. It was read twice, first at normal speed and then at dictation speed. It was at that time when the B.B.C. established its reputation for accurate and honest news reporting. The inscription above the entrance to the Savoy Hill studio's "Nations Shall Speak Peace Unto Nations", reflected those high ideals and standards. Yet another interesting item read each day was the Fat Stock prices which reflected the strong agricultural base of our economy at that time.

Today, the disc jockey is a well-known personality on both radio and television. The species was unknown before World War Two but that is not to say that we did not enjoy many music programmes played on the ubiquitous gramophone record. The first so called disc jockey was I believe Christopher Stone. He played a wide variety of popular music and became very well known in so doing. Dance tunes which he helped to popularise were "Oh Dona Clara", an Italian song. One which we children sang as we skipped to and from school across Broomfields was "C.O.N.S.T.A.N.T.I.N.O.P.L.E." an easy way to learn our alphabet while at play. Valencia and The Stein Song featured strongly in his repertoire. About 1930 a very popular song which was often played was "They are Changing the Guard at Buckingham Palace, said Alice". My abiding macabre memory of it was of hearing it as I slowly ascended the stairs to pay a final visit to my mother who lay dying.

We were one of the first families in Elmdon Heath to possess a wireless set. Because of that, Father always ensured that when an important event was broadcast he relayed it to the rest of the inhabitants in the locality. There were four such events each year which were important and which captured everyone's attention, — the Cup Tie, the Boat Race, the Service of Remembrance at the Cenotaph and the Schnieder Trophy Air Race.

The Boat Race was far more popular then and it was strongly supported by all of the school children. I always supported Cambridge who invariably won. The Air Race was held in various countries as each strived to win the very prestigious event. To win was to show that winner could control the skies, a much sought goal in the '30's. When the race, was held here it was flown over Southhampton Water. The broadcast of each race consisted of quiet periods suddenly shattered by the thunderous roar of high powered engines as they screamed and banked sharply round the course markers. The excitement became almost too much to bear as each listener strained every sense to capture each sound and comment by the excited commentator. Britain, rightly, was the most successful of the countries competing then with our Supermarine machines. Our ultimate success resulted in a contract from the Air Ministry for a fighter based upon the design of the winning aircraft. That design became the world famous Spitfire, most of them built here at Castle Bromwich. The period 1939 to 1945 proved the importance of winning those races earlier.

On the 7th November our household listened intently at five o'clock for the greeting, "Happy Birthday Stanley Beavan", on the occasion of my big day. Four days later a more sombre programme was relayed from the Cenotaph as the Act of Remembrance was held. The Armistice was remembered on the 11th each year, no matter which day on which it fell, unlike the current practice. At precisely eleven o'clock on that day everyone stopped whatever they were doing and stood stock still for a full two minutes; all with heads bowed, caps and hats removed by man and boy. It was an eerie sensation as postures were held in the one assumed on the stroke of eleven o'clock. The whole scene was accompanied by the tolling of the church bells and the sounding of the maroons which were normally used for alerting workers of the time to start or finish work. When the service fell on a Saturday or Sunday it was relayed by father from our bathroom window to everyone in earshot.

The new means of communication gave instant access to world events, it also

# THE WIRELESS ARRIVES IN ELMDON HEATH

introduced many personalities to the listener. Those that spring immediately to mind are Stewart Hibbert, Commander Stephen King-Hall, Uncle Mac, all of whom I have referred to previously. Others, most entertainers, were Billy Cotton, Jack Payne, Jack Hilton, Henry Hall and Elsie Caryle. Apart from the B.B.C. another station was established in Luxembourg which was financially supported by large firms who could also advertise on it, something not allowed in the B.B.C.'s Charter. It gained a wide recognition and was known as Radio Luxembourg. Programmes which I recall were, Guy Lombardo and his "Oxydol", Pioneers, Carters Little Liver Pills, and not to be forgotten were the "Ovalteenies". A very popular programme aimed at children. There was a signature tune which we all sang, it began, "We are the Ovalteenies, We are little girls and boys," and it went on to extol the virtues of the product.

Many British artists who became household names were Claude Dampier who played an upper class twit, and the Weston Brothers also did the same thing, one sang, the other played a piano. Fred Emery, who we later found to be a very fat, tall man, and who invariably smoked a large cigar, played a xylophone and cracked jokes while doing so. Leslie Sarony, another Music Hall artist who successfully converted to the new medium, sang funny songs which were often too risqué for the puritanical B.B.C. One of his songs "The Pig Got Up And Slowly Walked Away" was banned, for many years. Flotsom and Jetsam gave, a very polished performance, one sang in a deep bass voice while the other sang in a higher pitch while at a piano.

Popular female performers of the time were "Our Gracie", — who else but Gracie Fields, — stage, films, wireless were all grist to her mill. Her marriage to an Italian film star at the outbreak of the war lost her many fans until many years after the war. Grace More sang classical as well as lighter material.

An impressionist of the time was Reginald Gardener who later went to Hollywood and became a film actor. One of his famous impressions was of a train entering the tunnel on the approach to Snow Hill station. A phenomenon on the original line was a high pitched note as if a metal plate had been struck by one's carriage. It did not appear to matter which carriage one was in on the train to experience the strange note. Reginald Gardener made a record of a railway journey in which be reproduced the once familiar, clickity clack of the wheels as they passed over the joints in the rail, — the swish of one train passing another and a train speeding through a station. His final *piece de resistance* was to accurately reproduce the sound as the train approached Snow Hill.

A very well known programme which is even now acknowledged as the first nature programme to be broadcast was the relaying of the song of a nightingale in the Surrey woods one late July evening in 1930. To cousin Jim and I it was not particularly exciting as we were serenaded to sleep most evenings by a chorus of them in Bills Moor. How times have changed in Elmdon Heath!

As the years passed, more people acquired wireless sets and the need for us to relay special events from our bathroom window became unnecessary. My father used the three valve battery set for many years until I bought a Ferguson set driven by the mains electricity. It removed the need and cost of recharging batteries and the hazard of spilt acid, always a possibility. Unfortunately the Ferguson became a victim of the Luftwaffe when they attempted, unsuccessfully, to bomb Solihull Gas Works. The loss of the wireless set was of no consequence in relation to the lives of the whole Pinder family in Cornxy Lane and another house in Alston Road.

A vivid and pleasant memory of Christmas, 1928 readily comes to mind when I write of wireless entertainment. My parents and I walked all the way from Solihull to Fred Pratley's home at Hockley Heath because the snow was so deep the Midland Red buses could not get through. A very enjoyable time was had by all, especially we children. As we were playing with Connie's toy farm we listened to the wireless played from a speaker up on the wall, suddenly we stopped playing as we heard what was to become one of the song standards of all time, it was "The Teddy Bears Picnic". It sounded very good then even from fairly primitive equipment and of course it now sounds even better from modern equipment.

At the end of 1939 and with the threatening situation which Europe then faced, everyone recognised that the wireless was here to stay and would play an ever more important role in everyday life and so it became throughout the five and a half years of war. Our successes and failures were broadcast each evening at six o'clock on the News. The nation's determination to win through was further encouraged by the very strong speeches broadcast by the then Prime Minister, Winston Churchill. They gave everyone the inspiration and strength to carry on despite our early setbacks. Needless to say, every set in the kingdom was switched on, loud and clear, on the 7th May 1945 when the end of World War II was declared.

## Chapter 20
# Fate Casts a Shadow

The dawn of the 1930's brought drastic changes in its wake. Following World War I, severe economic and employment problems faced both victors and vanquished. Despite my father's working class background his paper was the Daily Mail which he read avidly each evening; he also took the large "C", Conservative view of politics and indeed voted that way. He was not best pleased at the prospect of a Coalition Government with Ramsay MacDonald at it's head when it was formed in 1930. I well remember him saying, "That won't last long! They will have to call another election very shortly and the Conservatives will be back". That happened, to his immense satisfaction.

The problems faced by the outside world were of nothing to that which my father was facing. The trauma was of such magnitude that, if fate so decreed, his life and the future of his family would change irrevocably for the worse. The illness of my mother was the cause of his distress. She fell ill the previous year but her condition had been hidden from me. Her condition deteriorated so that Dr. John Whitehouse had her admitted to the General Hospital in Birmingham. In those days there was a deep fear by most people of going into hospital and to "go under the knife!" The bad conditions that had prevailed in hospitals only a few years before in the previous century were still vivid in the minds of those who were sent to them. She was operated upon, which I later learnt was an attempt to remove a cancer.

My father and I paid regular visits to her while she remained in hospital. My memories of those visits are of very dark and sombre wards where everyone, both staff and those patients who were able to get out of bed, moved around the wards in utter silence with little joy on their faces. Such conditions did not inspire confidence in either my father or myself. A sense of doom descended as we alighted from the bus in the Bull Ring. As we made our way along the streets to the hospital my father was constantly steering me past and between the many men who were staggering, or laying on the pavements, the worse for drink. Many were minus a limb, some with more than one missing, all of them the legacy of the war a few years before. There was a good deal of shouting and swearing which accompanied the unsteady walk and gait of those who tried to find another pub or maybe, their home. Other men who had no wish to dwell upon their condition and what might have been, stood in the gutters, a tray hung from their necks, on which were boot and shoe laces, matches, packets of pins and needles and anything else which could be sold to earn a little something to support their families. Many of those men had been unable to find work or hope since their demobilisation at the end of the war. Lloyd George's boast that on their return the world would be "fit for a man to live in", seemed to be a very hollow one as they now stood in all weathers trying to make a few pence.

At last my mother returned home, much to my relief and joy. She did not look well but the doctor assured us that she would regain her strength and become her warm, serene and loving self once again. It soon became evident that such improvement was wishful thinking. Early in 1930 my father told me that a very important man would be paying us a visit to examine Mother to try to find out why she was not getting better. That evening Dr. Whitehouse arrived with another man and almost immediately went straight upstairs to Mother's bedroom accompanied by my father. When they came down, the stranger, — who my father later told me was a specialist —, spoke a few kind words to my father, who was obviously very distressed, and left. The following minutes left a deep impression upon me as my father broke down and wept bitterly as he stood with head on arms, looking down into the fire. After a while he managed to regain his composure and told me as gently as he could that my mother was going to die!

A nine year old finds it difficult to appreciate or understand the ramifications of such a simple statement. I realised that the future would be very bleak without her love, affection and constant endeavours to make our home a place of comfort and peace. I was about to lose one of the two people most dear to me. From that moment I left my childhood behind and entered the world of reality.

After that fateful visit my mother never came down the stairs and she died in June 1931 and was buried in Elmdon Churchyard near to many other members of our extended family.

The domestic routine now changed dramatically. My father and I slept in our home, 59, Damson Lane, but spent the rest of the time with my grandparents in their cottage. For me, apart from the sleeping aspect, the daily routine was not such a departure from that since we had moved from our cottage in Lugtrout Lane. I still dashed to and fro between the two homes, scrumping apples and plums as I did so. Mrs Churchill who lived next door but one, did the household chores for us twice a week.

For some time before my mother died, and also when she could no longer care for us as she wished, Polly Wright, the daughter of Mrs Butler, Gran's sister, came and cooked all our cake, bread and pastry requirements for the week. She was a very good cook, one who had been trained as had my mother in the art. A short time later, Emily Luker, Auntie Pem's daughter married Bill Jew and while they looked for a place to live, they came and lived with us and she took over as housekeeper. Before her marriage she had worked for one of the Jackson family, I believe he was the brother of Barry, he of Birmingham Repertory Theatre fame.

I well remember their wedding. My father and I were invited to the reception in

Elmdon church before its extension, c1938.

The George in the Tree at Balsall Common. The week before the event it had rained heavily and all the rivers in the neighbourbood had flooded. Our means of transport was by pushbike and our route was through Hampton-in-Arden, down Marsh Lane, over the packhorse bridge and ford to the main Kenilworth road. When we arrived at the bridge it was several feet below a raging torrent of water. Not to be deterred, we struggled up the railway bank with our bikes, walked along the track for some distance, descended back to the lane and successfully completed our journey. It was beneath that same railway bridge that my cousin Hector was drowned in the '30's when bathing with his twin brother, Horace.

The sale of the Elmdon Estate after the first war meant that its workers had to find alternative work. Uncle Harry, a gamekeeper on the estate took a job at Castle Ashby in Northamptonshire. From there they moved to Bourn in Lincolnshire before settling at Bestwood Hall in Nottinghamshire. His employer there was a member of the Baden-Powell family. My uncles' lot during those years had not been easy and in an effort to help Uncle Harry and Aunt Ethel, their eldest son Horace came and spent some time with us until their fortunes had changed for the better. He was about 14 in 1929 when he came to us and he began work as soon as he arrived. He went to work for Joe Davis as an errand boy on the bread round with Joe. I was pleased when he came as we got along very well and we both enjoyed the countryside. Unfortunately, his time with us was cut short by my mother's illness when he returned home.

A pleasant incident one warm summer evening illustrates his country skills. We had gone for a walk up Damson Lane and were talking when he suddenly stopped us in our tracks and said "watch this!". He then stepped over the verge by a field gate where Coppice Road now joins the Lane, bent down, and when he stood up he had a hen pheasant in his hands. Even though we were in earnest conversation his inherited skill had enabled him to see the bird sitting tightly on her eggs and he knew that if she was sitting "tight" he could do what he did do. We admired his skill as he carefully replaced the bird back on her nest and we continued on our way.

As the situation now changed so drastically, Uncle Harry immediately reciprocated by offering to take me with his family during my school holidays each August. The offer was readily accepted and I spent several summers with them.

My first was at Bestwood. The following year it was at Swinnerton Park in Staffordshire. I enjoyed two holidays there. His son Lesley and I formed a very good friendship and we spent many hours helping his father.

Cousin Barbie, the eldest daughter, had begun working away from home as a governess though she often paid frequent visits to see the family, dressed in a smart uniform. While they were there, Audrey, who was the same age as me, was taken ill and died. We were all devastated as she was such a pleasant girl. It had a profound effect on me as we were so close. Swinnerton was the last place I enjoyed with them. In the years that followed they moved on to Eccleshall where their last daughter, Masie, was born, they finally moved to North Wales. Ronnie, one of the sons, followed in his father's footsteps and keepered until quite recently.

My parents had planned to own a shop when the opportunity presented itself. Father had taken all the necessary steps to purchase one of the new shops that were to be built on the junction of Slater Road and Wydney Road at Bentley Heath. They had planned to open it as a tobacconist and paper shop. My mother's illness and my fathers efforts to seek a cure had cost him dear, although he did not begrudge any cost just so long as it was worth while and she survived. His loss of savings meant that he resolved to continue with his job at the gas company. After the traumas of the past two years we slowly got back on our feet. I was now 12 years old, and my life had taken on a fulfilling routine. School, paper rounds and wide leisure activities. Home, whether it was Gran's or our own, were merely places in which to sleep or eat, consequently, my father must have been very lonely. He was still only about 40 and in the best of health. We were eating our breakfast one Saturday morning when he asked me if I was doing anything that evening. A strange question but my response was "No". He then told me that he would like me to meet someone that evening, I was taken completely by surprise. Although puzzled I happily agreed to join him.

In the early evening we rode to Solihull and much to my surprise stopped outside a small cottage opposite Mill Lane School. The cottages were of Elizabethan origin and formed part of the original nucleus of the village. Alas! Like so many other aesthetic, valuable and interesting buildings, that once formed part of the tranquil village, they were demolished in the name of "progress". We now have the dubious delight of Mell Square. Before World War II Drury Lane was a warm, sunny and quiet lane. Today, when attempts are made to merely cross it to gain access to the car park, one is swept off one's feet by a hurricane. So much for progress!

At the cottage, we rested our bikes against a wall and mounted the steps to the front door. Before knocking, my father said "Now listen, lad, I want you to meet a lady who I have been seeing for sometime. I want you to see if you like her. If you do, I may marry her and then she would become your step-mother. I want to make sure that we can all get along with each other"! What a responsibility for a lad who had been given no previous warning and I had not realised that he had sought a replacement for my mother. The door was opened at his knock by an old lady. My immediate thought was "This cannot be the person he has told me about!". We were invited in with a greeting of "Hello Joe. So this is Stanley!". I took her knarled, outstretched hand with a hesitant "Pleased to meet you". We were divested of our overcoats and ushered to the side of a blazing fire which provided most of the light perculating into the dark interior. When my eyes became accustomed to the dim light I could see a much younger woman standing near the other side of the fire. I was still trying to come to terms with the reasons for us being there, and consequently I felt embarrassed when confronted by "the lady". I was relieved to see that she felt as nervous as I did, which was of some comfort. We were introduced by my father. "This is Mrs. Pat Webber, the person I told you about, Stay". (He always used that form of endearment when he wished to show affection for me, or to put me at my ease.) He then introduced the old lady as, "Pat's mother, Mrs. Reynolds". From that moment I always knew her as, "The Old Lady", I later found that everyone else did too.

After my initial reserve I found that I liked Pat, (a pet name, she had been baptised, Harriet Kiziah.) Unlike the feelings I had for her, I forever held a fear of her mother. There was always a sense of menace in her presence. A short while after our arrival a stooped, white haired old man came in from the small kitchen beyond the living room. He was ignored by the old lady but my father quickly greeted him with a warm and friendly "Hello Jim. How are you then?" The reply was a subdued, "Hello Joe, I'm alright thanks". Whereas the greetings between my father and the old woman had been proper and a little stiff, here was a warmth and understanding which I would later understand.

As the evening wore on, Pat told me that she had a little boy who was upstairs asleep. She told me his name was Frank and that he was four years old. I was assured that I would see him next time we called. An incident then occurred for which I was ill prepared. A silence fell on the gathering, suddenly, the old lady looked me in the eye and ordered me, yes, ordered was the only term that could describe it, "Go to the Outdoor round the corner and get me a bottle of Milk Stout". I was nonplussed, I had never been treated in such a manner before by anyone. I sought some escape by looking at my father, but found none, he did not wish to "rock the boat", at that stage. I concurred with the command out of fright. The hadrian was the epitome of the Victorian parent whose attitude was "Children should be seen but not heard". My 12 years did not save me from that approach. The evening passed and I was very pleased when Father announced that we should leave. We donned our overcoats and with a deep sigh of relief, I could not get down the steps fast enough and on my bike for home. After a short time, I told my father I was sure that I would grow to accept Pat into our home and he should go ahead and marry her. After enduring the distasteful procedures demanded for a divorce at that time from her absent airman husband, they did indeed marry in August, 1938. Once again 59 Damson Lane became a real home again.

Pat had a younger sister of whom we saw little. A nursing sister by profession, her name was Lucy. In later years when I got to know the Reynolds family much better, I was disturbed by the treatment meted out to the pitiful old man, Jim. He was required to carry out many menial tasks around their home with little or no appreciation being shown. It occurred to me that the old chap seemed to lack the ability to converse with anyone, or to be interested in activities as one would expect of a man of his age. I mentioned this to my father and he gave me the reason for the situation which existed in the family.

As a young man, Jim, had been a tall, active and happy man and well known in the village. He had worked as a labourer all his working life and was rarely out of work. One fateful day his life-style was shattered by a calamity all too common then.

Together with other men he was engaged in digging a trench. As was so often the case, the trench had not been shored up properly and in consequence, had collapsed together with several tons of soil onto the men in the trench. Three men were buried under the debris. Despite frantic efforts by their workmates and many others, two of the men were brought out dead and the third, Jim, barely alive. He had escaped serious physical injury but had sustained serious injury to his head which was to change his personality completely. No longer the outgoing, happy man everyone knew so well, now a shadow of his former self. He became retiring, uncommunicative and not an easy man to get along with. A measure of the trauma he had experienced was manifested by his thick, black hair turned completely white the day following the accident. Because of his condition he could no longer be employed in his former job which only served to aggravate his sense of loss and presence. In those days there was little chance of compensation for people who suffered such injuries, they were left to fend for themselves as best they could. His situation was further aggravated by the attitude of his wife. He was treated as someone deranged and was effectively banned from the main living room to the scullery, even at meal-times! There was no sharing of family life or the warmth that may have helped him to recover some of his old happy personality.

In later years when his circumstances became known he was often offered jobs as a nightwatchman. They were a common sight for many years when major work was carried out and there was danger to the public. They were employed to maintain the lamps that were placed along the length of a trench or on scaffold each night. They also made infrequent visits to the workface to check that all the tools and materials were safe and not stolen. Jim did many of those jobs throughout the '30's and even as late as the early '50's before he became too old and the world became a much more dangerous place.

When a major site was established, either building, gas, electric or sewer mains laying, a large hut or other shelter was erected on the site. It was made secure as a store, but more importantly, it served as a rest room for all the workers on the site. At the commencement of the job, a metal brazier was positioned at its entrance, a fire was lit in it and the fire was constantly refuelled with coke, day and night, until the job was done. Around the fire were seats made from lengths of substantial planks of wood and often the odd wheelbarrow up ended also served the same purpose.

There have been many occasions when I was very pleased to see Jim sitting in front of a blazing fire on a cold, frosty night, with invariably a large black kettle simmering on the side of the fire. Many workers, policemen, postmen and others were very thankful that such a haven existed, there they could sit and relax a while with a steaming mug of strong tea before going on their way much refreshed. Anyone fortunate to be hailed by Jim into the inviting shelter, always left it feeling right with the world, and their presence had served to pass the time for Jim and helped him to enjoy the time spent back in the community.

## Chapter 21
# We Gain Our Wheels

For centuries the horse had provided man with his means of transport. He was prime mover of heavy loads and his partner in sport, games and war. The end of the 19th century witnessed the demise of that relationship. The architects of The Industrial Revolution were those who began the process. James Watt and Stevenson invented and developed the railway system, initially here in England and then very rapidly, they were installing the iron road across many continents. Later as Victoria's reign approached its glorious close, Ludvig Daimler in Germany invented the internal combustion engine. The combination of speedier methods of transport sounded the death knell of the long established horse drawn method.

The new forms could readily be installed in a carriage. It was noisy, smelly, slow and frequently broke down, but did not require a large field in which to live and feed. It did not pollute the roads with manure. Replenished frequently with oil, both refined and unrefined, a competent driver could complete many more tasks than had previously been possible with a horse and cart.

It was not long before the internal combustion engines, of various sizes, were installed in bicycle frames, they then became motor-cycles. Larger engines mounted on four wheels were then used to haul heavier loads. By fitting a pair of wings on a three wheeled vehicle, and fitting a propeller to it, man's long held ambition to get airborne could be achieved in an aeroplane. Then in The Great War, after considerable slaughter of both man and horse, the British put an engine in a large steel box, which moved on tracks and could be steered. The tank was born.

At the end of that war, it was imperative that industry and commerce reverted to a peacetime production programme so that we could maintain our global supremacy in world trade. Many of the companies who had thrived on government contracts during the war, were found wanting in management skills when faced with competition in the open market. They soon ceased to trade and many well known names in the motor trade were lost.

The Midlands, because of its industrial base, became the centre of the motor trade. Many jobs were created in it until the recession in 1929. It then became very difficult for small firms to continue to trade and many fell by the wayside, while others merged with their competitors. Three well known companies which ceased trading then were Lanchester, Bean and Swift. My cousin Jack worked at the Lanchester factory in 1930. On some of his visits to see Gran, he told us he could see that the firm would close shortly and he was going to find another job. He moved to the Austin Motor Company at Longbridge. The move there helped him to understand why firms like Lanchester were unable to compete. At the Austin factory, German engineers were installing giant drilling machines to drill the cylinder blocks en masse for a new small car. Shortly after he started work there, the new car was launched, known as the Austin 7, and the cost, £100's!

Another very good vehicle manufacturer was in a precarious situation, the Sunbeam Company by name. It made push-bikes, motor-cycles, and cars, all to a very high standard. Despite their difficulties they were able to stave off the inevitable because they enjoyed a much envied position in the market. Apart from their high quality domestic vehicles, they also produced world record breaking motor-cycles and cars. They were pre-eminent in the Isle of Man T.T races early in this century and then became world beaters with their Blue Bird world record breaking cars. The Birmingham Small Arms, (B.S.A.) Company held a similar position but they survived because of their arms industry. They stopped making a four wheeled car but continued with a 3 wheeler as well as their famed motor-cycles and push-bikes.

Cousin Jim had for some time ridden a 1930, 250cc, B.S.A. motor bike. It had a saddle tank, three speed hand change gears, and acetylene lighting. It had a very good performance but that could not be said of its lighting system. I recall with some amusement a trip we made to Aston on Clun in Shropshire to his girl friends home. We took off on a fine autumnal Saturday morning, through Bewdley, Cleobury Mortimer and along Clee Hill to our destination. We left for home rather late on Sunday afternoon. Everything went well until we approached Redditch. The late sun had fallen below the horizon and a thick mist was beginning to form. We stopped and lit the lights before continuing the journey. Despite Jim's knowledge of the route, we both soon recognised the inadequacy of our lighting system. At each bend and corner we strained all our senses to remain on the road.

White lines and cats eyes had not been thought of then. On several occasions we did not react quickly enough and careered across the verge and into the ditch with the bike on top of us. Extricating ourselves, we hauled it back up onto the road, made sure no damage had been done, started it, remounted and continued on our way. We arrived back at Elmdon Heath much later than expected much to our parents consternation, but to their relief we had not suffered any injuries other than our own slight lack of confidence. Other than similar incidents, neither of us were involved in a major accident or suffered a serious injury.

Les Nocks field at the back of Walnut Tree Cottages which had served us well as a playground in our childhood now became a test track on which we tested and practised on our motor-cycles. Jim's B.S.A. which he rode each day on the road also served as his competition machine. Log books issued with each vehicle at that time gave the history of the owners and many other details, The log book for Jim's bike

# WE GAIN OUR WHEELS

Cousin Jim astride his competition 250cc, B.S.A., c1937.

revealed that it had once been owned by Margaret Cottle. She was the official trials rider for B.S.A. and had won many trophies and competitions on that particular machine. A status symbol indeed and a standard difficult to live up to, as we later

The B.S.A. flat tank model. A version of which I attempted to modify unsuccessfully.

found. I now began a search for a machine, of any condition, on which to learn all there was to know about a motor-cycle and what was required to keep it servicable. As I had only recently started work and my weekly wage was a mere five shillings (twenty-five pence), I could not afford a road worthy machine. I at last found a B.S.A., 3 speed hand change, with a flat tank and oil pump mounted on the tank. It was of about 1927 vintage, had no lights, but ran very well. Soon after we acquired a round tank version of the same machine, but at least ten years its senior, with a belt drive instead of chain. We could now boast a stable of three machines. The round tank was the cause of some amusement one fine Sunday morning.

My cousin, Jack, who had once owned a Douglas motor bike, brought his fianceé to have Sunday dinner with our grandparents. In the field, we had been riding all morning on the round tank machine until its tank was empty of fuel. We were about to wheel it off the field when Jack and Olwen came to watch our technique in the saddle. "Come on then, show Olwen how good you are. I have been telling her about the T.T. riders of Elmdon Heath!" A little shamefaced we had to admit that we could not oblige him as we had run out of petrol. As a couple of impecunious youths we were unlikely to be able to afford any more until next pay day, did he have any idea's? He gave it some thought and came up with the suggestion that because of its age, it may run on lamp oil! With considerable scepticism on our part, despite his greater experience, we stole a pint out of Gran's large can. The tank was filled, and with bated breath, Jim kicked the engine into life. Everything seemed to be normal apart from a little more smoke than usual, but as most engines tended to smoke in those days, we were not worried by it. Jack now encouraged Olwen to take a ride on it. With trepidation and a look of concern she acquiesced, to Jack's surprise. After explaining what the various levers and controls did, Jim held the clutch in and put the machine in first gear. With considerable encouragement and not a little help she moved off. All went well at the start then suddenly the engine began to race, emitting clouds of blue smoke and an obnoxious smell. Innocent of the vagaries of internal combustion engines, Olwen was at its mercy; even the rest of us who raced to her aid, and with our considerable knowledge of such machines, could not stop the racing engine or the spinning rear wheel. At last Olwen fell off, the bike fell to the ground and continued to spin on its axis emitting clouds of smoke and an ear shattering scream. I dashed over and turned off the petrol tap, but even then nothing happened for some considerable time. Eventually the engine began to spit and cough and then abruptly stopped. Meanwhile, we had all collapsed to the ground laughing and chiding Olwen for her lack of control! Needless to say, that episode taught us not to try to run petrol engines on paraffin. The aftermath was that Jack regained favour with Olwen at the cost of a port and lemon at the dance on the following Saturday.

After that episode our stable of machines increased rapidly. First, a 1913, Triumph 2¼ hp, belt drive but with a Sturmey Archer three speed hub in its rear

# WE GAIN OUR WHEELS

An example of my first motor cycle, a Velocette, 250cc, two-stroke, Model G.T.P.

wheel similar to those that were later fitted to pedal cycles. The next acquisition was a superb example of a Raleigh. All black with a red lining and footboards gave it a very elegant appearance. It had a 2½ hp, outside flywheel, side valve engine. Then Jim heard of a bike at Kingsbury which someone wished to dispose of. Off we went on his Beesa, with a length of rope. On inspection we found that it could not be driven so we had to resort to towing it home. With Jim on his bike and me on the well used New Hudson, for that was what it was, we started for home. All went well until we arrived at the pillory on the hill in Coleshill when the rope snapped. Tying a knot and shortening the rope to a dangerous short length we continued on our way. We made it to Elmdon Heath almost no distance between the two machines because of the many knots that had been made in the rope. It became another bike in our collection but it did not meet our standards as a grass track machine. I forget what happened to it.

I have referred to "round tanks, flat tanks and saddle tanks", all of which could be found in use throughout the '30's. In general, round tanks were the first to be widely fitted. In about 1920 the flat tank was adopted by the manufacturers and it soon became the norm and continued in use until the late '20's. The '30's saw the saddle tank rapidly replace it and it has continued in use ever since. An exception to the rule was the Scott motor cycle. It was an unconventional machine in several respects. The frame of the machine did not have the usual front bar but relied upon the sloping cylinders of its water cooled, 600cc engine. The cooling radiator and round petrol tank also formed part of the unconventional framework. The rider had foot-boards and leg shields and more often than not, the machine was harnessed to a side car made by the same firm. The whole made an excellent combination for the family man and was very popular. Yet another unusual machine was the large 600cc, P. M. Green Panther. The P. M. were the initials of the manufacturers, Phelan and Moore, who also produced a small, conventional 250cc machine.

The 600cc Panther's engine served the same purpose as that of the Scott (it also formed part of the frame) in all other respects it was a conventional machine.

Jim and my interest in motor cycles was matched by several of our contemporaries and so a small, exclusive club was formed. Enthusiastic young men who enjoyed each other's company, each owned a motor cycle, and most were competent mechanics. We rode all that were in good order and road worthy, the others gave us immense pleasure in races and trials in conditions way beyond their design parameters.

My first road machine was a Velocette model, GTP, 250cc, two stroke machine. A very safe and reliable machine and a good looking one too. I passed my driving test on it the first time. The test had recently been introduced in 1934, but prior to that, one could take any machine out onto the road irrespective of one's capabilities.

My father was very reluctant for me to possess a motor-bike. "They are very dangerous things, if you are involved in an accident it is either your head or your legs that are severely damaged. What is more, it is no good you saying that you are a good rider, how good is the other person?" When he relented and allowed me to get my first bike he constantly instilled into me to try to imagine what the chap round the corner was going to do. Had he been more articulate he may have encouraged me to use intelligent anticipation. His teaching has held me in good stead for the 50 odd years that I have driven in many parts of the world. He always extolled the virtues of the Douglas, "Dougie's" that he rode during the Great War as a dispatch rider. After a year riding my trusty, if unexciting, Velo, I changed it for a 1936 Douglas and side-car. A familiar combination of the time. All blue colour scheme with a lot of chrome. The machine was an "In-line", 500cc flat twin side valve engine with aluminium cylinders and heads, an unusual feature in those days. In the event they did not meet the requirements for their purpose. After a short time I experienced blown head gaskets because the head bolt threads stripped under pressure from the constant explosions in the cylinders. Although the Dougie provided very smooth riding conditions I experienced what could have been two serious accidents with it. The first was when the throttle cable frayed and stuck open as I started away from the kerb by the Malt Shovel one evening. Fortunately my grass track experience stood me in good stead and I simply did a "Wheelie" down the High Street of Solihull at about seven o'clock in the evening! I don't think

## WE GAIN OUR WHEELS

I could get away with a performance such as that today. The next incident occurred when I was on my way to work in Brook Lane, Kings Heath. My route took me down Robin Hood Lane, under the railway bridge, and round the island. On this occasion I was half way round it when the bolt holding sidecar to bike snapped. Immediately my left leg was trapped between the bike and "chair". Once again my track experience helped me to avoid a serious incident. Needless to say my confidence in the machine had suffered and I changed it for a machine which did not cramp my style as the combination had done.

My next bike was a 350cc New Imperial. It had a unit construction engine, that meant the gear box was an integral part of it. It had a single upswept exhaust pipe and a red and black colour scheme. It was very sporty with a good turn of speed. It was while I had it that I lost control on the road for the first time. I worked in Knowle and on a cold, frosty morning I applied my rear brake too harshly and the machine slowly slid from beneath me and we both slid ignominiously along the kerb to stop opposite the doorway of The National Electric Company's shop where I worked.

The informal club to which I referred consisted of 5 regular members. The machines which we initially used when the club was formed were:

Cousin Jim. B.S.A. 250cc.
Charley, "Wag", Smitten. B.S.A. 250cc, side valve.
Jimmy Timms. B.S.A. 350cc overhead valve tourer.
Fred Perkins. Royal Enfield, "Bullet".
Me. Velocette 250cc two stroke GPT.

Other chaps joined us occasionally. Our usual meeting place was either outside the cottages or in Solihull, at one end of The High Street. Outside The Malt Shovel was a favourite, opposite the entrance to Ramsgate was the other. Both venues had their particular attractions, the former for the beer, the latter for the fish and chips from the shop where the Yorkshire Bank now stands.

There were two chaps who used to occasionally join us at those venues. Ron Pickering with his now classic B.S.A. 499cc, "sloper". This was considered even then as one of the best models ever produced by the Small Heath factory. A conventional machine except that the engine was set inclined in the frame. A long stroke engine which when slowly ticking over blew smoke rings from its single exhaust accompanied with a mere murmur from the engine. In that state it belied its capabilities. I once rode one down the Meriden Mile at 75 miles an hour with no effort! Superb machinery. Another chap with Channel Island blood in his veins, used to show off with his 350cc Aerial, "Red Hunter".

The father of Wilf Backhouse, one of our boyhood friends, owned a very notable and rare machine, an Austin Brough with side-car. The Brough Motor Cycle

The Austin Brough minus side car.

Company manufactured only 2 models, they were model S.S.80 and a S.S.100. The former had a 800cc engine and the latter a 1000cc engine. They were both, "V", twins and manufactured to the highest standards, in fact they were recognised as the Rolls Royce of British bikes. The cost of that perfection was high and out of reach of many of the motor cycle fraternity.

A competitor to Brough emerged in the '30's, it was the H.R.D. Vincents. Although very good and more sporty machines than the Brough, they were known to us as "plumbers jobs", because of the many copper pipes that seemed to wind round the cylinders and other parts. Other large, "V", twins which were used to haul large private and commercial side-cars were Royal Enfield 990cc, A.J.S's and B.S.A.'s.

At this particular time car manufacturers were in difficulty, money was short and there was a world recession. In an attempt to overcome low sales, Austin at Longbridge and Brough designed and produced a combination which was aimed at the family man. The machine was a 4 cylinder Austin engine built into a Brough frame. It had many advanced features for the time. Self starting as for a car, shaft drive from the gear box to 2 rear wheels. The whole was finished in the conventional black. For those able to afford it, it provided a very good means of getting one's family about, but the cost proved to be too high and not many were

# WE GAIN OUR WHEELS

A typical trials scene.

built. The design encouraged another well known motor cycle company to produce a more attainable machine which became very popular, The Aerial Square 4. It was virtually a conventional machine except that it also employed a four cylinder engine, but they were built in a square format and not in the conventional, "in line", format.

Cousin Jim and I spent all of our spare time and cash improving the performance of our stable for grass track and trials competitions. Jim's prime machine was his "Beesa", and mine was the flat tank which I had acquired for the purpose. warm summer evenings or cold winter ones were the same as we strove in our labours. Stripping engines down, cleaning and polishing and replacing original items with high performance racing items.

Valve cams were replaced with "high lift" one's and stronger springs. Carburettor jets and needles, magneto gears and sprockets and chains all received our attention. So did the cylinder heads, inlet and exhaust ports, valve seats, pistons and their rings were all polished to a high gloss with many hours of elbow aching work.

Because my machine was an old one and it had not cost me very much I was willing to try to improve its performance by carrying out very advanced techniques on the engine. To do that I reduced the weight of the connecting rod and flywheels by drilling a number of holes in them. The theory was that the engine would achieve higher revolutions for the same petrol/air mixture, and therefore higher performance. Such modifications could be included in the original design specification for competition machine, it was different matter when they were introduced into a early model. My experiment needless to say did not work. With modifications completed and the engine reassembled, I wheeled the potential world beater into the field for its test ride. The petrol was turned on, carburettor "tickled" and with throttle and ignition levers set for a start condition, I slammed my foot down on the kick-start. Nothing happend. Again and again with no response. Had I miss timed either valves or timing? I kicked once again and suddenly the engine sprang into life. After a brief wait, with tongue in cheek, nothing untoward occurred and everything appeared to be O.K. Now the real test began. I sat on the saddle, pulled in the clutch and put it into first gear. Opening the throttle carefully the bike and I moved off very sharply which gave me immense pleasure. With increased confidence I began to blip the throttle and change gear in normal fashion, then it happened. Half way round the track in second gear and engine speed rapidly increasing to change to a higher gear, calamity! Suddenly there was an anguished scream and rough noises emanating from beneath the saddle, we came to an abrupt halt. With a wry grin I wheeled my now dead experiment back to the shed. As the cylinder was removed it was obvious that the engine had been subjected to pressures and forces for which it was not designed. The lightened con rod had been twisted into a long "S", and the piston was no longer recognisable as such. The engine was a complete write off, but I had gained valuable experience from the exercise.

The members of the club were constantly seeking improved performance from their mounts and therefore changed them several times over the ensuing years. An Aerial "Red Hunter", B.S.A. "Gold Star", and two Rudges, both with side-cars, were just some of those changes. The latter two were both acquisitions by cousin Jim. The first was an old machine of about 1930 vintage, a 499cc, 4 valve, open push rod engine with an aluminium torpedo "chair". That outfit could perform well but it certainly showed its age. We used to have some hair raising experiences with it. Because of our determination to get the most from the engines, we frequently timed them beyond their original specification's. That was so with the early Rudge. On many occasions, both Phyl, his girl friend, and I, or anyone else who happened to be seated in the side-car, had to resort to a fire fighting role. Sometimes when starting or when moving off from a temporary halt, the engine would burst into flame from the carburettor. A shout from Jim to "put the bloody fire out", meant that the person in the chair grabbed an always present piece of old rag from the nose of the chair, and rammed it into the flaming air inlet of the carburettor. After ensuring that all was well, Jim would with some misgivings, kick the engine into life again and we then sped off as if nothing had happened. After some time he became disenchanted with the constant need to "put the fire out",

Cousin Jim, his mother and fiancée Phyllis on the 1930 Rudge torpedo side car.

beneath his saddle and replaced the aging combination with another one of more recent vintage. This was a 1934 Rudge "Special", with a very nice Watsonian launch side-car. The whole in black and gold with a cream and brown livery on the chair. The Watsonian was recognised as only second in style and quality to the very popular Steib as fitted to the excellent B.M.W.'s. Later that was replaced with a Morris 8 car and then a Riley "9".

Meantime I had enjoyed riding my New Imperial but because I too was now coming under the influence of petticoat rule, had also to consider my passenger. With Jim's move to four wheels I took the opportunity to acquire his combination, knowing its history and capabilities. I quickly found it to be a far superior machine to the Douglas. It gave me very good service and Hilda and I spent many happy hours touring the local countryside and visiting places of interest.

In the latter part of 1939 I was working in Anstey, a short distance outside Leicester and apart from a short time when I lodged in a cafe there, I travelled back and forth each day. Sometimes it was via Coventry where I frequently encountered problems passing the trams in narrow Earl Street, and then on to Leicester and then Anstey. I eventually used the Knowle, Meriden, Nuneaton route which evaded the traffic problems in the larger towns. Each morning, clad in Stormguard coat, waders, cap, gloves and goggles my journey began. After removing a canvas cover

The 1934 Rudge Special with Hilda in the "chair".

from the outfit, I tickled the carburettor, adjusted air and timing levers, lifted the exhaust valve lifter, — otherwise, the high compression of the engine could well have meant an injured knee or worse —, I kicked the machine into life. Lowering the exhaust valve lifter to its normal position, and engaging first gear I swept out of the now double gates of Walnut Tree Cottage. After a days work I sometimes decided to change my route home to go past the ancient monument in Kirby Muxlow and home. One particular journey was memorable in that as I passed the monument there was an unusual metallic sound from beneath the petrol tank and then the engine spluttered to a halt. On inspection I found that the nut securing the four inlet tappets to their support had come off and the whole assembly had collapsed onto the cylinder head. Looking closely around the bike I found the missing nut and after refitting it I was on my way again. At the time, my future wife was working in a house in Blytheway and she always knew what time I had arrived back in Solihull. As with all our machines, the Rudge's engine had been honed to perfection by adjustments to ignition and valve timing among other improvements. Because of them, it frequently back fired. Each evening as I descended the hill over Sandels Bridge and throttled back the engine, it produced a series of loud explosions which was characteristic of both Rudge Specials and Ulster's; the sound alerted her to my return and our meeting later in the evening if it was a Thursday.

The only accident in which I was involved during my time as a motor cycle rider

The author in Stormguard.

was on a Sunday afternoon as we took a gentle ride through Packington. Riding along Somers Lane one Sunday afternoon we came upon a car parked on a blind right hand corner. It had been left there by a learner driver wbo was enjoying a picnic with his family in a field nearby. Just there, the road narrows, and at that precise moment "Murphies Law", decreed that another car should approach from the opposite direction! I was forced to take immediate action to avoid a serious accident. My first reaction was to remove my right hand from the handle bars and my right foot from the footrest; almost a subconscious action to protect both limbs. My next decision was purposely to ride the nose of the side car up the sloping back of the offending Hillman Minx. As we slowly came to rest, the Austin 12, which was coming from the opposite direction ploughed along the side of me, ripping off the right foot-rest and bending the right handle bar.

The result of the coming together of myself and the Austin was the removal of its hub caps and a one inch score line along the side, from front to back. The damage to my bike was to the foot-rest and handle bar and the front mud-guard bent onto the front wheel. The damage prevented the immediate use of gear change, throttle and movement as the front wheel would not turn. There was damage to the back of the Hillman where my side car had ridden up it. Hilda and I suffered no injuries apart from Hilda's camel hair coat being ripped across the right elbow.

The noise of the collision and the loud denunciation of the "idiot", who had parked the Hillman in an obvious blind spot, brought the owner and his family sheepishly from behind the hedge. The farmer and the father of the learner exchanged documents, meanwhile, the mother of the young offender accused both me and the farmer of careless driving! At that, Hilda's Welsh desire for fair play caused her to take the mother to task in no uncertain fashion. She upbraided both mother and son for being the cause of the accident and took great pains to point out the near serious injuries to my leg and arm. Eventually the shouting and the tumult died and after carrying out roadside repairs we were able to continue on our way. In our wake we left a very chastened father and son to a fate worse than death from the tongue of their female "guardian", if that's the correct description! Shortly after that incident I sold the outfit in anticipation of being called up to serve in the Royal Air Force.

Jim and I bought our machines from two sources along Barston Lane at Eastcote, his from a garage and mine from the son of the owner of the Malt Shovel pub. It was a popular drinking venue for most of our small club. The landlord was a Mr. Littleford and his son Godfrey. The father had spent all his early working years in the car industry in Coventry and had retired to the quiet life of a country pub. Godfrey had followed in his father's footsteps in that he went into the motor cycle trade. He had converted a small outhouse by the side of the pub into a show room and workshop. Godfrey's interest exceeded the normal involvement of someone selling and repairing the machines; he raced them in major road races like the Ulster Grand Prix and also competed in the now defunct Southport sand races. He was also a good trials rider. He raced a Rudge "T.T. Repleca".

Cousin Jim competed in various trials and grass track events around the locality. Grass track races at Monkspath, Maxstoke and Lillishall and trials on Weatheroak and Fish Hill's and also at other venues. I played a small part in his efforts by acting as his mechanic. We could be found at the former competitions throughout the summer and the latter during the cold, wet days of winter. As we went about our daily tasks during the week we yearned for the weekends, their excitements and thrills. The distinctive odours of Castrol, "R", and Mobile, "D", were constantly in our nostrils during the greater part of the 1930's.

Lillishall was undoubtedly the best grass track in the area. It was the largest of those we visited and provided a wide range of challenges,it would now be

The T.T. Replica Rudge.

considered as a scramble course. A particular sight and sound of the course was the effort of the "big port", A.J.S.'s to master the first hill in the circuit. A gentleman by the name of Arthur John Stevens, (A.J.S.) began to build motor cycles early in the century and produced a very good range of machines over the years. The model of which I write was produced in about 1926. It had a flat tank, a 350cc, engine with overhead valves which were operated by exposed push-rods. The single feature which made that model so different from other machines was its single exhaust pipe, it was of a much greater diameter than that usually employed. The large pipe together with the special silencer produced a very distinctive "bark", when the engine was being worked hard. The raucous sound could be heard above the rest of the field, right round the circuit. It was obviously a good design feature because despite the age of the machine, it regularly won races against much newer machines.

Yet another aspect of the sport which attracted Jim and I was the Dirt Track. There were two local tracks in the '30's, one in Hall Green, (it also served as a dog track), and the other was at Brandon, near Coventry. The machines raced in the events were much different to any other. Conventional road machines were used in Grass Track, Trials and road races whereas, the Dirt Track bikes had to meet a much different criteria. A major influence on the design and preparation of those machines was the type of track. It was an oval some three hundred yards in total length and the surface was loose ash. To meet the special conditions, the bikes

A racing, 750cc, Douglas, "Dougie".

employed components specifically designed to fit the bill. Their petrol tanks were a mere two pint can strapped to the cross bar, the engines were of either J.A.P. or Rudge design with extra strong chains driving large special sprockets, the final one on the rear wheel almost as large as the wheel itself. There were no brakes, the engine served as a means of stopping at the end of the four or five circuits of each race. Because of the special conditions, most of the riders played a major role in the final. design of their particular machine. There was one notable exception to the J.A.P. and Rudge powered machines, it was one designed and built by Douglas. A 750cc, flat twin, overhead valve, in line with the frame similar to their long established road machines. However, the larger engine required a longer frame to accommodate it. Because of the type of track on which they would race, it could not be extended as far as sound technological design would permit so the gear box for that machine was mounted immediately underneath the saddle. The machine could also be fitted with a side-car for entry in three wheel outfit road races such as those at Donnington Park and Brands Hatch. Imagine if you can, charging round either small, tight, slippery dirt tracks, or the much faster, but also often slippery road circuits with the primary chain from engine to gear box flapping around at a very high and unstable speed, right underneath one's posterior! Despite the problems, it was reasonably successful in both competitions. The machine and its riders always held a special place in my desire to see them win because of my own "Dougie", associations.

# WE GAIN OUR WHEELS

When Jim and I were not participating ourselves, we frequently spent many happy hours at Donnington, watching both car and motor cycle racing on the original course. During World War II it was taken over by both Army and Air Force and when it reopened the perimeter track used by the aircraft to move around it was used as the race track. Events which appealed to us were the three wheeler ones, as not only did motor cycle combinations race, but also three wheeled cars such as the highly regarded Morgan. The J.A.P. 750 or 1000cc, air cooled or water cooled vee twin engines were fitted to the front of the low slung chassis's. They always gave a good account of themselves, and for many of us, were the highlight of the days racing. The particular makes of motor cycles which formed the major competitors were also well known commercial manufacturers such as BMW's, Nortons, Velocette's, and Excelcior's. These were their "Manxman" machines.

An unusual machine which enjoyed a very high reputation both as a road machine and competition machine was the Scott. They were either 600 or 750cc, twin cylinder, two stroke, water cooled engines mounted in the frame to form its main front member. Because of their large engine capacity they were invariably used as combination machines for road use. However, on the track, they were often ridden as solo machines. They were readily recognised as they raced round because of the high pitched exhaust note which earned them the nickname of "Bee's in a Can", for obvious reasons. We also enjoyed the car races there, however, toward the end of the decade it became a foregone conclusion which car would win, either an Auto Union, Mercedes and occasionally a B.M.W./Fraser Nash. The German government began to provide unlimited support and sponsorship for those marquee's as a means of enhancing their prestige and the development of their war machine. It always remained a puzzle to us that our own government did not do the same thing. Nevertheless, I was later to enjoy riding a captured B.M.W. "Combo" over the Western Desert. So much for government support!

In the period of which I write conditions on the roads were much different than those of today. Whereas we have to cope with an escalating traffic problem and falling driving standards on a superb motor-way system; then the road surfaces left much to be desired and the vehicles were no match for many of them, nor were the drivers and riders. A steep incline presented a formidable obstacle to both vehicle and its occupant. Liveridge Hill on the Stratford Road near Lapworth presented such a challenge and my father and his pals spent many happy Sunday afternoons before World War I watching the efforts of pleasure drivers coming to grief on it. The prospect of an exciting and often, profitable, afternoon's sport was a strong inducement for them.

They waited at the bottom of the hill, smoking their Black Cat or "Willie" Woodbine cigarettes, passing the time of day and awaiting their quarry. It was not long before a distraught rider or driver found their vehicle could not cope with the climb before it. My father often regaled us in later years with tales of helpless drivers struggling to make their pride and joy behave as it should and as the manufacturers boasted that it would. Eventually a "crie-de coeur" would take them to a perspiring and angry driver unable to persuade his car or motor cycle to climb the hill. The lads who had been anticipating such a request would then put shoulder and hands to the task of helping to get the reluctant vehicle and its passengers up the hill. Sometimes if it was a large car with several passengers, the driver was advised to reverse it and to attempt the hill in reverse. Even that was not always possible in those days as not all vehicles could boast a reverse gear! Some of the cars that encountered problems in those early days had names that are but a memory now. French Bouton's, English Beans and Clyno's were some. Motor cycle's and side cars were often in trouble, especially the Scotts if the wind happened to be blowing up the hill so causing a following wind; that condition invariably caused them to boil.

On occasions the lads were unable to assist the stricken drivers. In wet weather the primitive electrical systems often failed, punctures were also a common cause in the newly introduced "balloon" tyres. Father often told us that "we often had to repair the puncture in the inner tube as many cars or motor bikes did not carry spare wheels". As dusk fell, father and his pals made their way home well satisfied with their efforts. Sometimes they were amply rewarded for their afternoon's sport.

## Chapter 22
# Welcome to the Fairer Sex

Christmas, 1935, was one of many milestones in my career, as I had reached the age of 14 when most of us left school in those days. I left that closeted world and launched into the wide world of work and other distant horizons. Little did I realise what challenges and surprises I would encounter in that world. Despite the depression, which was deep in the mid '30's, I had been offered and accepted my chosen profession of electrical engineer. My free time was taken in motor cycle sport and I saw little chance of any other activity becoming an important aspect of my life, how wrong I was.

Although my early life had been rather male orientated, an only child, cousin Jim as my closest contemporary both geographically and literally, I had not ignored the girls who lived near us at that time, for Ivy Davis lived opposite and cousin Rosie Street next door. The Peachy girls lived with their family in one of the Keepers cottages up on the canal bank toward The Gossies. These were later joined by the Maynard girls when their father came to work down at the gas works. On the odd occasion when I gave them any thought, I saw their skin was smooth unlike my spotty one, their voices were more pleasant and they took more care over their appearance. At about the age of 13 my voice broke and suddenly they began to attract me in a different way than before.

A short time before this, Dennis Cockayne, a lad about my age, came to live in one of the houses which had been built on Gran's top garden. We became firm friends and spent quite a good deal of time together. They had lived in one of three small cottages which stood behind the shop on the corner of Lugtrout Lane and Hampton Lane at Catney. We were soon to become competitors in the pursuit of girls of our age who lived near to us.

The first of those girls was one Mary Adkins, the daughter of Ron, who worked on Billy Markham's farm, and who lived in the cottage which had been the head keepers cottage where cousin Jim's grandparents had lived. The cottage was a little way along a path beyond the school in Elmdon park. Because we were both "cocking our hats" for her, each of us played gooseberry when we met her in the park. Those meetings by perforce were always surreptitious because her father's demeanour was of one who would tolerate nothing which would affect his families well being. It must be said that we also provided moral support for each other in this new experience. After a while I became disenchanted with the joint approach and took the initiative and gained the advantage, Dennis quickly realised what had happened and gracefully left the scene. Our innocent friendship lasted for about four months before she went to work in Yardley, from then we decided to go our own way. Dennis and I now resumed our chase for other female company. We set our eyes on a girl who lived a few doors above his house. She was of our age and the daughter of a Mr. King who had an electrical shop in the row of small shops which used to stand between Mill Lane and Drury Lane along the Warwick Road.

At about this time my attention was diverted from the pleasant game of "sparking" because of more pressing concerns such as starting to work, entering into further education — with The British Institute of Engineering Technology — and I also became more involved in my motor cycle activities. After a while I regained my interest in girls, I believe it was because Jim had for some time been going out with a girl who was later to become his wife. Before she came on the scene, he had been interested in Helen, who worked in a house in Ashley Road as a domestic servant. I must point out that many of the girls were employed in that work between the two world wars. When Phyllis, for that was the name of Jim's future wife, came on the scene, unfortunately Helen was left at a loose end. All we lads possessed a fairly high moral standard where the opposite and weaker sex was concerned. Our approach to them was always with respect and probity. With those conditions in mind, Jim felt that he had to "let down" Helen as gently as possible. Because of our close relationship he no doubt thought that I should help him to do just that. Helen was a very good looking and stylish girl, as were all his girl friends, that being the case I was not slow to step into his shoes. Smart, petite and fashionable, she hailed from Liverpool, unlike many other girls who came from the Welsh valleys to escape the poverty there. She was very proud of her brother, a cartoonist featured each day in the Daily Mirror. I remember some of his work made very forceful comment on the Spanish war which was then making the headlines.

Helen was the first girl I took home to meet my parents. Christmas, 1936 and the people she worked for would not release her for the two or three days to go home as they had a full programme of entertainment and required her presence. As she was allowed a few hours off on the afternoon of Christmas Day I invited her home to enjoy tea with us; I was overjoyed when she accepted the invitation.

It transpired that my father was not going to be available so it would be a quiet evening with my grandmother. I met her at the gate of the house where she worked and we walked to Elmdon Heath on a cold and frosty afternoon. When we reached Gran's door I ushered her into the warm, cosy and welcoming room. The fire had been stoked high and now there were flames licking up the wide chimney throwing a warm glow over the festive scene. As I helped her remove her overcoat I found she was wearing a stunning ice blue dress, dark blue stockings, and blue, high heeled court shoes; she made quite an impression on both myself and Grandmother. The greatest impact was yet to reveal itself. When she shook hands with Gran, I noticed, as did Gran, that her finger nails were painted a deep, mauve colour which completed a very pleasing and sophisticated picture.

Imagine if you can the effect of such a picture upon an old lady whose whole life had known little more than life just above the poverty line, and who had only glimpsed ladies dressed in such finery during her service in the big house! Little had she believed that anyone so dressed would be a guest in her humble abode. Her easy acceptance of the situation gave me much satisfaction and indeed, considerable pride that she was able to carry it off. The time we spent with her went very well and then it came time for Helen to return to her chores. Shortly after that visit she returned home to Liverpool.

My next involvement with a girl was once again one in domestic service. I met her at a dance at The British Legion, they were held on most Saturday evenings. They had been a regular feature in the old Public Hall in Popular Road until the new British Legion building offered better facilities. Most of the young people could be found at the dances. Jim and Phyl were regulars with their friends, Bill, George and Bess Mabbot. I was always the butt of many jokes at those functions because of my height, six foot three inches, – there were not many girls anywhere near that. They were invariably shorter and the sight of me cavorting around the floor with someone much shorter was the source of much merriment. I became interested in my next girl as she was at least five foot ten inches tall and therefore we did not present an spectacle as we glided around the floor. She refused to provide us with her name but insisted upon us calling her "Yorky" for obvious reasons, – she spoke with a strong Yorkshire accent. We enjoyed a brief friendship merely because of our compatible height and for no other reason. Very shortly after that friendship came to an end I met the girl who would later become my wife. Her name was Hilda. She had come up to Birmingham from the Welsh valleys to find domestic work like so many of her contempories. Her first job was with the Durnell family. He was the manager of Lewis's in Birmingham and they lived in a large house on the Warwick Road which has now become the St. John's Hotel. In the days when she worked there only the centre section of the present complex was the family home. She returned home for a spell in 1937 before returning to the Brown family who lived in Blytheway.

A steady relationship developed between Jim and Phil, and they got engaged and shortly after, in 1938, we did too. A big occasion and a costly one too. I sold my New Imperial motor bike to bolster my liquidity so that I could afford the ring. Shortly after our engagement, in August of that year, we spent a holiday at her home in Wales. I recall it very well as the weather was kind to us and we spent a very happy time with her family. It's a great pity that engagement anniversaries are not recognised as are weddings; if they were, we would have celebrated our Golden Engagement three years ago as we celebrated our Golden Wedding anniversary in May 1991!

We motor cycle fraternity were now faced with a brutal choice, – should we forsake our religious dedication to the two wheeled, smelly, noisy and expensive love of our lives for the two legged, sweetly perfumed, chatty and expensive one? James and I had done so. Wag Smitten was going strongly with the manageress of Wimbush's cake shop. It was one of several shops recently built on the corner of Warwick Road and Station Road at Knowle. Jimmy Timms was also very involved with Elen who later became his wife. By the time we all went off to war in 1939 we were either married or nearly so. We all returned safely except for Jimmy Timms who had been rendered deaf by his experience.

I should perhaps draw a picture of our different characteristics. Cousin Jim was always a very energetic person, but also someone who would not suffer fools gladly. His desire to compete supports my assessment of him. Wag Smitten was a quiet person who always gave a great deal of thought to what he said or did. Jimmy Timms was an enigma. He was slightly deaf and a little older than the rest of us. He possessed a dry humour and a musical bent. A halt in the conversation or an awkward moment and he would save the day by a quip or funny remark. His other accomplishment was made manifest by him playing a tune on a set of coins taken from his pocket or with a single coin played on the spokes of a motor cycle wheel. At his home in the council house along Cornyx Lane from Wharf Lane was an organ on which he played with some vigour. Each time that I walk along the path which leads from the Civic car park to where it emerges on the High Street where the Gardeners Arms once stood; I still see his back and bright red hair under a flat cap, chasing up the dark alley to work at the bakery. The author at that time was a tall, lanky chap, black hair brushed back and held in place with a liberal application of a very well known recently introduced hair, dressing. It was a product of the Chemico factory at Shirley, and it would shortly find worldwide fame as it became identified with members of the Royal Air Force, it's name of course Brylcreme. Unlike Jimmy, I was taciturn which may have been the result of loosing my mother at an early age.

Hilda, my girl friend and later, wife, did not enjoy a very happy early life. Her father was a coal miner in the Welsh coal field. They were a family of seven, and with industrial unrest, including the General Strike of 1926, life was far from easy. Her father was once offered the post of teacher at a school but chose to earn his money down the mine. He obviously possessed considerable intellect but chose not to make use of it. Sadly he denied the chance of a better education to his daughter. Hilda was pressured by her teacher to take examinations for high school, the offer was refused because she knew that her father would not have agreed to the plan. As far as he was concerned her future was as so many girls at that time, to go out to work at the first opportunity to earn money to support the family. In Wales in the early part of this century, the hiring and firing of labour was no different to that which my grandmother experienced in the middle of the 19th century.

For generations, men, women and children were hired for labour by farmers and landowner's at the local fairs which were held on Lady Day, (in the Spring), and at Michaelmas, (in the Autumn). The men and boys were engaged for work on the land for farmers and large estates. The women and girls were taken also for work on the farms but also for domestic work in the farm houses and in the houses of the large estates, the Manors, Halls and such like. It was customary for the Lady Day Fair to hire workers and the Michaelmas Fair for labour to be disposed of and likewise, for labour to leave their employers. In the former, once a person had agreed conditions and pay and had accepted a proffered coin, — usually a shilling —, a contract had been entered into by both sides. In the latter case, termination of employment had been agreed by either side before the forthcoming Fair.

My grandmother, who had attended a Dames school, often used to recount to me how her parents had taken her to a Lady Day Fair where she was hired in her first job. They had taken great care to coach her in the best way to speak when questioned and to act demurely so that "You can get the best offer"! On that occasion she was successful. My question when we were chatting in front of the fire was "Didn't you feel shy and awkward standing there being inspected and asked difficult questions"? "Yes", she did feel embarrassed the first time, "but as it was the accepted procedure she took consolation because every other girl and lad had to face the same ordeal".

Later when Hilda and I discussed her early years she told me that she too had to endure the same ritual when she had started work. She was hired to work on a farm near Talgarth, a small village on the edge of the Brecon Beacons. Like my grandmother, she also felt very nervous standing there not knowing what the future held for her. What is revealing is that she was offered about the same wage as my grandmother had been offered 70 years before.

The demeaning process all country folk had to undergo to obtain a job then was matched only by the paltry wages they were offered, and were forced to accept if they were to avoid starvation. The common practice at the time was to agree a 6 months contract for a given sum, in Gran's and Hilda's case it was £6's, or £12's for the whole year! That gave them 5/- a week, (25 pence). It was agreed that the employer provided lodgings, keep and food and usually care if they fell ill. On the farms there were many other "perks", such as free milk, butter, cheese and produce including the gleaning's off the corn fields after the crop had been carried. That was a valuable supplement to the workers feed budget for their own livestock. Finally, but by no means, least, there was the "tied cottage, a cottage which belonged to the farmer or employer so long as the worker remained healthy and capable of working in his job. If for any reason, the health, skill or conduct became suspect, both the worker, breadwinner and head of family could quickly find himself and his family without anywhere to lay down their heads. Although it was gratefully accepted, it was also recognised as a "sprat to catch a mackerel".

The girls were ostensibly taken on to work in the house on household duties, however, often when they were taken on by farmers or farmers wives, the duties also involved work on the farm itself. Needless to say, this was not mentioned during the negotiations when the contract was agreed. In Hilda's case she was expected to milk the cows, by hand of course, as it was long before the introduction of the ubiquitous milking machine. She was also expected to feed the poultry, clean the dirty farmers boots, chop the wood for the fire and many other menial tasks. Such subterfuge was not uncommon when jobs were at a premium. The unfortunate girls who found themselves in such a situation were committed to either six or twelve months of repetitive drudgery until they found a method of release.

Hilda and her mother devised a scheme in which she would escape from her enforced hard work which was much too hard for a young, inexperienced girl of 14. Her mother contrived an excuse and she was eventually released and she returned home for a short time before taking a job at a boarding house in Weston-Super-Mare. She remained there for a season before she came up to Solihull where she eventually became a naturalised Silhillian.

As in most situations there were many excellent employers as well as the bad ones. I recall very well my elders and others who had worked "up at the Hall". When people worked for Squire Alston at Elmdon Hall they were treated very well and all of them extolled the conditions in the Hall. Many still speak with affection of those times and the satisfaction and pleasure of working for the Squire, and for the local farmers, namely, Charley Lea at Foredrove Farm and Les Nock as his successor, Billy Markham at Whar Hall Farm and many others.

## Chapter 23
# "An Electrifying Experience"

School days came to an end at Christmas, 1934. On the day following Boxing Day that year I started out to earn my living as an apprentice electrical engineer with cousin Arthur Street. He worked for Tommy Gibbs who had an electrical business and who had a small office cum store at Hampton-in-Arden. The small wooden building occupied a site next to the station and I am sure that it had, at one time, been the booking office in the early days when the railway first came to the village. Tommy and Arthur had both once worked for Walker Brothers in Birmingham before Tommy set up in business on his own. Walkers were held in very high regard by the trade and their employees. It was they who set a standard which other electrical traders had to follow if they were to succeed. Arthur had attended night school to extend his technical knowledge and in so doing, gained his City and Guilds Certificate in Electrical Engineering. He maintained those standards in all his work and insisted that I attain them also. Tommy's business was like so many others at that time. The rapid expansion of industry and the building of many houses required a similar rise in firms capable of installing the new source of power. Gas had been available for many years and was the accepted form of lighting on the streets, in the home, for heating, cooking and industrial use. The general public were still very sceptical of the new source of power. My Father encapsulated the general approach in one of his succinct quotations, "You can't see it, hear it, or smell it, but you can die if you touch it!" That approach discouraged many from using it when it first became readily available.

On my first morning, I called next door to meet Arthur before leaving for Hampton and my first meeting with Tommy Gibbs. My father had warned me that Arthur had a quick temper and so I should "show willing when you are asked to do something". I became familiar with his irascibility, especially if he had had one over the eight the night before. With one hand I knocked on Ginties back door, while in the other, I proudly carried the canvas tool bag presented to me by my father's work-mates at the gas office. The door opened and Arthur emerged, his first action was to hand all his tools to me, how pleased I was to have the bag. He also instructed me to carry two accumulators which he was taking to be recharged in the office at Hampton. It came as quite a shock to me that I was expected to carry all the tools and accoutrements of the trade every time we moved from one job or place to the next one. All of them had to be accommodated on the handle-bars of my bike. As

I have always been tall, the space between saddle and handlebars had been taken up riding it without the addition of so much more on board! I became accustomed to the chore of packhorse when we travelled to each job, no matter how far from Hampton or our homes. I cannot imagine such a situation being accepted today by tradesmen in any trade. Imagine my chagrin then when I found that I was required to carry all the material for each job! On the odd occasion when no more room could be found on my handle-bars, Arthur grudgingly deigned to carry the odd item on his.

The development of large housing estates proliferated round Birmingham and Solihull in the 1920's and '30's. Locally, Tommy Gibbs had been successful in obtaining work in the electrical installation on many of the estates. Those which readily come to mind are the Partridge estate at Yardley, The Redland Road estate, this was shared with Les Banks who operated from his home in New Road. Then there was the whole of Blytheway and the houses from its junction with the Warwick Road toward Sandalls Bridge. Mr. Brueton, he who built the Avenue, also built Blytheway. He lived in a large house set back behind Malvern Hall and had many interests in several well known engineering companies in Birmingham. There were also all the houses along Brook Lane in Olton. So most mornings, a self assured, not to say, cocky, electrician and his rather lanky, overloaded mate, could be seen trundling along the local lanes to a job. I loathed the Yardley job as it was so far from Hampton and there were so many hills along the Coventry Road. We always found time to stop at a small cafe where the Arden Hotel now stands. My enthusiasm for the job quickly paled in those circumstances. It was not only the fatigue arising from the travelling between jobs and home, it was also the conditions encountered when working on skeleton houses. It was frequently cold and wet, and after struggling to the particular site, we were then faced with the task of working in very difficult conditions.

I received little encouragement from Arthur, more often constant criticism. The situation changed for the better however when Tommy won the contract to instal electricity in the Isolation Hospital at Catherine-de-Barnes. A major job which involved all the buildings which made up the hospital complex; scarlet, diphtheria, typhoid and smallpox wards, the latter the most feared at a time when all of the diseases were common and many people died from them. There was also the Nurses home, laundry, garage and boiler room and workshops. As the whole of the work was carried out by just Arthur and I, it was hard but very interesting. The health aspect was of constant concern but fortunately neither of us was laid low by the fevers that were cared for there.

Apart from the run of the mill work on the housing estates there was other much more interesting work too. The conversion of many factories in the centre of Birmingham from the old 110 volt, D.C. system to the nationally accepted 250 volts, A.C. In one of those factories, Arthur and I came perilously close to losing our eyesight. The Brightside Plating Company was where we nearly caused serious damage to equipment and injury to ourselves. Whenever we were involved in a change over from old to new installations in a factory, the need to keep the shafts, pulleys and belts turning was always paramount to meet the output levels. To meet that requirement we invariably attempted to make the change over without disconnecting the main supply to the premises.

On this occasion we had completed the task of rewiring and all that was required was to connect the new installation. We were in the small, dark and cramped confines of a transformer house. This is where the main electrical supply is converted into various levels for use in the factory. Arthur was at the top of a tall pair of steps with a candle which he had stood on the top of a large mains switch. I was at the foot of the steps with another candle awaiting his demands for tools. The power on which we were working was 440 volts, 3 phase and the switch-gear was metal clad and earthed. Arthur was in the process of removing a live wire when there was a blinding flash, a loud explosion and he was catapulted over my head to land heavily in a heap on the concrete floor against a transformer. In the poor light he had misjudged the space between wire and switch box. He was lucky to escape electrocution or serious injury by the fall. The result of the accident was to bring the whole factory to an abrupt halt. Where there had been incessant noise of machines and men there was now an unearthly silence. After a second or two we staggered to our feet, (I had also been thrown off mine), and made for the door and fading daylight. Once outside we were soon met by anxious workers who had run to see what had happened. Shortly afterwards, stern management came striding purposefully up the yard to demand an explanation.

The wire touching the metal switch had caused an intense flash of light which had temporarily blinded both Arthur and me. Gradually, with much feverish wiping of our eyes, our sight slowly returned, and we were able to assure all assembled around us that we were O.K. and the power would quickly be restored. That was done and then the recriminations began. Firstly we were accosted by the workers because the failure had reduced their valuable piece work money, and secondly, the manager informed us that his output had fallen for that day. The work in progress at the time were cycle rims for the Hercules Cycle Company.

The incident occurred near the end of the working day and after ensuring that the night shift had power we left for home. The factory was at the bottom of Summer Lane and so we made our truly, weary way up the Lane to catch a train at Snow Hill station for Solihull. On the journey we both suffered from sore eyes and I felt as if I had tears in mine. When I arrived home my father wanted to know why it looked as if I had been crying? When I told him what had happened he tried to make me go to see a doctor, but I resisted and felt that after a good nights sleep, all would be well. The same thing happened to Arthur and he took the same decision as me and did not seek medical help. I slept soundly but the following morning when I was called,

I found that I could not open my eyes. Panic! I quickly realised that the previous days event had done more damage than I had thought. After a minute or two and with some careful attention to them they slowly began to respond to the light from the bedroom window. With difficulty, I dressed and made my way down stairs with a copious stream of tears running down my face. Even then I resisted my father's plea for me to see a doctor. With difficulty I ate my breakfast and then made my clumsy way next door to see how Arthur had fared.

I had long ceased to knock and wait to be invited in, I simply knocked and entered like one of the family. The usual routine was for him to be getting ready to go to work. Not that morning, he sat at the table vainly trying to stem the flow of tears, with little success. As in my case, his parents had tried to get him to see a doctor but he too had rejected such a need. Retrospectively, I believe that we both felt rather embarrassed that our condition was the result of his carelessness and by seeking medical help we would be acknowledging it. After a struggle he at last was ready and we departed for work.

After what can only be described as a very sober and tearful ride we eventually arrived at the Hampton office. Our condition had delayed us and we were late for work which was unusual. Tommy was waiting for us and our excuses. His first words when he saw me was "What on earth has happened to you?. He had obviously not been informed of our previous days experience. My rejoinder was "Wait until you see Arthur!". Needless to say he was not amused as he had visions of claims arising from the firm for loss of earnings because of the stoppage. After a great deal of discussion, much of which I was not prithy to, we set off to earn our wages for the day.

With more interesting work I settled down and resolved to succeed in my chosen profession. Alas, after a mere 18 months Arthur found a better job with the City of Birmingham Electric Supply Company, this was long before nationalization, – and left Tommy's employment. I was still very young although I had gained considerable confidence in my trade from very good tuition by Arthur. Because of that, and as I now owned a motor-cycle, Tommy decided to make me an "improver", which meant that I had not completed my apprenticeship, but I was competent to do work on my own. Not long after achieving that milestone I also became disenchanted and left without having another job to go to. That was a very reckless move at a time when there was a recession and many people were out of work. I found an alternative source of income one Sunday morning in The Malt Shovel at Eastcote. On most Sundays we found our way there after a trial or just a ride round the country. During a conversation with Godfrey, (the son of the landlord), I mentioned that I had given up my job. He at once asked me if I would like to work for him in his workshop by the pub. What a golden opportunity, to be paid to do what we had been pleased to do for nothing as a hobby! I accepted with considerable alacrity. I enjoyed the work, stripping the various machines, cleaning

## "AN ELECTRIFYING EXPERIENCE" 191

and repairing them and helping Godfrey tune his T.T. Replica Rudge for an event. Despite my initial enthusiasm, I found as so many before me, and since, that one loses something in being paid for a pleasure. So it was in my case and to maintain my interest and enjoyment in motorcycle sport I reluctantly left Godfrey's employ. I was not without work for very long, I quickly found a job with a chap by the name of Edward Lucas who had started up a small electrical business from his home in Lodge Road in Knowle. The name of the business was The National Electric Company and it would become a very respected and profitable one.

The small house in Lodge Road was used as home, office and store for the business. Very soon after starting up, he and his wife, opened a very small shop in The High Street. It was located between The White Swan pub and Eric Lyons butcher shop. The charming pub now houses a bank in a modern building, and the small shop has been enlarged to become a furniture shop. The small shop which was run by Mrs. Lucas sold a wide range of electric goods, some very fine lamp shades being just one line, also radios and other items. Names of some of the electrical appliances which were on sale were, Vatric, Hoover and Goblin vacuum cleaners, Creda, Belling and Ferranti fires and cookers, and a wide range of Swan cooking utensils and kettels. The latter company was owned by Bulpitts who were friends of the Lucas's and who lived on the junction of Widney Lane and the short extension of Browns Lane in Bentley Heath. One of the fond memories of the small shop for me are the distinctive smell of silk lamp shades which permeated it and of the many cups of tea and sandwiches which Mrs. Lucas, "Duck" to her husband, plied me with on the many evenings when we worked late into the night. Many evocative memories come to mind each time I pass by that place.

The business proved to be a success and the niche which we recognised as a shop, became too small for the expanding concern. It so happened that two cottages lower down The High Street, between a cobblers shop and Chester House, (at that time it was an antique shop), were being converted into two shops, and Ed. Lucas bought one to display the wide range of appliances and goods for sale. Although the business was doing very well, I think that there may have been a liquidity problem and therefore Ed. and I did all the fitting out of the shop ourselves. The work involved was carried out each evening after the days work. My father did not approve, he thought that I was being "put upon"! I realised that he was concerned for my health as we did work long hours during that period. Nevertheless, the temporary lights burnt late in the new shop in the latter part of 1937 so that it would be ready for the Christmas trade of that year. We did it and it served as an electrical shop for many years. The other shop of the pair opened as a sweet and tobacconists. The shop was owned by a German and his wife. It was not a particularly busy shop and when either Ed or I required assistance on a job we often recruited him to help us. We got on very well despite his seniority, he was at least 50, and was a soldier in the German army during the First World War, and me as a mere youth of 18 years. Sometimes he tended to show his teutonic background but I was well able to handle that situation. At the outbreak of World War II the shop was sold and he and his wife returned to Germany.

A passage led to the back of the shops along the side of the sweet shop. It was more than adequate for the Morris 8 car that Ed used. When he changed it for a Standard 8 and then a Hillman Minx just before the outbreak of the second war, it still coped very well with those cars. Incidentally, he paid £175 for the Minx in 1939, used it throughout the war, then sold it in 1946 for £325! A very good deal indeed. From his profit in that deal he bought a Standard Flying 12. This was a larger car then the others and the narrow passage now became difficult to negotiate.

The small amount of traffic that used The High Street before the war, and immediately afterwards, presented few problems when we wished to get in and out of the passage. However, to reduce the risk of an accident, Ed always drove past the entrance and then reversed into the passage, closing the large wooden door afterwards. On rejoining him after my service in the Royal Air Force he allowed me to use the Standard when I needed to carry equipment to a job or when I was required to get to a job at unusual times. I had assured him that his pride and joy was safe in my hands as during my service I had driven every type of vehicle from a Jeep to large lorries like Scammels, A.E.C.'s, Maudsley's and Crossley's and trailers. All of those in conditions and over surfaces far more primitive than ever to be encountered in this country. The only formidable manoeuvre which I experienced when attempting to drive a car up the passage was with a large 1947 Rover 14. There was very little room but I made it, repaired the radio and returned it to the customer without a scratch.

Ed. Lucas had begun his venture, as had Tommy Gibbs, when the need arose to meet the ever increasing electrical installations in the burgeoning housing developments. In addition to those which Arthur and I worked on when in Tommy's employment, there were now a whole lot more for Ed. Moreton Road in Shirley, Brook Lane in Kings Heath as well as Colebourn Road which originally led off Brook Lane opposite Wake Green Road. The largest of the developments was the one on Cranmore Boulivade estate. As with many at that time, it was built to house the people wbo were being moved out of the slums of Birmingham, Little did we know that Hitler would soon be doing that too! Apposite to that, on Sunday morning, the 3rd of September, 1939, I had gone to the shop as on a normal working day because we had arranged to work that day to catch up with the builders on the Cranmore Estate. Also as usual, Ed was late in rising and I was left kicking my heels waiting for him. At about 10.30 he came down to join his wife and I as we listened for the anticipated news from Downing Street on whether there would be a war. There was a cinema organ playing, not unusual as that was a very common but enjoyable form of entertainment then. The music was interrupted at intervals to announce that the Prime Minister would be making a statement at 11.00 o'clock. At the appointed time, the music ceased and for a moment there was an eerie silence as we waited anxiously for the message. Alvar Liddell, one of the senior B.B.C. announcers introduced the Prime Minister, and after a short pause Mr. Neville Chamberlain informed the many avid listeners that morning that, "I have had no message from Adolph Hitler that he was going to pull his troops out of Poland and return to the status quo. As a result, we are now at war with Germany". The wireless went dead and we just stood and looked at each other, perhaps fear and excitement in our eyes. Fear in Ed and his wife's eyes for he had served in the Great War and realised what war meant. Excitement in mine because although my father had often said that he never wanted there to be another war after his experiences during the last one, like many of my contemporaries, I sensed travel, excitement and yes, danger. After some idle chatter of what, or what not, would happen, Ed and I departed for the job in hand on Cranmore Boulevade.

Before World War II a Mr. Slater lived in a large house in its own grounds on the corner of Station Road and Widney Road in Knowle. One of his interests was the development of a small estate off Widney Road. Ed was a friend of Mr Slater and had secured the wiring contract for the houses to be built. When I joined Ed there were still a few houses left to be wired in Slater Road and a new development to be known as Hurst Green Road had been started. Work on these houses was curtailed for the duration of World War II; when the work was restarted. Council houses were also built on the land, as they were in Mill Lane at the junction with Salter Road.

Ed Lucas was a highly qualified electrical engineer and his knowledge and professional acumen was recognised by many. Such recognition was invaluable as it opened doors to many specialised fields in the science. In 1938 he offered me a staff appointment with the company. He told me that I would be paid weekly on a flat rate of £2.15 shillings, there would be no overtime payment but I would be paid if I fell ill. The important aspect of the appointment would be that I would enjoy enhanced choice of jobs and would become his close associate on all the special work which he did. When I told my father, he was against my accepting such a post. He thought that it was a subtle way of obtaining cheap labour. Despite his rejection of the offer, I accepted it and was not sorry and never had cause to regret that decision. My acceptance resulted in a considerable change of attitude by Ed and his wife toward me. It would not be putting it too strongly to say that from that moment I became their surrogate son. The consequence was that whenever he was called out to a special job he always took me with him.

The work was very interesting and demanding, and it appealed to me because of that. My father continued to take an opposite stance on the basis that he thought that I was being exploited. He was unable to recognise the value to me of a special relationship which gave me access to a mine of knowledge and expertise not offered or available to the average electrical engineer at that time.

The mystique associated with electrical energy was similar to the obscure medical profession. It was soon recognised by the latter that the former could be of great value in effecting cures for many ills of the human race. From 1900 many items of electrical apparatus were introduced in the treatment of patients. To name but a few — "X" ray, Dythermery ray, shock, heating, and many others were increasingly accepted as forms of identifying, curing, or elevating the ills of both mankind and also the animal kingdom. Some of the establishments that employed the new aid to recovery were, the Eye and Dental Hospitals, Dudley Road and the New Queen Elizabeth Hospitals, and many of the veterinary surgeries also employed the full range of devices. Yet another area of health care which used a wide range of electrical devices was the physiotherapist. Miss Stubb's, who had a clinic above the row of shops in Dorridge, she was the better known of our local physios. She had quite a collection of items, some of which had seen many years of service, others were right up-to-date. The older items of her electro/medical equipment frequently broke down, often at the most inopportune times. I spent many hours getting dry warm baths used to ease arthritic pain back into operation. They consisted of two hinged bowed, metal capsules, each of which had nine carbon filament electric lamps attached to one side. The lamps, (the carbon filament was the first type of lamp commonly in use), developed considerable heat when lit. The modus-operandi was to wrap the patient's, legs in blanket and then to place them between the capsules which were then closed together to form a bath around the affected area. It is not difficult to see that constant use would quickly cause problems with what at the best of times were fairly delicate lamps and wiring.

I found many faults at different times with them. Another item which gave problems was a metronome, — it had electrical connections which could be alternatively electrified with low levels of energy to provide an interrupted shock treatment to specific areas of the body. I also often attended the vet's surgery which was housed in the first house next to what used to be Samuel Davy's estate agency in Wilsons Road. The large lamps above the operating table seemed to be a source of trouble. It was there that I learnt of the precautions one took when working in an environment where oxygen was in frequent use.

Because of the encouragement given to me by Ed Lucas I was determined to succeed in my chosen profession. To do so I recognised that it required a great deal of effort and in particular, theoretical and academic standards to reach the desired goal. I enrolled in a correspondence course with The British Institute of Engineering Technology in the subjects of Heat, Light and Power to achieve my purpose. The outbreak of war in 1939 brought my plans to an abrupt halt and I did not fulfil my ambition until much later, but then not in Electrical Engineering but in Electronics.

The work in which I was involved just prior to that war was in preparation for the forthcoming fray. Most of the work was installing light and power into newly built

## "AN ELECTRIFYING EXPERIENCE"

shelters in manufacturers premises, one of whom was Pattisons, (the very well known and esteemed local bakers and restaurateurs), in their main bakery in Birmingham. The same type of work was carried out in many of their shops around the city. I emerged from their shop in Moseley Road in Moseley on the evening of the 1st September, 1939 to see a paper sellers board outside the shop proclaiming "Poland Invaded". An involuntary shudder ran down my spine as I realised that the crunch had come and my planned future would now change drastically.

In that month I happened to be working in a factory in Union Street in the city centre. I was in the process of converting the old installation from 110 volts, D.C. to 220 volts, A.C. By that time most of my friends had been called up or were volunteering for the armed services. Earlier in that year I had made tentative overtures to the R.A.F. with the intention of joining them as an Observer. At the time I was awaiting instructions regarding my request when I received a letter informing me that if I still wished to join the R.A.F. I should report to the local recruitment office. After discussing the subject with my family and Hilda, my future wife, I took the decision to make an effort to join. At the earliest opportunity I attended the local office in Dale End, on the 5th of September, only to find the doors tightly closed and a notice to the effect that the system had been inundated with applications and the office would next open on the 17th. On that date I tried again and as I arrived at the door, with a long line of hopefuls behind me, they were again slammed shut. I breathed a sigh of relief that I had made it. Once inside it took about two hours to go through the various tests and routines. One of the tests was to assess my abilities and suitability for a particular job. I had decided to forgo my original aim of becoming an observer and chose that of wireless operator. My job of electrical engineer posed no problem and in fact made my choice an easy one for the R.A.F. to accept with some confidence. With details finalised, I was presented with the Kings Shilling, a formality which sealed one's fate, and I was also informed that my "calling up", notice would follow in a short time.

At the end of that day, I returned to the shop in Knowle to tell Ed that I had taken the only course I considered open to me in the circumstances and had joined the R.A.F. He was not pleased. We had discussed the options open to me on several occasions and he had always tried to dissuade me from making what he considered a hasty decision. I knew that he wanted me to stay with him, he had already taken advice on my being put into a reserved occupation. Our trade and profession lent itself to such action. My pride would nct allow me to shelter under what I considered a way of avoidance of service for the country. Yes, immature patriotism, but not out of place in the days when we still felt immense pride in being British; an attitude not so obvious today!

That evening I told both my parents and Hilda that I had enrolled in the R.A.F. They received the news in silence, I knew that they did not wish for me to anticipate the call up before it came. I had earlier said that I wanted to fly and that at least when I was a member of a small team in an aircraft, we could take individual decisions when faced with a tricky situation, unlike the poor soldier in a trench when ordered to, "go over the top!", I am sure that they like me, recognised that I was stretching the argument to suit my own preferences. Discussion soon came to an end because none of us wished to dwell on the forthcoming events.

My calling up papers arrived on the morning of the 10th October, 1939 in forming me that I was to report to R.A.F. Station Cardington in Bedfordshire on the 19th. That day happened to be a Thursday, but more importantly, it was Hilda's birthday. On the evening when I received the notice I made a point of seeing Hilda although she was not free to come out of her place of work, the house in Blytheway. It was with very mixed feelings that I broke the news to her. Such news was not the sort of birthday present I had hoped to give her. We spent a very glum evening until I bid her goodnight and left with a heavy heart.

The 19th arrived and off to war I went with many others. After a month at Cardington being taught the rudiments of taking orders, no matter how stupid or ridiculous, plus the art of looking after oneself, and the ability to march in step with one's comrades. A month after such diversions I was sent to Yatesbury in Wiltshire, No. 2, Wireless Training School where I was trained as a wireless operator. I left there in May 1940 to begin what was to become five and a half years of service both in the U.K. and in the Middle East until I was demobbed in January 1946. On one brief 48 hours in 1941, also in May, Hilda and I were married in Elmdon church. It was not for another four years or so that we would set up home in Solihull and begin to live a normal life. Fortunately, all of my friends and mates were also able to return home and live almost normal lives.

Hilda and I were allotted a prefabricated bungalow on a small estate which was built on farm land opposite the Rover factory on Lode Lane in June 1946. Cousin Jim and Phyl were also lucky to be housed in one. We were in No. 3, Oleander Lane and they were in No. 00. After 25 years, some of them tumultuous, many of them happy and rewarding, we became family men and looked forward to a happy future.